THE LIFE OF ST. THOMAS BECKET OF CANTERBURY
BY
John Dobree Dalgairns

THE LIFE OF ST. THOMAS BECKET OF CANTERBURY

Published by Magisterium Press

New York City, NY

First published circa 1876

Copyright © Magisterium Press, 2015

All rights reserved

Except in the United States of America, this book is sold subject to the condition that it shall not, by way of trade or otherwise, be lent, re-sold, hired out, or otherwise circulated without the publisher's prior consent in any form of binding or cover other than that in which it is published and without a similar condition including this condition being imposed on the subsequent purchaser.

ABOUT MAGISTERIUM PRESS

Magisterium Press is a Catholic publishing house that loves to spread the word and love of Jesus Christ to everyone, Christians and non-Christians alike.

It ought not to be hard to read the character of S. Thomas of Canterbury, nor to understand for what cause he shed his blood. Ranke, with simply honest endeavour, has comprehended both. Speaking of Henry, he says: "He did not choose to allow the Church freedom of election to high ecclesiastical dignities; he would not permit her excommunications to proceed without the supervision of the State. Not only did he insist on the right of the civil tribunals to judge ecclesiastics for great crimes, which would otherwise have been left unpunished, but in the sphere of spiritual jurisdiction he claimed for the State the right of being the highest court of appeal, instead of the Pope."

Of S. Thomas himself the same historian says: "Becket was not actuated by the same unbending obstinacy which characterizes most of the champions of the hierarchy." All this is quite clear and simple, and ought to be seen by anyone who takes the trouble to study the question. S. Thomas died for the liberty of the Church. It was only after great struggles with himself, with early prejudices and affections, that the saint saw nothing was left for him but to lay down his life for the cause of Christ and His Church. History alone ought to enable even a Protestant to understand at least the momentousness of the issue. Henry wished practically to sever England from the Holy See, and to cripple the spiritual power of the Church—the only power on earth, besides material force, which the king and his wicked barons respected. Now, wherever the Church of a country is enslaved by the State, and separated from Rome, one of two things follows. In a country like ours at this day, which believes in no Church, the State allows the wildest and most ridiculous licence of opinion. In a believing nation, on the contrary, as England was then, the State wields the authority of the Church for her own purposes, and enslaves the intellect and the soul of its subjects, as Russia does now. It was to avert the latter degradation from England that S. Thomas died.

Now, really it is not too much to ask of men who write on the subject to see that this was something worth dying for, even though they may prefer the present supremacy of the Queen, and its consequences. Above all, men who profess to write history ought at least to state that for which he did die, and not something totally different, or ludicrously short of it. What he shed his blood for was to prevent England, Ireland, and half France from becoming in the twelfth century what Moscow is now: this was a cause worth dying for. Most writers, on the contrary, and even some Catholics, represent him as contending only for clerical immunity from secular tribunals; which was only the occasion, and a very small, though not unimportant, part of the contest. The worst offender, however—who is most offensive, precisely because, from his qualities of head and heart, he ought to know better—is Dean Stanley. Any one reading his lecture on the murder of Becket in his "Memorials of Canterbury" might suppose that the saint died because of a squabble between the sees of Canterbury and York, and because he excommunicated the Brocs for poaching on his manors and docking the tails of his horses and mules. The Dean's conception of S. Thomas of Canterbury is worthy of being placed side by side with the Becket of the Ingoldsby Legend of the "Prior of Birchington." It might seem invidious to notice what, after all, is only a lecture *ad populum*, if it were not a type of a whole class of compositions which tend perhaps more than any other to falsify the truth of history. The fact is worth dwelling upon.

It is said that all languages in their infancy are sensuous. To barbarians all abstractions are concrete, and all ideas are images. "In their High Dutch," says Gustav Freytag of the Germans in uncivilized times, "as it rolled sonorously, with varied, harsh inflexions of voice, from their lips, there still clung to nearly all the words the primitive sensuousness of the expression, just as when it was first educed from the soul. Abstractions, words for conceptions, unclothed of all sensible image, were almost wholly wanting." It seems as if literature in its decrepitude returns to primitive infancy. Images take the place of thought. History becomes picturesque, and nothing more. When the weary soul has given up the search after the truth, which is the right key to the understanding of the great world drama, it takes to vivid painting of the outside of facts. Very beautiful are Dean Stanley's pictures, for instance, of the Council of Nicaea. The chestnut woods, the sloping hills, the tranquil lake, the snowclad Olympus looking over the scene—the whole landscape is before us. Then we have Arius, "tall and thin, in his long coat with short sleeves, and his hair in a tangled mass," confronted with Athanasius, "the small insignificant young man, of lively manners and speech, and of bright serene countenance." We take in all these details, and are thankful. The reader is bewitched with the diorama unrolled before his view; but if he recovers from his intoxication, and asks for the inner meaning of it all—if he begs for the truth wrapped up in all these images, Dean Stanley's answer is that there was absolutely none. "When we perceive the abstract questions on which it turned—when we reflect that they related not to any dealings of the Deity with man, not even, properly speaking, to the Divinity or the Humanity of Christ, nor to the doctrine (for all these points were acknowledged by both parties), but to the ineffable relations of the Godhead before the remotest beginnings of time, it is difficult to conceive that by inquiries such as these the passions of mankind should be roused to fury." According to Dean Stanley, the question was one of words. Now I maintain that this is simply untrue. The question was whether Christ was eternal God. If "before the first beginning of time" (I am using the Dean's words) the Son was not, then He was not God. Surely this is not so very unintelligible a question. Is God an abstraction? What the Arians denied was no less than the Christian conception of God. Surely it is perfectly conceivable that indignation should be roused when a party of men calling themselves Catholics not only denied the first elements of the faith, but did their best to force their views upon the Church. Furthermore, the honour of Christ surely justifies a little enthusiasm. It is only when the sad infirmity of the dreamy latitudinarianism, which has not the courage to believe, has seized upon the mind, that the heart ceases to burn about a Christ, who is too shadowy to be worth fighting for. To represent the question as unimportant is simply to speak what is untrue. For Heaven's sake, let us have a little solid truth, instead of all this lively untruth. Chestnut groves and vivid photographs are but poor substitutes for a real knowledge of the bearings of the great contest.

S. Thomas has fared like the champions of the Christian idea of God. Here also the grand inner motives of the combatants are ignored and concealed; and we have in their stead a picture of the event. In this case, however, the offence is greater. The picture is so cleverly managed, that a strong light falls precisely on those parts which make it vulgar. Now I submit that this is to falsify history. If the relative position of events is altered—if what in the acting of the very deed was thoroughly in the background, is, on the contrary, put into the front, then I maintain that the picture is false. There is an old German painting of the marriage of the Virgin, in which the artist has put two dogs into the foreground. Now, even granting the fact of the presence of the dogs, we should hardly call the picture a real representation of the event, if the animals were painted to the life, and the graceful form of the Virgin was only dimly seen in the distance. Thus, to make history true, little things must keep to their place, and great things must not be slurred over. By a wilful neglect of this rule, the narrative becomes positively false. It is a cheap and easy artifice; for in all events, however great, there are many things commonplace and out of keeping with our notions of dignity. The reality aims at neither the romantic nor the picturesque. All death-beds, for instance, have degrading details, though death is the grandest event of life. Much more is this true of a murder, and even of a martyrdom; and it is an unworthy trick of writing to attempt to take away the sympathy of the world from heroism, because the victim does not wrap his robes about him with the dignity of the virgin in the Greek tragedy. It was an artifice which we might have expected from Mr. Froude, but which pains us in Dean Stanley.

Even if the old Adam had come out in S. Thomas during that terrible scene, it would not have been wonderful. That the martyrdom was well-nigh "an unseemly brawl" we utterly deny. Dean Stanley has managed to make it appear so by the shabbiest ingenuity. He has laid stress upon and thrown into prominence things which formed so small a part of the event that they are hardly noticed by the spectators. Even these he has distorted. S. Thomas knew that death was inevitable, and he came to meet his murderers, offering himself as a victim for God's Church. His only wish, however, was to die in his own cathedral, before God's altar and at the foot of the crucifix. Accordingly, when his murderers tried to drag him out and despatch him in secret, he resisted. At this moment occurred the circumstance of which the Dean has made so much. Herbert of Bosham says: "Taking hold of the other knight by his coat of mail, he shook him off so strongly that he *almost* threw him on the pavement." This our author converts into the following words: "In the scuffle Becket fastened upon Tracy, shook him by his coat of mail, and, exerting his great strength flung him down upon the pavement." So insignificant a part of the deed was this circumstance, that not a single spectator mentions it; it was known long afterwards by Tracy's own confession. It is this which the Dean of Westminster exaggerates, and on which he makes the event so turn as to give him a right to call it a scuffle and a brawl. Again, he makes the Archbishop, "heated to anger by the fray," use "a coarse epithet." But does Dr. Stanley know what word S. Thomas used? We suspect not; for he does not cite Gamier, the only French contemporary author, for the circumstance; and the Archbishop did not speak Latin. This, however, is of little consequence. The crime itself of Reginald was not such as would admit of being spoken of in the society of ladies in a drawing-room. S. Thomas, however, was being murdered, and was not in a drawing-room. This was precisely a point in which the great struggle came forth in all its nakedness, unclothed of conventionalities. The Church and her excommunications were the only barrier interposed between defenceless virtue and lawless power. S. Thomas was the guardian of Christian morals, and it was in defence of that very power which enabled him to protect the weak and to punish the violent that he was dying. "Are you going to excommunicate us all?" was the cry of FitzUrse at their last interview. Now that the great champion of virtue stood unarmed face to face with the licentious nobles, who were the representatives of brute force and coarse lust, it was no time for mincing words. Dean Stanley's aim is evident. He has wished to vulgarize S. Thomas. So far his success has been perfect. His conception of the Saint is thoroughly vulgar.

Unfortunately for himself, he has condescended to argue in a note. He has pleaded for his client, Henry VIII., in the following terms: "It is this part of the narrative, that was—not altogether without justice—selected by Henry VIII., representing him (Becket) as having fallen in a scuffle with the knights, in which he and they were *equally aggressors*." For the sake of one so worthy of respect as the Dean of Westminster, we wish that these words had never been written. A more dastardly and cowardly murder than that of the Archbishop of Canterbury was never perpetrated. To make it cease to be a murder, it would have been necessary to show that it was not premeditated, and that it arose out of the expression cited by the document. Never, however, was murder so deliberately planned. The four knights cross the sea to kill the Archbishop. They put on their armour for the purpose. Humans and victim alike know that he is to die. The only difference between them was as to where it was to be done. Hence, and hence alone, arose what Dean Stanley and Henry VIII. call a scuffle. I deny the justice of the disgraceful plea in every possible sense.

It is hoped that the following account of England's great Martyr will enable the reader to understand the simple grandeur of the life and death of S. Thomas. It is especially to be commended, because the author treats her subject in a thoroughly Catholic spirit, and dwells on the Saint's devotion to our Lady and on his secret life with God.

J. B. Dalgairns.
    The London Oratory,
Feast of SS. Nereus and Achilleus, 1868.

THE AUTHOR'S PREFACE.

FEW biographies are supported by such ample contemporary records as that of S. Thomas of Canterbury. Fewer still are drawn from such sympathetic sources. Within fifty years of the martyrdom twenty-five lives of the saint were published, of which no less than twelve were by his intimate friends, who were witnesses of some part, at least, of what they narrate.

Of these, John of Salisbury, Herbert of Bosham, and William FitzStephen were his clerics. John, the first scholar of the day, and afterwards Bishop of Chartres, had been associated with him in the service of Archbishop Theobald, and now stood in the relation of an attached old friend; who freely used his privilege of contradicting, advising, or blaming him to his face. Herbert, though much younger, was the chosen monitor on whom he imposed the duty of pointing out whatever he might think wrong in his conduct. FitzStephen was his fellow-citizen, held a confidential position in his chancery, assisted when he heard causes, or conducted them at his bidding, acted as sub-deacon when he sang Mass, and strengthened and consoled him at Northampton by his counsel and courage.

Benedict, William, Gervase, and Alan were his monks. Benedict was chosen, as one of his most intimate friends, to write a record of the martyrdom and the first miracles. William entered the monastery during his exile, but was admitted to the habit, and ordained deacon by him a few days before the martyrdom. Gervase, whose life of the saint appears in his chronicle, tells how his holiness had excited his affection, and his kindness had attracted him, and how he was granted the habit by him the very year he was consecrated Archbishop, made his profession to him, and received Holy Orders from him. Alan wrote a short life as a supplement to the still shorter life by John of Salisbury and an introduction to the saint's letters, which he collected and arranged. His selection for this task, and the positive tone in which he gives details of conversations and facts omitted by other writers, leave little doubt that he had been closely connected with the saint, and had gone abroad with him. He was a Canon of Benevento, and he probably got this preferment from S. Thomas's great friend, Lombard, who was Archbishop of Benevento during the three years that intervened between the martyrdom and Alan's return to Canterbury in 1174.

Grim was a cleric of the province of Canterbury, and having come to see his Archbishop on his return from exile, stood by him in the cathedral till his arm was nearly cut off in protecting him from Tracy's sword. One of two anonymous lives is commonly ascribed to Roger, a monk of Pontigny, who was S. Thomas's personal attendant; and the other, generally known as the Lambeth MS., is by an eye-witness of the martyrdom. Ralph de Diceto, Archdeacon and afterwards Dean of S. Paul's, in whose chronicle S. Thomas's life has a place, stood among his clerics close to him at Northampton, and mingled his tears with theirs when the probability of his being put to death by the king was suggested. Giraldus Cambrensis, with whom he must have had at least official relations, mentions in his history, with affectionate interest, details omitted by the other writers, especially as to how he spent the last few days of his life.

The simple narratives of writers in such familiar relations to the saint are very touching. The affection with which they linger over every trifle connected with their much loved friend, outweighs their veneration for him as a martyr. They recall the incidents impressed on their hearts without any attempt at formal eulogy or hiding his foibles. His brilliant career as chancellor is dwelt on with a touch of natural pride, though his subsequent contrition for this unclerical life is not passed over. The foolish vanity of his early youth and his unsullied purity are mentioned in the same breath. His hasty retort to the king at Woodstock, his weakness in shrinking from contention which led to his fall at Clarendon, his rising spirit at the insults offered him at Northampton, the sinking of his courage from time to time, and his bursts of passionate feeling, are all recorded. Nay, even that last temptation to fly the night before the martyrdom is not passed over, though the final triumph of grace in his supernatural humility, meekness, and sweetness during his conversation with the knights in his room, and the calmness with which he goes to the Church where he knows death awaits him, are duly recorded.

These natural details, while they make us intimately acquainted with S. Thomas, show us the work of grace in his heart, and thus bring him down, as it were, to our own level. He does not stand before us, like S. Anselm and most other saints, at an unapproachable distance, but inspires us with personal affection like S. Philip Neri and S. Francis of Assisi.

Besides the foregoing lives there is a metrical one, which is valuable for its accuracy and completeness. It was written in French by Gamier, a monk of Pont S. Maxence, who came to England within two years of the martyrdom, collected the details of S. Thomas's family, birth, and history from his personal friends, and among others from his sister, the Abbess of Barking, and formed them into a romance in the style of the time, which was very popular in its day.

A rich mine of information also exists in the numerous letters which have been preserved. In the Vatican there are above five hundred written by himself and the principal persons with whom he was connected between 1163 and 1170. Many of these were deposited there by himself, and the rest were collected by Alan within a few years of the martyrdom. In the Bibliotheca Veterum Patrum are three hundred and three letters of John of Salisbury. In Corpus Christi College, Cambridge, there is a volume of letters of Herbert of Bosham; and in the Bodleian a very old MS. which contains Gilbert Foliot's letters.

S. Thomas's letters were first published by Lupus in 1682. Above forty years ago the Rev. Dr. Giles reprinted them and the letters of John of Salisbury and Gilbert Foliot, and also nineteen of the biographies, or such fragments of them as he could recover. Since 1878 a well-arranged collection of the whole, under the title of "Materials for the History of Thomas Becket," has been in course of publication by Canon Robertson, and since his death by Mr. Magnusson, with the authority of the Master of the Rolls.

The first editions of the present work were compiled from the biographies and letters of S. Thomas published by the Rev. Dr. Giles, the Rev. Richard Hurrell Froude, and the Rev. John Morris, S.J. The present edition has been carefully compared with the original lives and letters, and corrected with reference to both chronology and numerous details. The references are taken from the Master of the Rolls's edition, so far as it is yet published, and the rest from Dr. Giles's edition as specially indicated. The references to Gamier are taken from Hippeau's edition; those by Gervase, Diceto, and Bromton are from Twysden's edition, and those to Giraldus Cambrensis from Wharton's "Anglia Sacra."

BIOGRAPHICAL SKETCH OF MRS. HOPE.

THE subject of this memoir was the second daughter of John Williamson Fulton, Esq. (1769-1830), whose family had been settled for some generations in the neighbourhood of Lisburn, Co. Antrim. Her mother was Anne, widow of Capt. John Hunt, of the Bengal Army, and daughter and coheiress (with her sister, Eleanor Sophia, wife of Lachlan Mackintosh, Esq., of Raigmore), of Robert Robertson, a member of the family of Robertson of Inshes. Born in 1809, at Calcutta, where her father, like his father before him, was an eminent merchant, she was sent at an early age to the care of relatives at Lisburn, but completed her education, after her parents' return, at their London house, 4, Upper Harley Street. In the fortunes of the Irish party of that time Mr. Fulton took an active interest, and its members were ever welcome to his house, as were also the Highland families to whose acquaintance his wife's Scotch extraction opened ready access. To the entertainment of this brilliant society Miss Anne Fulton contributed her share as a finished pianist, a painter of no mean skill, and a well-read and intellectual companion. Doubtless, the friendship of such men as O'Connell, Lawless, and other leaders helped to develop in her that independence of thought and generous loyalty to what she believed right and truth, which won and kept for her through life the friendship of many whose opinions differed widely from her own. In 1831 Miss Fulton married Dr. James Hope, a young but already distinguished physician, of brilliant talents, unfailing energy, and deep religious feeling. Her whole powers and acquirements were devoted to literary, social, and charitable pursuits under his guidance, and to aiding, as an amanuensis and otherwise, in the publication of his works. These latter, with the important discoveries they announced, and the skill, attention, and tenderness displayed in his medical practice, rapidly increased his reputation and his fortune. In twelve years from Dr. Hope's first settling in London, as a young man of twenty-seven with only one friend, he had become Physician of St. George's Hospital, Fellow of the Royal Society and of the London College of Physicians, with an income of £4,000 per annum, and one of the most successful and distinguished physicians of the day. But the exertions involved had undermined his constitution, inducing pulmonary disease, and in 1841 Mrs. Hope was left a widow, with one son nine years old.

Her first care was to compose a memoir of her husband (Hatchard, 1842), which, for its lucid arrangement, facility of expression, and complete treatment of the subject, together with its intrinsic interest, attracted attention far outside medical circles, and ran rapidly through four editions.

She next devoted herself to the education of her son. In the autumn of 1842 she addressed to him a series of letters, which she has described as "an attempt to antedate the period at which self-education usually commenced," and to inspire "those motives of religious hope and duty, which alone are sufficiently powerful to stem the strong current of human corruption." Shortly afterwards the letters were published ("Hope on Self-Education," Hatchard, 1842), and went through two editions. Eleven years later, when she had become a Catholic, she remarked of this work that it had "one great defect," namely, the current assumption "that man, by his own efforts and by intellectual cultivation, can educate himself independently of the grace of God. I often think of this as being a branch of the tree of knowledge, by eating which the Devil promised to make our first parents' as Gods.'"

Shortly after this, evidences of the anxieties and labours of the preceding years appeared in a delicacy of the chest, which obliged Mrs. Hope to resort to Madeira, where she passed every winter from 1842 to 1850. During this period she continued to watch over and aid in the education of her son, whose own consumptive tendency kept him a good deal, off and on, in her company at Madeira. In addition to directing and accompanying his studies in history and English and foreign literature, she pursued actively her own. These became directed to Church history and doctrine owing to dissentions then rife in the Anglican congregation at Madeira. Hitherto, a deep sense of the paramount importance of religion, a reliance on constant prayer, and an endeavour to order all her actions according to the will of God had, indeed, been at once the principle and the consolation of her life, as of her husband's, but she had comparatively little studied the constitution, progress, and dogmatic theology of the Church. But now, circumstances brought also to her notice the Oxford movement, and to her society some of its choice spirits, and she recognised it as a duty to her son, no less than to herself, to explore to the best of her ability the new field of enquiry opened out to her. One who knew her well in 1848-9 has "a vivid recollection of her" at this period as "a woman, earnest, intellectual, helpful, and gentle, with one object in life—the welfare of her son."

By the year 1850 she had virtually completed a work of considerable magnitude and research on the first three centuries, which she called "Fall of the Roman Empire and Rise of the Christian Church," but it was not published, because of her gradually growing conviction that she might before long leave the Anglican Body. Three years later she remarked that she still expected to turn the work some day to account, because there seemed to be a growing demand for works of religious history, but that she should have to re- write it "in a much larger spirit, *i.e.*, with reference to the whole theology and history of the Church, and not so exclusively in reference to those points which are connected with the Protestant controversy."

The doubts above referred to as to continued membership with the Anglican Communion appear to have grown up out of her long studies rather than through the representations or influence of any particular individual. Her historical investigations having led her to regard the See of Rome as the one source of jurisdiction, the sacraments and orders of any communion, such as the Anglican, separated therefrom, could possess at best but doubtful validity. In 1851 the Rev. Frederick

Hathaway, then Incumbent of Shadwell, near Leeds, and twenty-five other Anglican clergymen appealed to Rome for a formal decision on this point, and after some delay were referred in reply, through the Bishop of Southwark, to previous Papal condemnations of Anglican Orders and Sacraments. On learning this fact, submission appeared to Mrs. Hope the only course, and accordingly she was received into the Church by Father Wells, of the London Oratory, on November 21st, 1851, at the Oratory in King William Street. On the Sunday following she was confirmed by Cardinal Wiseman, and received her first Communion at his house in Golden Square. Thus ended, calmly and without excitement, a period of eighteen months spent in prayer, self-humiliation, and penance with the one purpose of finding the truth, and which brought its reward in the undoubted conviction of the imperative necessity of the step she took.

In this separation from the Church of England and all thereby implied, she was spared to a very great extent the alienation of family and friends, which too often accompanies such sacrifices for conscience' sake. Her closest friends, she soon afterwards wrote, had addressed her "in such terms of unchanging love and regard that I feel their love may be a snare to me." Practically, however, her life became henceforward more solitary. For the occasion of her reception she came up from Oxford, where (and at Littlemore) she had been residing, to the Community of the Filles de Marie, at 4, Vicarage Place, Kensington, and after revisiting Oxford to wind up her affairs and spend Christmas with her son, she returned to Kensington, and passed there nearly the whole of 1852. Her conversion brought her to the notice of Cardinal Wiseman, Dr. Grant, Bishop of Southwark, Mr. Oakeley, and others of less note; but what she most valued was the friendship of Mr. W. G. Ward and his wife, which became a pleasure and resource in many succeeding years. She also made the acquaintance of Father John B. Dalgairns, of the Oratory, who ere long became her spiritual director and principal literary adviser. Still, the position was one of profound isolation, old sympathies and currents of thought arrested, new ones not yet formed, the solitude of a religious House unbroken except by an occasional brief visit from the Superior, her only recorded pleasure the Chapel. To one who for long had been in delicate health, the events of the past year had naturally been an especially severe strain, and resulted in the recrudescence of old maladies and the appearance of new. But a heavier trial still supervened in the departure for India, on February 8th, 1853, of the son who had been the care, as well as the companion, of so many years, and in whom all her earthly thoughts and occupations had centred. "God has separated us that we may both love Him more," was her comment respecting it. On the following day she herself sailed for Madeira, in the hope that rest and climate might restore her shattered nerves and constitution.

She now endeavoured, according to the recommendation of S. Francis de Sales, to put away thoughts of regret, not crushing or struggling against them, but passing on gently to think of other things. Promptly she turned her attention to the religious education of the Portuguese, which had long been suffering from the effects of the political troubles, the decay of religion, and the advance of infidelity which had marked the nineteenth century in the Peninsula. A school was soon established at her expense, in which religion was made the first requisite, though reading and writing were not neglected. The numbers were limited, by her resources, to sixty children, but it became at once a great success, and continued for many years. A few weeks later she also opened a second smaller school at one of the country villages near Funchal, where she resided. Besides this, she completed and sent off to Father Dalgairns the MS. of her first work as a Catholic, "The Acts of the Early Martyrs," which she had begun in the preceding year on understanding that a light popular account of the subject would be useful to the Oratorian Schools of Our Lady's Compassion. Finally, she took in hand the translation of the life of Doña Marina d'Escobar from the Spanish, a very rare book lent her by some Capuchin nuns in Madeira, for a copy or translation of which F. Faber had advertised in the preceding year. At this period she rose at 5 a.m., was at Mass by 6 a.m., and retired to rest at 9 or 9.30 p.m. After a pleasant interlude of three summer months in England, passed between King William Street, Edgbaston, and the hospitable roof of the Wards, at Old Hall Place, she returned to Madeira, to her schools and literary pursuits, added to which were the care of an invalid friend who accompanied her, and the arduous duty of relieving the sufferings of the poor around her during a severe famine which visited the island.

The middle of 1854 saw her on her way to England, having bid adieu for ever to Madeira, which may be said to have done its work, and so transformed the tendency of her ailments that henceforward she suffered less in a cold than in a warm climate. For upwards of two years she was now settled at Edgbaston, in order to have the advantage of the direction of Father Dalgairns, then attached to the Birmingham Oratory. Numerous proposals of literary work soon presented themselves. Through Father Hutchison, of the Brompton Oratory, came a suggestion from Lady Arundel and Surrey that she should write a series of Old Testament stories, steeped in Biblical phraseology and lore, and as attractive to children as Robinson Crusoe or Miss Edgeworth's tales. This idea, though admirable itself, seemed to her beyond her power owing to her insufficient knowledge, as she thought, either of the Bible or of dogmatic and mystical theology. Later on Father Hutchison suggested that she should write a Church History down to the present time, in two volumes. She pointed out the dryness of such a bare abridgment, and suggested a history of Europe from the Church point of view, but broken up into several separate works for different countries or periods, to be worked out by different writers under some very competent editor. Acceding to this, he pressed her to undertake the whole, under the editorship of Mr. Allies, then about to be Professor of History at the Catholic University. She declined so formidable an engagement, which would have taken ten or twelve years, but in her "Conversion of the Teutonic Race," published eighteen years later, may be recognised the realisation of her idea so far as related to the Franks, English, and Germans. Eventually, in June,

1855, she undertook, at the instance of F. Dalgairns, to write a short life of S. Philip Neri, suited to the frequenters of the Oratories in London and Birmingham. It was not to be very learned, because F. Dalgairns had a much larger work on hand, but she felt none the less that it would be a work of time, because leisurely meditation, calm thought, and prayer were essential to realise and develop the many deep spiritual truths which must be set forth.

Meanwhile, in February of the same year, appeared at last her "Acts of the Early Martyrs." Father Faber styled it "very fascinating"; the Catholic reviews spoke of it in warm terms, but the fact of the present issue of a seventh edition constitutes, perhaps, its best testimonial. As both this work and her subsequent ones are remarkable for the childlike faith in which miracles are woven by hundreds into the tale, it may be interesting to give here, in a somewhat condensed form, an answer she once made to a friendly critic on this score:—

"Though I do not pledge myself to the historical accuracy of every miraculous fact which I have narrated, yet I do believe them to be true *in the main*. Further, I cannot agree that the miracles were 'objectless,' nor do I think that the apparent object of a miracle can be used in any way as a test of its truth, since it does not belong to weak ignorant creatures like ourselves to judge whether, in common phraseology, it is worth God's while to act in a certain way. Following this style of argument, many have rejected the facts of the Incarnation and Atonement, and the doctrine of a particular Providence. Finally, I do mention them as common events, because, notwithstanding their extraordinary character, they are only such as the analogy of Christianity would lead us to look for under similar circumstances. As to the historical evidence: some of the lives, *e.g.*, that of S. Cecilia, rest on good historical evidence, while others, *e.g.* that of S. Catharine, are not so undoubted in all their detail; for S. Catharine being, like S. George, one of the great saints of the Eastern Church, her life, like that of S. George, has been so worked up by contending heretical and schismatical bodies that the true details are difficult to ascertain. My reasons, then, for believing in miracles generally, and in these more particularly are:—First: Because the power of working miracles was one of the promises which our Lord made to his Church, and, therefore, no one has a right to disbelieve this promise more than any other. He not only gave this power to His apostles and first disciples, but He expressly said that it was one of the 'signs which should follow them that believe'—in other words, it was one of the signs of His true Church. In another place He declares the unlimited nature of the power which He committed to them, 'If you have faith, etc., you shall say to this mountain "Remove from hence hither, and it shall remove; and nothing shall be impossible to you" ' (Matt. 17-19). This first reason ought to be conclusive. My second reason, however, is that it is not *reasonable* to reject the concurrent testimony of all classes of persons of this period, whether Christian or Pagan. The former speak of the working of miracles as quite common, while the latter persecuted the Christians for working them by magic, as they said. My third reason is that there is no doubt magic was very common in those days, and one can scarcely suppose that our Lord would have allowed the servants of the Devil to possess a preternatural power which he withheld from his own children, to whom he had actually promised it; not to say that what the Devil does or is allowed to do is generally a counterfeit of our Lord's works and of the graces which He bestows on His Church. My fourth reason is the extraordinary work which was performed by the Church during the first three centuries in the conversion of the Roman Empire. One of the early writers says that to have converted the whole world without miracles would have been the greatest miracle of all. This reason shows that the miracles were not objectless. Conversions are constantly connected with the miracles. The miracles, too, must have had a great effect in giving courage to the martyrs, and in preserving many a coward soul from apostasy. These four reasons are those upon which I more especially rest my belief in the miracles which I have narrated. But there is a fifth reason which, like the first, applies to the working of miracles at all times up to the end of all things, namely, the essentially supernatural character of the Christian religion itself. It is founded on the supernatural fact of the Incarnation, and the supernatural element which is imparted to human nature by its union with the Divinity in the person of Jesus Christ pervades the whole religion in such a way that it may be called the very breath of life on which its existence depends. Not that all Christians have the power of working miracles. It belongs to the extraordinary class of gifts, and very few ever attain to the sanctity it involves. But this gift is only another and a higher manifestation of that supernatural power which dwells in all baptised persons who are in a state of grace, and which attests its working in us all by the common everyday answers to prayer. Miracles may be divided into two classes, those in which God directly interposes and confers extraordinary favours on the objects of his love, and those in which the miracle seems to flow from the saintliness of the person who works them or with whom they are connected. Most of the miracles in my book will come under the former class, but many, such as the death of S. Cecilia and the preservation of S. Agnes, belong to the latter, and these will be seen to have even higher objects than the others, since the purifying and elevating to higher states of virtue those who are Christ's children may be deemed superior to the first conversion of sinners."

The period of residence at Edgbaston, though full of mental activity and marked by a growing yearning for definite separation from the world, was also one of growing nervous debility and disease. At length the imperative necessity for change and repose obliged her, in October 1856, to break up her home at Edgbaston and take refuge at the house of "Les Dames du S. Coeur de Marie," Rue de la Santé, No. 29, Paris, a religious community which admitted a few lady boarders. Here she was enjoined by her Confessor, Père Chervaux, S.J., to lay aside all thoughts of a religious vocation until the attacks of nervous fever, to which she had for the past eighteen months been liable, had passed away, and in no case to contemplate more than entering some third order. Here, suffering many vicissitudes of recovery and relapse, unable to put forth the already completed Life of S. Philip, and prohibited from all continued intellectual effort, but still gradually improving, she remained until June 1857, when she had the joy of a visit from her son, who returned from India on leave. This, unfortunately, proved all too brief, as the outbreak of the Mutiny obliged him to return after a stay of only three months.

On his departure Mrs. Hope once more took up her abode with the Filles de Marie at Kensington. Unfortunately, the improvement in her health proved of brief duration. In April, 1858, her increasing debility culminated in a seizure which had many symptoms of paralysis, but was eventually pronounced to be a peculiar affection of the nerves of the spine, which, with other maladies acting and re-acting on each other, practically confined her to the sofa for the remaining twenty-nine years of her life. Carriage motion was always most prejudicial, but under favourable circumstances she sat out in the open-air, or could even walk very short distances.

In the course of 1859 she was at length able to bring out the Life of S. Philip, but under considerable disadvantages. The life was cast in chronological order on the plan of that of Gallonio, and thus differed from the narrative by Bacci of S. Philip's virtues, gifts, and miracles, of which an English version by F. Faber was already published. Originally she had felt great difficulties in the task, and had taken proportionate pains to overcome them. In 1855 she wrote: "Several points in S. Philip's character and vocation have been puzzling me sadly. I cannot tell you how difficult it is to write his life. My way of writing a biography is to put myself in imagination in the place of my hero. But how can I put myself into the place of a saint, whom a modern historian has called Thaumaturgus?" In 1856 the Life was completed, but the medical restrictions upon her working obliged her to put the manuscript aside. Now, when she sent it to the publisher, he objected to its dimensions as inconvenient, and required it to be either lengthened by seventy pages or reduced by fifty. Unequal to the mental effort involved in the former alternative, she chose the latter, with deep regrets at parting with what had cost her so much thought and prayer. Still the reception of the book was extremely favourable.

At the close of 1859 the Filles de Marie were unable to accommodate her, and she passed some time between Mayfair, Torquay, and other places. By the middle of 1861 the fresh air and soothing climate of Torquay were proved to suit her better than any other, and she fixed her residence there permanently, relinquishing, to her deep regret, the advantages of the spiritual direction, and the personal literary counsel, of Father Dalgairns. Here she was once more able to secure the comfort of a house of her own, of which the vicissitudes of her health had deprived her since leaving Madeira. Perhaps its chief advantage in her eyes was that she was able to have a private chapel and Mass weekly, or oftener if, as sometimes happened, some priest was her guest. But she also soon gathered round her a pleasant circle of friends, some of them the Catholic clergy and laity of the locality, among whom may be named Canons Agar and Brownlow, others her relatives or visitors from London.

The next fourteen years, excepting one break in 1864-6, were passed at Torquay, and devoted, as far as health allowed, to the studies which resulted in her next two publications. The first of these, the Life of S. Thomas a Becket, appeared in 1868, and placed popularly before the public the results of deep research, especially as regards the causes of the martyrdom. The second, the "Conversion of the Teutonic Race," or as she afterwards preferred to style it, "The Apostles of Europe," came out in two volumes in 1872. Its materials were almost entirely in German and Latin, and it has been styled "the greatest of Mrs. Hope's works, solid history and romance in one." The general character of the Teutonic nations, their proper place in the Aryan family, and their relations towards Christianity and Roman Paganism, as well as towards Rome and the world in general, together with the circumstances of the conversion of the English, and its contrast with that of the Franks, were here grasped with clearness and insight, and under the latest lights of modern criticism effectively portrayed. The book thus filled up a blank to general as well as Catholic readers. The *Dublin Review* termed it "a growth of individual intellectual labour, fed from original sources, and fused by the polish of a discerning and cultivated mind." Even the *Saturday Review* was specially complimentary, and while deeming her acceptance of the miraculous in hagiography too free—a point upon which her defence has already been quoted above—says that "as long as she is without this magic circle, Mrs. Hope uses her faculties, and uses them to good purpose. She has gone to the right sources, and she has used the right method, on many of those branches of knowledge, the scientific treatment of which has been reserved for our own day."

The break in residence at Torquay, already alluded to, was caused by the return of Mrs. Hope's son from India on three years' furlough (1863-6), and her sojourn with him for two years in London. Designed primarily for his advantage, this change was the more welcome in that it enabled her to renew personal intercourse with Father Dalgairns and a large circle of friends who had long been out of reach, and to draw more freely upon the centres of modern thought. It may here be interesting to mention that Mrs. Hope's conversion never caused any break in harmony with her son, though he remained a member of the Anglican Church. Until his departure for India in 1853, she still followed his studies with sympathy and aid, and subsequently she maintained to the last a voluminous correspondence with him, which is remarkable no less for keen appreciation and deep study of the great problems of Indian and English politics, which she habitually discussed, than for earnest insistence on the moral and religious aspects of life. Although her severance from him for lengthened periods was, perhaps, the severest trial of her life, she always insisted on his completing the service to which God had called him, but the three years' furlough of 1863-6, together with briefer visits to England in 1872, 1878, and 1880-1, enabled the mother and son to keep touch with each other in advancing years and changing circumstances, and imparted to her letters a freshness of knowledge and sympathy which might otherwise have been unattainable.

The pleasant task of describing the Conversion of the Teutonic Race discharged, Mrs. Hope was induced by Dr. W. G. Ward to become a contributor to the *Dublin Review*, and between 1872 and 1879 above thirty notices and articles are from her pen. Among the latter may be mentioned those on "Jervis on the Church of France" and "On the Jansenistic and Gallican Movements," Ranke's and Green's Histories of England, Simon de Montfort, and Mr. Froude's attack on S. Thomas à Becket. Her being selected to make the Catholic defence in the last case may be deemed a special compliment.

At the close of 1875 she removed from S. Mary's Lodge, in the centre of Torquay, to the Hermitage, a villa in the more bracing suburb of S. Mary Church, having good grounds situated between the parish churchyard and the Dominican Convent and Church of Our Lady and S. Denis. She had a little door opened in the garden wall, and was thus able to walk across to the church almost every Sunday. She took great interest in her garden, and was able to walk in it at times, and to sit out in the summer. The priest, Canon Brownlow, had known her for some years, and took great interest in her literary work. He used to hear her confession at her house, as it was too great an effort for her to walk to the church twice in the week, and then she went to the early Mass and Holy Communion on Sundays and holidays. For the last two or three years of her life she was unable to go out so far, and used to receive Holy Communion at home. For many years she had been accustomed to say the Divine Office every day.

In 1878 appeared her last published work, "Franciscan Martyrs in England," which was compiled from original sources, and designed to supply, as regards the Franciscans, a record of the first burst of the storm of persecution in England, which had been hitherto comparatively neglected in favour of that of the second persecution under Elizabeth. Her remaining years were passed in further researches along familiar and unfrequented paths, for which her mental powers, no less than her familiarity with the Latin, French, Italian, Spanish, and Portuguese languages, rendered her specially qualified. Of these researches her notebook of works taken out from the London Library bears striking evidence, but only the revised Life of S. Thomas now published, and a few disconnected literary fragments remain.

It may not be inappropriate here to insert the following remarks by Canon Brownlow:—"My recollections of Mrs. James Hope extend from 1863 until the time of her death in 1887. For the last twenty years of her life I knew her well, and from the time she came to live at the Hermitage I knew her intimately. What struck me most in my first acquaintance with her was the calm, even, correct manner in which she expressed herself. It was said of her with truth that she 'talked like a book.' She rarely had to correct herself. Historical subjects were those in which she took most interest; and in forming her judgment, and, especially if she intended writing for the Press, she always verified her references with scrupulous care. Even in works intended for the young, such as 'The Early Martyrs,' she would not allow a new edition to be published without making corrections wherever fresh discoveries had brought to light facts which suggested a modification of what she had written before. She had a wonderful power of generalising and forming an accurate judgment of individuals and periods from a mass of apparently contradictory evidence, making due, but not exaggerated allowance for the motives and prejudices of each witness as he gave in his testimony. She had strong sympathies and antipathies, both religious and political; but she was very rarely unjust, even to those whom she disliked. She had a strong sense of justice, and would put herself to great inconvenience to resist an injustice; and if she thought she had done anyone an injustice she would never rest till she had made reparation. In later years she found her hand could no longer hold the pen easily, and she had to employ an amanuensis. But her power of criticism and accuracy of thought remained unimpaired almost to the last. On the day she died, when she could no longer speak plainly, she made me understand that she wished me to send to the Prior of the

Carthusian Monastery at Parkminster some notes that she only finished the day before, collating his copy of 'Maurice Chauncey's Narrative' with her own, which was a better edition. Sometimes she would say that she thought her time for writing had come to an end. She regarded it simply as a talent given her by God, which she was to use for his glory as long as she could. It was especially in deference to Father Dalgairns that she began to write her Catholic publications; but though his death in 1876 was one of the greatest trials she had, she did not think it right to lay aside her pen. I think it was her constant spirit of prayer that enabled her to face all sorts of historical and intellectual difficulties without prejudice to her own faith and piety, and to be of great service to those who needed her sympathy and advice. Her reading was very miscellaneous, and in a great measure guided by what she thought would be interesting to her son in India. She had a marvellous memory for personal domestic history, and could tell all about the ancestors and collateral branches of every family of her acquaintance. Frugal and even austere in the simplicity of her life, she was most generous in her charities. Young people were especially attracted to her by her ready sympathy and firm and wise counsel. Though her life was entirely spent on the sofa, yet she knew enough of society to be able to give valuable advice to those in the midst of the world. Her conversational powers made her very attractive to people of literary tastes. The late Archbishop Ullathorne never came to S. Mary Church without visiting her, and many other distinguished ecclesiastics valued her friendship. At all times her affection for the Fathers of the Oratory remained constant. Whether they came from Edgbaston or London, the sons of S. Philip were equally welcome."

In the winter of 1884 she had a severe attack of bronchitis, which warned her that she must be very careful to avoid cold. It is characteristic of her keen interest in passing events, that she was for several days much worse during this illness from having been incautiously informed of the death of General Gordon and the fall of Kartoum. After this she continued much the same in health, although with increasing age her strength gradually failed, and she had less power to rally from any slight indisposition. She had made all arrangements for her death long beforehand, made her will, written out directions about her funeral, at which she particularly requested that no flowers should be used, and was very anxious that the Catholic service should be used at her burial beside her husband in Highgate Cemetery.

Her life went on much as usual until the second week in February, 1887. On the Monday she received Holy Communion as usual, but the priest noticed that when he said 'Ecce Agnus Dei,' she gave a little start. She told him some days afterwards that it seemed as though a voice said to her, 'It may be a long time before you receive Holy Communion again,' and she disposed herself as though it were her Viaticum. On the Wednesday she seemed to have caught a cold, and on Friday morning she sent for Canon Brownlow, and said, "I want to make my confession as if I were at the point of death." Still, she seemed far from being so ill as she had been before. On the Saturday morning her medical attendant said she was in a very critical state, and she received the Last Sacraments with great calmness and devotion, making the responses herself. In the afternoon she received the Last Blessing, and, clothed in the Carmelite habit which she had prepared for her shroud, while the commendatory prayers were sounding in her ears, she gave up her soul to God, at about five o'clock on Saturday, February 12th, 1887.

A solemn Requiem was sung for her soul at S. Mary Church, and her body was then taken by her niece, Miss Mackintosh, and Canon Brownlow, to the Oratory at Brompton, where the fathers kindly allowed it to remain all night in the church that she loved so well. The next morning, after Mass, Father Antrobus, Canon Brownlow, and some of her relations followed her to the cemetery, where she rests, after her forty-six years of widowhood, beside the remains of her husband.

She had looked forward with pleasure to the hope of soon again seeing her son, Sir Theodore C. Hope, K.C.S.I, C.I.E., whose career as Public

Works Member of the Governor-General's Council she had followed with the keenest interest, and who was about to return home for good. But Providence ordered it otherwise, and afforded her another opportunity of submission to the holy will of God.

LIFE

OF

S. THOMAS OF CANTERBURY.

CHAPTER I. ENGLISH MARTYRS—THE NORMAN CONQUEST.

THE continuous succession of martyrs in the Catholic Church is at once her glory and a proof of her union with Jesus. For since love is the one great commandment of the Gospel, and there is no greater love than that a man shall lay down his life for his friends, it is only reasonable to expect that He who laid down His life on Calvary for those whom He loved, should ever be inspiring the souls in whom He dwells with the same spirit of love, which shall make them willing to lay down their lives for Him. Accordingly, in every age and every clime the Church has brought forth martyrs, even from S. Stephen, who first trod in his Lord's blood-stained footsteps, down to that noble band of bishops, priests, and laymen, nuns, mothers, and young girls, who in China and other Eastern lands at the present day joyfully lay down their lives for love of Him.

To this army of white-robed martyrs, England has sent her full quota; but she is distinguished from all other Christian nations, not so much by the number of her martyrdoms, as by the length of time over which they have extended, embracing nearly fourteen centuries, from S. Alban, who was beheaded at Verulam A.D. 303, down to Dr. Oliver Plunket, Archbishop of Armagh who was hanged at Tyburn A.D. 1681.

In the bright roll of English martyrs the name of S. Thomas of Canterbury stands out preeminent. Our Lord gave to His apostles, as their bond of union with Himself, the threefold cord of faith, morals, and government, all equally a part of the divine deposit, and all equally necessary to the preservation of Christian Unity. For experience has shown that, while the threefold cord cannot be broken, no sooner is any one of the cords severed, than the other two collapse, and the bond of union is lost. The Church, therefore, has always been equally careful for the preservation of each, and each has had its martyrs. S. Thomas was a martyr more immediately for the apostolic government; but he openly declared that on it depended the due transmission of the supernatural powers which Christ has left to His Church, and, consequently, the preservation, through grace, of both faith and morals in Christian unity. His memory inspires a peculiar feeling of mournful regret, because his blood was shed in order to retain for the English Church this priceless inheritance, which has since been lost to it by his faithless and cowardly successors.

Besides the higher interest which attaches to S. Thomas as a martyr for the love of his Lord, a secondary interest may be found in his life from its connection with two critical periods of English history. For, in the first place, his contest with Henry Plantagenet may be regarded as the first act in the great national struggle to throw off the cruel tyranny of the Norman conquerors; and, in the second place, the pretensions which Henry Tudor advanced with such fatal success in the sixteenth century, were only the counterpart of those which Henry Plantagenet had failed to wring from S. Thomas in the twelfth.

In order to understand more clearly the cause for which S. Thomas died, it will be desirable to cast a glance over the history of the age immediately preceding him, as well as that in which he lived.

The Saxon monarch's of England are remarkable for the attention they gave to legislation and the interior organization of their dominions. They seem to have had the same reverence for long-established custom and right which characterizes the modern Englishman; for instead of aspiring to initiate new laws, they were satisfied with collecting in a written form and enforcing those of their predecessors—of Ethelbert, the first Christian king; of Offa, king of Mercia; of Ina, king of Wessex; and of Alfred. The last of the Saxon codes was drawn up by S. Edward the Confessor, and hence his name has been associated with national rights which, in fact, date from above four centuries earlier. In this code the rights of each individual, "high or low, laic or cleric, churl or earl, who they were and what they were, and their relations and duties towards each other and towards the king," all were distinctly marked. The extent and limits of the sovereign's power were, moreover, expressed in the coronation oath, which in its latest form was drawn up by S. Dunstan. Hence it came to pass, that at that time in no other country in Europe were the liberties both of the nation and the Church so clearly denned and so carefully guarded as in England.

Thus had the English nation been trained for centuries in the appreciation of law and right, of constitutional duties and liberties, when suddenly, in a single day, they found themselves transferred to the despotic sway of the ruthless Normans. No words can adequately express the extent of this calamity, for it would be difficult to find in the pages of history a revolution more complete, or fraught with more utter misery to the conquered race.

The Normans were the last of the northern barbarians who overran the more civilized countries of Europe. They had been easily induced to receive the Christian faith, but they long retained the spirit of their Pagan ancestors. They were remarkable for personal courage and military discipline, which made them almost invincible; but they were scarcely less distinguished, even in those rude times, by their licentiousness, rapacity, vindictiveness and cruelty. William, their duke and England's conqueror, was well fitted by his talents to be their ruler. He was their superior in some respects, for his life was not stained by drunkenness and licentiousness; he did not give way to fierce bursts of rage for every trifle, or take pleasure in cruelty for its own sake; and he could perceive and acknowledge the rights of others. But his master passion was the love of power, and his other passions seemed to be conquered and restrained only to give it freer scope. When his will was crossed, no scruple of conscience, no thought of solemn oaths, of justice, or the rights of others, no shrinking from cruelty, arose to check him; and fire and sword, cruel mutilations, life-long imprisonment, the axe, the halter, or the stake, were employed to enforce submission, and all the more unrelentingly because they were calmly and deliberately adopted.

Though William had conquered England by his sword, he professed to hold it as the heir of S. Edward the Confessor. Accordingly, at his coronation he took the oath usually taken by Anglo-Saxon kings, swearing on the Gospels that he would defend the Holy Church, forbid all rapine, and govern according to law. A code of laws still exists bearing the title, "Les leis et les custumes que li Reis William granted al pople de Engleterre apres la cunquest de la terre: iceles meimes que li Reis Edward sun cusin tint devant lui."

But notwithstanding this solemn oath, a writer of that day tells us that "all things divine and human were governed according to William's absolute will and pleasure, all were subservient to his caprice and commands." He would not allow any of his barons or tenants to be punished for their crimes, as the law directed, without his express permission; and hence his Norman followers committed the greatest outrages with impunity. The Saxon nobles, too, were forced to give their beautiful, gentle daughters, and the widows of their murdered relatives, in marriage to the ruffians and low-born adventurers who had flocked to William's standard. Every Norman seized what pleased him, and so great was the pillage, that when the Conqueror and his army returned in triumph to Normandy, his Norman subjects gazed in wonder at the treasures he had won, and exclaimed that England might be called another Araby for gold, and the very granary of Ceres for fertility, since their duke had brought thence more wealth than could be found in thrice the extent of land elsewhere.

As for the lands which he had promised that all the freemen should "hold in peace and quietness," he divided the English into two classes, namely, those who, having borne arms against him, were to be completely dispossessed, and those who, having been loyal to him, were to be allowed to keep a small portion of their estates, his rule appearing to be, that the higher the rank of the owner the less mercy was to be shown him. Thus, before many years had elapsed, the whole race of English earls and greater thanes had disappeared, and almost the whole soil of England belonged to the conquerors.

Besides these spoliations, William marked out a district in Hampshire, full fifty miles in circuit, dotted with sixty churches, each with a village clustering round it, and this he appropriated for his own hunting-ground. The poor villagers were driven off, the churches and houses were levelled with the ground, and the whole tract was turned into a forest and given up to the wild animals which were necessary for the pastime of which he and his race were passionately fond.

But his cruelty in war surpassed all his other acts, and all that had ever before been known. To prevent the English being helped by the Danes, he laid waste the eastern coast of England and converted it into a desert many miles in width. He also laid waste, in the depth of winter, the country north of the Humber, burning the forests, the fruit-trees, and standing crops, killing all the cattle, levelling the houses to the ground, and driving the wretched inhabitants before him. For nine years the whole tract between York and Durham was a desert, and even twenty years later many fertile lands remained untilled.

The clergy fared even worse than the laity. The monasteries were robbed; Church lands were seized; heavy taxes were imposed; military service was required of the bishops; on one pretence or other, within two years all the English bishops and abbots, except S. Wulfstan, Bishop of Worcester, were removed, and for fifty years after no Englishman rose to any ecclesiastical dignity. These sacrilegious acts, however, did not touch the Church's life. But they did not satisfy William's ambition. He was resolved to cut off the English Church from the great catholic body, to constitute himself her supreme head and governor, and thus to bring her into complete subjection to his will. With this view he would not allow a Pope to be recognized, or an appeal to the Pope's authority to be made, or a papal bull to be received or obeyed, without his permission being previously given. And within the realm, no bishop or abbot was to be elected without his sanction; nor were the bishops to make laws for the Church, or to reform public morals, or to censure and excommunicate great offenders, or to give judgment in the ecclesiastical courts, except with his leave. In fact, he resolved to rob the Church of her supernatural treasures, and to turn her into a mere human institution, deriving its mission from a lay sovereign, and exercising its high office of binding and loosing sinners, dispensing the sacraments, and teaching Christian faith and morals, in obedience to his will alone.

The Norman barons and their retainers naturally followed the example of their duke, so that England was overrun with the victims of their violence and cruelty. Wretched objects, maimed of hand, or foot, or nose, or ears, or blind of one or both eyes, were met on every side. Crowds of nobles and yeomen, with delicate women and children, took refuge in the wildest solitudes, and lived as outlaws. Unburied corpses were seen in all directions, and through the land there rang the cry, "Never had England such sorrow and distress. The rich men moaned, and the poor men groaned, but he was so hard that he recked not the hatred of them all."

So terrible was the general suffering that the conquerors even were appalled at their own crimes. Some threw up their blood-stained wealth, and, returning to Normandy, entered religious houses and spent their lives in penance. Others tried to sanctify their ill-gotten possessions by building the fair abbeys and ministers which were for centuries the glory of England. Even the stern William had tits of remorse. For the last twelve years of his life his peace of mind was gone, and on his death-bed he exclaimed, in the agony of remorse, "Innumerable are the awful sins with which my soul is burdened since my blood-stained youth."

The Conqueror's successors followed in his footsteps. Each swore to maintain the ancient liberties of the nation and the Church, and each broke his pledge. Rufus surpassed the others of his race in tyranny and wickedness, so that, as a contemporary chronicle says, "Normans and Englishmen, clerks and laity, were in such misery that they loathed their very lives."

But his great object was the persecution of the Church. He hated religion, he prided himself on scoffing at God, and he used to say that he had pitted himself against prayer. His father had aspired to control the Church, but he was resolved to destroy her altogether. He would not allow any synod to be held, or any ecclesiastical censures to be published, or any cause to be tried in the ecclesiastical courts. Whenever a bishop or abbot died, the king's commissioners took possession of the bishop's palace or the abbey, turned out the clerics or monks, seized every valuable and all the manors, racked the tenants, put a stop to the usual alms and hospitality, and then kept the bishopric or abbey vacant; or if it were filled, it was put up to sale and given to the highest bidder, without the least reference to moral character. William Rufus thus kept the Archbishopric of Canterbury vacant for four years; and when at last, being supposed to be dying, he was induced to appoint S. Anslem to the see, he refused for two years more to let him receive from the Pope the pallium, without which his mission was invalid; and finally he banished him the kingdom.

Though this tyranny was directed against the clergy, it fell even more heavily on the laity. The poor, the sick, and the afflicted, were deprived of their usual alms and consolation; the schools were closed; the guilds and trade associations were broken up, for in that age religion was interwoven with all the ordinary affairs of life. Besides all this, when the Church was not allowed to censure and excommunicate open sinners, and when all causes were taken out of the ecclesiastical courts, where alone justice could be obtained, and were transferred to the king's courts, where gold or favour influenced the judgments, all check on wickedness was removed; for if a man was rich or powerful, or in favour with the king or the barons, he could commit murder or robbery or any other crime, without fear of punishment.

Henry Beauclerc, Stephen and Henry Plantagenet, all followed the Conqueror's example. They swore that the Church and the nation should enjoy all their ancient liberties, and the charters which they signed to that effect may still be seen; but, notwithstanding, they governed according to their own will. Thus time passed on, and as king after king mounted the throne, precedents of tyranny were formed. The royal customs began to be spoken of as if they were just rights; each king insisted on exercising the same power as his predecessors had done; and thus the old Saxon liberties, though clearly defined in written laws and ratified by charters, were in danger of being superseded by the innovations of these Norman tyrants.

In this terrible emergency, when the spirit of the nation was so crushed down by suffering that none dared to resist the oppressors, the Church came to the rescue. Soon after the Norman Conquest S. Gregory VII. was called to fill the Chair of S. Peter. His pontificate was one long struggle against the pretensions and usurpations of the Emperor Henry IV.; but notwithstanding his own great trials and critical position, the loud wailing cry from England touched his paternal heart, and he both wrote letters of remonstrance to William, and sent his legates to check, and, if possible, remedy the grievous wrongs. S. Wulfstan, Bishop of Worcester, too, though threatened by William with removal from his see, ceased not his efforts to relieve the poor sufferers; and by his eloquence and the power of his sanctity he put a stop to the horrible traffic, which was carried on at Bristol by the sale of the Saxons as slaves. The Norman Archbishops of Canterbury also, animated by the love of God, stood up against their own countrymen on behalf of the Church's laws and of the flock entrusted to their pastoral care. S. Anselm incurred William Rufus's bitterest hatred by refusing to wring a large sum from his people, who, he said, were already impoverished by the royal exactions.

Both he and Archbishop Theobald suffered exile, as confessors of old had done, for this holy cause; while to S. Thomas was granted the privilege of laying down his life "for the name of Jesus and the defence of the Church."

CHAPTER II. BIRTH, PARENTAGE, AND EDUCATION.

S. THOMAS of Canterbury was born on the feast of S. Thomas the apostle, December 21st, 1117, in a house in Southwark, which stood on the site occupied till a few years ago by S. Thomas's Hospital, erected in his honour. He was the son of Gilbert Becket, a native of Tierrie in Normandy, and his wife Matilda. There is a pretty legend which says that S. Thomas's mother was a Saracen princess, the daughter of a Saracen emir, who had taken Gilbert captive on his way to the Holy Land; and when after a time Gilbert made his escape, the emir's beautiful daughter, who had fallen in love with him, ran away from home in pursuit of him. The only words she knew, of any language but her own, were "London" and "Becket," and these she repeated constantly till, falling in with some pilgrims returning to England, she was taken by them to the city where Gilbert lived. There she wandered through the streets repeating "Becket," till at length she met Gilbert's servant, Richard, who had been his companion in captivity; and when Richard recognised her he took her to his master, who, touched by her love and constancy, had her baptized, and then married her. This romantic tale, however, is not mentioned by the personal friends of S. Thomas, several of whom wrote his life, and therefore it can scarcely be considered true. On the contrary, his friends say that both his parents were natives of Normandy, who settled in London. S. Thomas, too, in his letters, says that his parents were citizens of London of the highest class. They were distinguished by both their birth and their wealth, and were not engaged in business, but lived on their own income. His father at one time filled the office of Sheriff, and, in common with all the citizens of the highest class at that time, had the title and rank of a Baron of the city.

The birth of saints has often been marked by circumstances foreshadowing their future greatness; and so it was with S. Thomas. Before he was born his mother dreamt that the river Thames flowed into her bosom. Another night she dreamt that as she was going into Canterbury Cathedral, to pray, her child prevented her entrance. Again it appeared to her that twelve very bright stars fell into her lap. And at another time she had a vision, in which it seemed that she was about to give birth to Canterbury Cathedral, in allusion, probably, to which, as soon as he was born, the nurse raising him up cried, "I have an archbishop in my arms." While he was still in the cradle, his mother dreamt that she was finding fault with the nurse for not having put a coverlet over the baby; and that the nurse answered, "Nay, my lady, he has a beautiful red silk one over him." "Show it me," answered the mother. Whereupon the nurse brought it and tried to unfold it, but she was not able to do so, and cried, "It is too large to be unfolded in this bedroom." "Come into the hall, and unfold it there," answered the mother. But it was too large to be unfolded in the hall. Then they went into the street, but still it was too large; and in amazement they went into "the great space of the open plain of Smithfield," but all in vain; for even Smithfield was too small for it, and a voice said to them that all England would not contain it.

S. Thomas owed much to his tender and pious mother. She was accustomed to weigh him from time to time, putting in the opposite scale bread, meat, clothes, and money for the poor; and, as the child grew heavier, she would increase her alms; and when she distributed them she would give them in our Blessed Lady's name, asking her in return to take her little son under her protection. In after-life S. Thomas used to say that from her he learnt to fear God, and to invoke lovingly Blessed Mary, the Mother of God, as the guide of his steps and the patroness of his life, and to place all his trust, after Christ, in her. From her, too, he inherited the tenderest compassion for the poor.

His love to the Virgin Mother was also increased by an occurrence which he himself related to Herbert de Bosham, one of his most intimate friends. While he was still a child he had a fever; and when he was recovering, it seemed to him that a lady, tall and beautiful, with a calm countenance, stood by his bedside, and, consoling him by a promise that he would get well, gave him two golden keys, saying at the same time, "Thomas, these are the keys of Paradise, of which thou art to have the charge."

His education was begun in one of the London schools in the neighbourhood of his father's house; but as soon as he was old enough he was removed to the care of Robert, Prior of Merton, of the order of Canons Regular, who was ever after his intimate friend and his confessor, and was present at his martyrdom. While he was at Merton, his father came one day to see him, and as the boy entered the room Gilbert fell at his feet, whereupon the Prior said indignantly, "Old man, are you mad? What are you doing? Your son ought to fall down at your feet, not you at his." But Gilbert, to whom his son's future sanctity had been revealed, said privately to the Prior, "Sir, I know what I am doing, for this boy will one day be great before the Lord."

As Gilbert was a Norman, his house was the resort of his countrymen, among whom were several persons of birth and position. One of these visitors was a knight, Richier de l'Egle, who was very fond of hunting and hawking, and used often to make S. Thomas the companion of his sports. One day when they were out hawking, they came to a footbridge across a mill-dam, at a place called Wade's Mill, between Ware and Old Hall Green. Richier, spurring his horse over the narrow path, reached the other side safely; and Thomas, who was daring and impetuous by nature, boldly followed, but his horse slipped, and both fell into the stream. The mill was at work, and the current ran strong. Still, the boy could easily have saved himself, had he not been eager to save also the falcon which had been on his wrist; and while trying to do so he was drawn almost under the mill-wheel, a cry for help was raised, the water was let off, the mill was stopped, and the miller, rushing out, rescued the boy, breathless and almost insensible. Another second and the Church in England would have lost her great champion and martyr.

When S. Thomas arrived at manhood, he went to Paris to finish his education. On his return home he applied himself to business, and filled the offices of clerk and accountant to the sheriffs of London.

When he was twenty-one years of age his mother died, and his father did not long survive her, leaving his family in straitened circumstances. S. Thomas now entered the service of a relative, Osbern Witdeniers, who was in high repute both among his fellow-citizens and at court. With him he lived three years, and in his service he acquired habits of business and a knowledge of the world which enabled him afterwards to manage the affairs of the State and the Church with such ability and success.

But it was not to the world that S. Thomas was called. A higher vocation awaited him; and as he toiled industriously at secular business the sweet lessons he had learned and the holy aspirations that had inflamed his ardent soul, when he dwelt in the Benedictine cloister at Merton, must often have come back to his memory. The Norman clergy who had frequented his father's house had been struck with his talents, and had often urged him to offer his services to Theobald, Archbishop of Canterbury. But S. Thomas's characteristic humility seems to have made him long hesitate to devote himself to the sacred office; and it was not till about A.D. 1142, when he was twenty-five years of age, that his scruples were overcome by a cleric called Baillehache, an intimate friend of his father's, who held a post under the Archbishop.

CHAPTER III. AT THEOBALD'S COURT.

ARCHBISHOP THEOBALD was at Harrow-on-the-Hill, then an archiepiscopal manor, when S. Thomas presented himself at his court. His first interview being deferred till the next day, he and his serving-man, Ralph of London, took up their quarters at the village hostelry. The tall, handsome figure of S. Thomas and his noble bearing, seem, in spite of his humble equipments, to have attracted attention; for the next morning his hostess told her husband she had dreamt that one of the new-comers had covered their parish church with his vestments. And the good man answered, "Perhaps it portends that one of them will some day be lord of this church and village."

That morning S. Thomas was introduced to the Archbishop. Theobald received him kindly, for he was a native of the same Norman village as Gilbert, and had known him well. Moreover, S. Thomas came to him well recommended, not only by Baillehache, but also by two brothers from Boulogne, Archdeacon Baldwin and Master Eustace, and by others of his household who had often partaken of Gilbert's hospitality. S. Thomas's natural gifts were well calculated to add force to these friendly encomiums. For we are told that "he was modest in speech, in person tall and elegant, easily led by good example, prudent beyond his years, combining the personal beauty of youth with the gravity of a more advanced age." Such was the force of his intellect, that he could answer questions of the greatest difficulty on subjects with which he had been previously unacquainted; and his memory was so strong, that what he had once learned he seldom found it difficult to remember and repeat, in this respect surpassing many who were more learned than himself.

In Catholic times the Archbishop of Canterbury was the head of the English Church, and had authority and power befitting his high position. His jurisdiction extended not only over all the bishops and clergy of the realm, but also over the laity in all matters regarding faith and morals. He held councils and enacted canons. All ecclesiastical affairs between his Church and the Holy Father, and between the Church and the State, passed through his hands. He was also Prior of the monastery of Christ Church, which was attached to his cathedral, and he had to govern that large community. In his palace there was a school for the encouragement of learning and education, and also a court of justice for the trial of all clerical causes and all infractions by the laity of the laws or rights of the Church. Moreover, he possessed many benefices, manors, fiefs, castles, and even towns and villages, the entire management of which devolved upon him. Thus his court was the resort of a host of persons of all classes, distinguished visitors and learned men from foreign countries, nobles and Church dignitaries, knights and clerics, monks, and students, tenants and suitors, besides a retinue of inferior dependents, and crowds of poor and infirm, who were daily fed, clothed, and tended by the princely charity of the Archbishop.

Such was the world into which S. Thomas was transplanted from the humble counting-house in the city. He soon perceived that though his previous desultory education had made him superior in general attainments to the other young clerics, he was greatly their inferior in learning. He at once set resolutely to work to remedy his deficiencies, applying himself especially to the study of canon and civil law; and before very long he had placed himself on a level with his associates. His zeal and fidelity were publicly praised by the Archbishop, while his modest and gentle manners, his pure life, and his great compassion for the poor, won him the approbation of all good men, and the friendship of many who remained faithful and devoted to him through life. Among the latter were King Stephen's brother Henry of Blois, Bishop of Winchester, the Archbishop's brother Walter, Archdeacon of Canterbury, and John of Salisbury, a priest of great reputation in Theobald's service, who became in after-years the confidential adviser and free-spoken monitor of S. Thomas.

But such evident superiority would naturally awaken the jealousy of inferior minds, and at this time began an enmity which unhappily lasted through the saint's life. There was in Theobald's service a cleric called Roger de Pont l'Evêque, who at their first meeting took a violent dislike to S. Thomas, and in derision called him Cleric Baillehache, in allusion to the person who had brought him to the Archbishop's court. Roger twice managed to have him sent away from the palace; but on both occasions he took refuge with his friend Walter, the Archdeacon, by whose intercession he was restored to favour. In 1147 Walter being made Bishop of Rochester, Roger succeeded him as Archdeacon of Canterbury; but by this time S. Thomas had gained for himself a position in Theobald's estimation, from which Roger's enmity could not dislodge him.

There were at that time several important questions pending in connection with the Church in England. One of these was as to the office of Pope's legate, which was then held by the Bishop of Winchester; but many difficulties arose from the legating authority being vested in a suffragan. Another question was as to the relative positions of the Archbishops of Canterbury and York. The Archbishop of Canterbury was Primate of all England, while the Archbishop of York had long borne the title of Primate of England. Hence disputes arose, and the Archbishop of. York even claimed the right to have his cross carried before him in the province of Canterbury. As these questions had to be referred to the Pope's decision, Theobald went to Rome in 1143, and S. Thomas was so fortunate as to be one of the retinue that accompanied him. But Rome was then in a troubled state; for the Romans were in rebellion, and as it so happened that three Popes in succession died within eighteen months, there was no settled government, and the affairs of England were not likely to receive much attention. It was not till Eugenius III., a Cistercian abbot, was elected Pope in 1145, that, through the assistance of S. Bernard, who took the part of Theobald against the prelates of York and Winchester, a decision in Theobald's favour was obtained. As Theobald had returned to England, the management of these affairs seems to have been intrusted to S. Thomas, and he would probably have thus been brought into personal communication with the great saint who was so powerful an advocate of his patron's cause.

But this was not the only business in which S. Thomas received lessons for his own future career. Stephen was a true Norman King, and tyrannized over the Church whenever his uncertain tenure of the throne allowed him to do so. When, in 1148, Pope Eugenius summoned a council to meet at Rheims, Stephen forbade the Archbishop of Canterbury to attend it. But Theobald knew well that in such matters his obedience was due to his spiritual superior, Christ's vicar on earth. He therefore managed to elude the guards whom Stephen had set to bar his passage, and appeared at the council, when the Pope received him with great honour, and publicly thanked him, "because," the Holy Father said, "he had come rather swimming than sailing." On this occasion, S. Thomas was again so fortunate as to be his companion. When Theobald came home at the close of the council, Stephen banished him the kingdom, and it was not till, with the Pope's sanction, he had placed England under an interdict that Stephen allowed him to return to his see.

There was another important matter in which S. Thomas took a prominent part. Peace had been concluded between Stephen and the Empress Matilda, with the stipulation that on Stephen's death Matilda's son, Henry Plantagenet, should succeed to the English throne. In course of time, however, Stephen wished to have his own son Eustace crowned as his successor; but Theobald refused to officiate at the coronation, and he was again banished the kingdom. At S. Thomas's suggestion he then referred the matter to the Pope, and sent S. Thomas to plead Henry's cause. The Cardinal-deacon of S. Angelo, knowing Henry's violent temper, took the part of Eustace, saying, "It is easier to hold a ram by the horns than a lion by the tail"; but, notwithstanding, the Pope forbade the coronation of Eustace. This decision in Henry's favour, we are told, was gained by "the subtle prudence and cleverness of Thomas, a cleric of London." It was about this time that Theobald allowed S. Thomas to go abroad for a year to study law at Bologna under the celebrated Gratian, and also at Auxerre.

Meanwhile S. Thomas's services had been rewarded by ecclesiastical preferment. He had been presented to the churches of S. Mary Littory, and Otford. He was also given a prebendal stall in S. Paul's Cathedral, and one at Lincoln besides several other prebends and churches; and in 1154, when Roger de Pont l'Evêque was consecrated Archbishop of York, he succeeded him as Archdeacon of Canterbury and Provost of Beverley. Thus, though only now ordained deacon, he possessed wealth and station which made him independent alike of both episcopal and royal favour. Still higher honours, however, awaited him, and to these he was soon after called.

CHAPTER IV. THE CHANCELLORSHIP.

HENRY PLANTAGENET ascended the English throne at the close of the year 1154. He inherited the passions of both his Norman and his Plantagenet ancestors, and his character caused grave anxiety to thoughtful men. The only chance of keeping him within bounds seemed to be to place near his person some wise adviser who should win his affections and influence his conduct. Henry, Bishop of Winchester, at once fixed on S. Thomas as the person best fitted for the task, and Theobald, after due consultation, recommended him to the young king as his chancellor. Henry was prepossessed in S. Thomas's favour by the success of his late mission and willingly gave him the chancellorship to Rome.

S. Thomas was thirty-eight years of age when, in 1155, he was raised to a dignity which, it was said, made him "second to the king in four kingdoms." He was very tall and handsome, with a large, quick eye, a slightly aquiline nose, and a calm, gentle countenance. His mind was at once subtle and powerful, his conversation was refined and sensitive; he had warm affections and sensitive feelings. There was in his character a genial spirit which drew men irresistibly to him, and in his actions a simplicity and loftiness which forced all to regard him as a superior.

Before three months had elapsed, a great improvement was visible in the state of England. During the civil wars, many foreign barons had been brought over by both parties, and these, as well as the English nobles, kept up large bands of soldiers. Many who had lost their castles or farms, had taken refuge in the forests, and roamed about living on plunder. The country was covered with forts and military camps; universal licence prevailed; and the general misery was very great. S. Thomas lost no time in forcing the foreign intruders to restore the land and castles to their owners; those who had been driven into the forests were enabled to return to their homes; marauding bands were broken up; the people resumed their peaceful avocations, and agriculture and trade quickly revived.

He also paid great attention to the administration of justice in the court over which he presided. No wrong that came to his knowledge was allowed to pass unredressed. The poor and oppressed found ready sympathy from him, while to the proud and tyrannical alone was he severe and unbending. He was also careful in the distribution of the large Church patronage which fell into his hands, bestowing it not by favour, but on deserving persons, and especially on poor clerics who had done good service.

But he felt that his best chance of doing good was through personal influence with the king and his nobles; and therefore, actuated by the highest motives, he united in a marvellous way the opposite characters of clerk and courtier, preserving the interior purity of the deacon, while he assumed the manners of the courtier, and spared no pains to win popularity. His natural taste for magnificence, and his love of sport, now helped his purpose, and were thus sanctified to the service of God. He kept hawks, horses, and dogs; he rode to the chase, or played chess with the nobles. Every day he invited many courtiers to his table; but as all who came unbidden were welcome, we are told that he ordered his hall to be daily strewed with fresh straw and hay in winter, and green boughs in summer, in order that the numerous knights who could not find room on the benches, might have clean seats on the floor, without injury to their beautiful shirts and valuable clothes. His table was adorned with vessels of gold and silver; the dishes and wines were of the finest quality; and the food was served with such profusion that crowds of poor were daily fed from his board.

His retinue was equally magnificent. Fifty-two clerics conducted the business of the chancery. A vast number of knights offered him homage, and entered his service. Many nobles, too, confided their sons to him; and when he had educated them, he would confer knighthood on them, and then either retain them in his own household, or send them home with honour to their parents.

All his actions were characterised by the same grand and generous spirit. When he was made chancellor, the king's palace in the Tower of London was dilapidated. He set so many men at work on the repairs that they were completed between Easter and Whitsuntide, which was then looked on as marvellously expeditious, and the king's treasury being at the time unable to meet the expense, he supplied the deficiency out of his own money. At another time ambassadors from the King of Norway having come to England, he sent to meet them, and took all their expenses on himself. Again, as the court had frequently to cross the Channel with the king, he caused three ships to be built and fitted up magnificently, and presented them as a gift to his royal master. As for himself, he would have six or even more vessels for his suite, in which all who wished to cross were given a free passage; and when he came to land he would pay the captains and sailors most handsomely. He treated all his dependants with the same princely liberality, providing carefully for their wants, never letting a day pass without making presents of horses, birds, clothes, plate, or money, and bestowing his gifts with such a grace that all the Latin world loved him and delighted in him. His popularity with the clergy, the nobles, the soldiers and the people, was unbounded. There was nothing they would not do at a single word from him, and such numbers flocked round him that the royal palace, was comparatively empty, and even the king sometimes was left almost alone.

He managed to gain an equal influence over the young king. Henry was quickly attracted by the wit and brilliant conversation of his chancellor, while the remarkable success of all he undertook won his confidence; and he soon became glad to leave all the business of the State in the hands of one on whose talents, devotion, and disinterestedness he could rely, and thus be more at liberty to give himself up to his favourite amusement of the chase. As he returned from the forest, he would often ride into the chancellor's hall, and sometimes, after drinking a cup of wine, would ride out again; but at other times he would jump over the table and sit down and eat with him. Occasionally, too, he would come to dinner, either for the pleasure of his society, or to see whether all that was said about the magnificent style of his living was true. When business was over, the king and the chancellor would amuse themselves like boys, and play many a prank together.

It happened that one very cold winter's day they rode through London, the king and the chancellor riding in front, and their attendants behind. The king saw a poor old man very thinly clad coming towards them, and said to the chancellor, "Do you see that poor old man? He is almost naked. Would it not be a famous alms to give him a thick warm cloak?" "A very good thought, and a royal one, too," answered the chancellor. Meanwhile the poor man came up, and Henry asked him if he would not like to have a good cloak. The old man, not knowing who they were, thought they were only joking. But the king, turning to the chancellor, said, "You shall have the merit of this great alms;" and laying hold of the beautiful scarlet and gray cloak which the chancellor wore, he tried to pull it off. But the chancellor resisted, and there was quite a scuffle, in which both were almost pulled off their saddles, on sight of which the attendants hastened up in astonishment to see what it could mean. Of course, the chancellor at last gave way, and the attendants laughed long and loud; but they did not neglect to offer their own cloaks to the chancellor, while the old man went away thanking God for the prize he had obtained.

Thus there sprang up the closest friendship between the King and S. Thomas, and S. Thomas used his influence solely for God's glory and the welfare of the Church and nation. But he frequently found it no easy matter to induce the King to do what was right; for Henry was a tyrant like the rest of his race, and he would often get into furious passions, and order whoever offended him to be cruelly punished; and in such cases S. Thomas was obliged to acquiesce for a time, waiting till the King's rage should have subsided before he could dare to plead for the culprit, since any attempt to cross Henry's will while the passion was on him, only made matters worse.

At that period two Popes claimed the papal throne, and Alexander, who was the one canonically elected, sent ambassadors to the Kings of France and England to claim their obedience. The bishops of France and Normandy met in synod, and after examining the elections of both the candidates, acknowledged Alexander to be the true Pope, and the King of France acquiesced in their decision. But though Henry had written a beautiful letter to Alexander, which won him the friendship of the Holy Father, yet he was very angry that the bishops in his dominions should dare to recognise either Pope except in obedience to his command. His wrath fell first on Gillot, Archdeacon of Rouen, who had received Alexander's envoys, and he ordered his house to be destroyed. S. Thomas prudently acquiesced, but added in a submissive tone, "My lord, the house which you have ordered to be destroyed, does indeed belong to Archdeacon Gillot, but it is the one in which I am living." Then the King, unwilling to incommode his favourite, and touched by this appeal to his friendship, countermanded his order, and he was soon after induced to pardon Gillot and restore all his property.

But the next day there came news that the Bishop of Le Mans had promised obedience to Alexander. Henry was now more enraged than ever, and his marshals went to the house where the bishop was lodging, and, turning his horses, his baggage, and his retinue into the street, compelled him to leave the court in disgrace. Then an order was drawn out for the destruction of the bishop's house at Le Mans; and when Henry had signed it, he held it up, saying to the bystanders, "I'll warrant the townsmen of Le Mans will hear something about their bishop." This happened at Nieumarkt, where the King of France also was at that time, and the consternation in both courts was very great. S. Thomas knew that nothing could be done while Henry's passion lasted; so he sent off the King's mandate, but he bade the messengers travel slowly, so as to take four days instead of two for the journey, which they promised to do. The next day he sent some bishops to the King to intercede for the Bishop of Le Mans, and when they were repulsed he sent other bishops, and at last went himself; but all in vain, for Henry was inexorable. The following day, S. Thomas did the same; and at last Henry, thinking the house must by this time be destroyed, consented to revoke his order. Then S. Thomas sent off a messenger, ordering him to ride day and night without stopping; and the man made such speed that he reached Le Mans before the bishop's house had been touched. When Henry heard of the stratagem and its result, he was very glad that S. Thomas should thus have prevented his committing an act which would have brought him into discredit, not only with his own subjects, but with the Pope and the French King.

But S. Thomas was not always equally successful, and often he was compelled to acquiesce in measures which he was powerless to prevent. A case of this kind occurred during the war of Toulouse, when Henry having levied an illegal tax on the clergy, under the name of the royal "custom of second subsidies," S. Thomas had to let the measure pass, though he did not sanction it.

Another more outrageous case of tyranny was that of Battle Abbey. After the victory of Hastings, the Conqueror founded this abbey, and with his usual disregard for the rights of others, endowed it with lands belonging to the Bishop of Chichester, and gave it a charter freeing it from episcopal jurisdiction. This gross wrong was a standing grievance to the Bishops of Chichester. During S. Thomas's chancellorship Bishop Hilary of Chichester asserted his claim to jurisdiction over the abbey; Theobald supported him; and the King, probably through S. Thomas's influence, favoured his cause. But when a royal council was assembled to give the final decision, Hilary "daring," as S. Thomas wrote some years after to the Pope, "to speak before the court about apostolic privileges, and to denounce the abbot as excommunicate, he was forthwith compelled to communicate with him in the face of all present, without even the form of absolution, and to receive him to the kiss of peace; for such was the King's pleasure, and that of the court, which dared not to oppose his will in anything."

Besides such cases in which Henry insisted on carrying out the "customs "of his Norman predecessors, it was no easy matter to induce him to fill up vacant bishoprics, the revenues of which, during the vacancies, he was in the habit of appropriating. Lincoln was vacant for seventeen years, and it was generally said there would never be another bishop; but at last S. Thomas got it filled. Exeter was vacant for two years, and it was with difficulty that Bartholomew, the archdeacon, was raised to the see instead of Fitz-Harding, an illiterate person whom Henry wished to intrude into it. Notwithstanding the united efforts of S. Thomas and Theobald, the sees of London, Bangor, and Worcester were all unfilled in 1161, when Theobald died. No wonder then was it that under such circumstances, S. Thomas "would tell the Archbishop and his friends that he was wearied of his very life, and that, after the desire of salvation, there was nothing he so longed for as to be able to disentangle himself without disgrace from the snares of the court."

In after years the charge was brought against S. Thomas that, as chancellor, he had encouraged the King to aggressions on the Church, which he resisted when he became Archbishop. The obvious answer to this accusation is Henry's invincible resolution, as shown in the subsequent struggle, to resist the least encroachment on the prerogatives which he claimed, so that S. Thomas could influence him only by not openly crossing his arbitrary temper. That he did all that was possible in other ways is proved by the fact that Theobald, on his deathbed, expressed the greatest confidence in his zeal for the Church, and his hope that he might be his successor, and in touching terms of affection begged to have the consolation of seeing him before his death.

But what was the source of S. Thomas's power over all who came within his influence? Though his natural gifts and talents, his magnificence and liberality, must have been attractive, yet the real source of his power was his supernatural virtue. In the midst of a licentious court, associating constantly with the profligate King and his courtiers, he not only preserved unsullied purity, as his old friend and confessor, Robert of Merton, declared, but he practised the mortifications of the cloister. While his table was covered with costly viands, his own fare was simple and frugal. His sumptuous style of living was redeemed by personal charity to the poor and oppressed. Beneath his splendid attire he wore a coarse hair shirt; and after a day of pleasure and luxury, he would pass the night on the bare floor, and receive the discipline from Ralph, Prior of Holy Trinity, or Thomas, a priest of S. Martin's. But not the faintest self-consciousness or assumption of superiority marred the purity of his self-denial. He always placed himself on the level of those with whom he associated, so that to all men he seemed like themselves. In God's sight alone was he unlike them. So completely was his inner life hidden that its full perfection became known only by chance, or through his confessors after his death.

By such ascetic practices he preserved humility, mortified sensuality, and maintained close union with God. It is not then to be wondered at that, being thus purified from passion and fortified by supernatural graces, his intellect should have been so clear and strong, his undertakings so successful, and his power of fascination almost irresistible.

In after-years he used to reproach himself for his chancellorship, and to accept the sufferings of his exile as a penance for the faults of this period. But the unanimous testimony of his friends and the silence of his enemies prove that he was preserved from great sins, and that the only ground for his self-accusation was, that the world had had power to charm his genial and sensitive nature, and had led him into venial sins and imperfections, from which even saints are not free while they are fighting their way to the high sanctity to which they are predestined.

CHAPTER V. THE CHANCELLORSHIP— *continued.*

BUT it was not at home alone that S. Thomas distinguished himself. Henry employed him also in delicate and important negotiations with his vassals, and with the King of France.

Henry had placed his eldest son, Prince Henry, under S. Thomas's charge, and wishing to secure the prince's peaceful succession to his large dominions, he ordered S. Thomas to make all the nobles of the realm do homage, and take the usual oath of allegiance to him. Such affairs were very often attended with great difficulties, but, to the surprise of everyone, S. Thomas managed to accomplish the business with perfect success in the king's absence.

Henry was also anxious to strengthen his position by a marriage between Prince Henry, who was then only five years of age, and the Princess Margaret, daughter of the King of France, who was only three; and, about A.D. 1158, he sent S. Thomas to negotiate the alliance. As it was considered desirable to impress the French court with a high notion of the King of England's wealth, S. Thomas had full scope for the indulgence of his taste for magnificence. He took with him two hundred men on horseback of his own household, besides soldiers, clerics, butlers, serving men, knights and sons of the nobility, who were performing military service to him, all armed and handsomely dressed according to their rank. He had also dogs and birds of all kinds; twelve sumpter horses, with a groom to each, and a long-tailed ape seated on the back of each horse; eight coffers to carry his gold and silver plate, and the utensils for his table; other coffers for his money, clothes and books; twenty-four changes of garment, foreign skins, elegant tartans, cloaks, carpets, and other stuffs for presents; and finally, eight waggons, each drawn by five horses, with a groom in a new tunic for each horse, a driver and a guard for each carriage, and a large dog "capable of conquering a lion," tied either above or below it. Two of the waggons were laden with beer as presents for the French, who "admired that sort of liquor, as a wholesome drink, bright and clear, of the colour of wine and a better taste;" a third waggon was used for the chancellor's chapel; a fourth for his chamber; a fifth for his kitchen; and the rest were filled with various necessaries.

When they entered a French village or castle, first went two hundred and fifty footmen singing songs after the fashion of their country. After an interval came the huntsmen with their dogs; then the waggons rattled over the stones; and at a little distance followed the sumpter horses with their grooms. After another interval came the squires, carrying the knights' shields and leading their chargers; then came other squires; then the falconers, with birds on their wrists; then the chancellor's servants; after them the knights and clerics riding two and two; and last of all came the chancellor, riding with some of his particular friends. As he passed, the people would exclaim, "What manner of man must the King of England be, when his chancellor travels in such state?"

In this splendid style S. Thomas travelled to Paris, where the King of France had arranged to receive him. Louis had ordered that the embassy should be entertained entirely at his expense, and had forbidden the people of Paris to sell them anything. But S. Thomas had anticipated him, and had secretly sent his servants before him to the neighbouring markets, to buy what he should require; and as he entered the quarters assigned him in Paris, they met him and told him that they had laid in provisions for one thousand persons for three days.

S. Thomas was lodged in the Temple, and here he entertained all comers with more than his usual princely magnificence. The fare was not only abundant, but also rare and costly; for a single dish of eels is said to have cost one hundred shillings. He scattered his gifts profusely, giving away not only the fine clothes he had brought for that purpose, but distributing also his gold and silver plate, horses, chargers, and sums of money among the nobles, knights, learned men, and servants of the French court. Louis and his nobles reciprocated his courtesy, and treated him with the greatest honour. The object of the embassy was gained; the marriage was arranged; and there sprang up between Louis and S. Thomas a warm and lasting friendship, which proved of great value to the latter when his fortune changed.

On his return from this embassy, S. Thomas performed a great public service by taking prisoner Guy de Laval, a notorious freebooter, whose predatory excursions were the terror of his neighbourhood. This was not, however, the only military exploit in which S. Thomas was engaged. One of the wrongs inflicted by the Conqueror on the English Church was the conversion of a large portion of the Church lands into military fiefs; and this led to the abuse, then too prevalent throughout Europe, and in which S. Thomas shared, of clergy leading their own troops into the field. It is only fair to judge S. Thomas by the opinions of the age in which he lived; and in that day his military deeds were not brought against him by his bitter enemies, nor did they enter into his self-accusations; but, on the contrary, they added greatly to the high estimation in which he was held at both the English and French courts.

The first war in which S. Thomas took part was in A.D. 1159, against Gilles, Count of Toulouse. He led a chosen band of seven hundred knights of his own household, who, in an army composed of troops from England, Scotland, Normandy, Aquitaine, Anjou, and Brittany, were conspicuous for their deeds of valour. Had his advice been taken, both the city of Toulouse and the King of France, who had incautiously entered it, would have been captured. But Henry hesitated to attack Louis, who was his liege lord, and, the French troops coming to the rescue, he was obliged to retire. His barons then refused to remain behind to hold Cahors and several castles that he had taken; but S. Thomas and Henry of Essex offered to garrison them with their own retainers; and afterwards S. Thomas, at the head of his own men, took three other castles and brought back the whole province to its allegiance to Henry.

Soon after, the seat of war was removed to the boundaries of the King of France's territory, between Gisors, Trie, and Courcelles. S. Thomas now took tip arms with all the ardour of his nature. He contributed not only his own seven hundred knights, but one thousand two hundred others, and four thousand serving horsemen, whom he maintained for forty days. He paid each knight three shillings a day, and his table was open to them all. He led them into battle, encouraging them, pointing out the path to glory, and directing their movements by signals on a small trumpet, so that his knights were always foremost in the fight. One clay he charged, with lance in rest and horse at full speed, against Engelram de Trie, a French knight, and dismounting him, bore off his horse in triumph. At the same time, he was so distinguished by unimpeachable faith and nobleness of spirit that, though he laid waste the French territories with fire and sword, Louis and his nobles regarded him with both admiration and friendship.

Thus years passed on, and each day S. Thomas's position became more and more distinguished. All prospered with him, whether at home or abroad, as a statesman, a warrior, or a diplomatist. The king, the nobles, the people, all loved and admired him, and none envied him. He lived in the fear and love of God, in charity and purity; and all his high fortune was powerless to mar his simplicity or make him proud. In the records of history it would be hard to find a more brilliant character than S. Thomas, or a more prosperous career than his up to the close of his chancellorship.

CHAPTER VI. ELECTION TO THE ARCHBISHOPRIC.

ARCHBISHOP THEOBALD died on the 18th April, 1161, and the see remained vacant for about thirteen months, during which time the revenues were entrusted, as usual, to the chancellor for the king's benefit.

About this time S. Thomas fell seriously ill at S. Gervase, in Rouen, and the Kings of France and England both came to see him. One day, as he was recovering, he sat up to play a game of chess, wearing a cloak with sleeves, which was then considered an unclerical dress. Aschetinus, Prior of Leicester, happened to be passing through Rouen, and called to see him; and S. Thomas always encouraged his friends to reprove him freely. Aschetinus, after saluting him, bluntly exclaimed, "What do you mean by wearing a cloak with sleeves? You look more like a falconer than a cleric. Yet cleric you are in person one, in office many: Archdeacon of Canterbury, Dean of Hastings, Provost of Beverley, Canon of this place and of that, and procurator, too, of the archbishopric, and, as the report goes at court, archbishop to be." Then the chancellor said, "I know three poor priests in England, any one of whom I would rather see promoted to the archbishopric than myself; for I know my lord the king so intimately, that, were I appointed, I am sure I should be obliged either to lose his favour, or, which God forbid, to set aside my duty to my God to please him." No doubt S. Thomas spoke his true feelings.

Not very long after this, in the spring of 1162, Henry ordered the chancellor to go to England on various matters of business. Before S. Thomas started he went to the Castle of Falaise to take leave of the king. Then Henry, drawing him aside, said, "You do not yet know altogether the cause of your journey. It is my will that you should be Archbishop of Canterbury." S. Thomas, looking down at his dress, which was very gay, answered with a smile, "What a religious man, what a saint you wish to place in that holy bishopric, over so famous a monastery! I am certain that if, by God's disposal, it were so to happen, the love and favour you now bear me would speedily turn to the bitterest hatred. I know that you would require many things in Church matters, as even now you do, which I could never bear quietly; and so the envious would take occasion to provoke an endless strife between us." But Henry had made up his mind, and would not be turned from his purpose. So, turning to Richard de Luci, the Grand Justiciary, who was going with S. Thomas, he said to him, "Richard, if I lay dead on my bier, would you not strive that my eldest son Henry should be crowned king?" De Luci replied, "My lord, I would with all my might." "I wish you to take much pains," rejoined Henry, "for the promotion of the chancellor to the see of Canterbury." And with these directions they parted and crossed to England.

In the following May, Hilary, Bishop of Chichester, Bartholomew, Bishop of Exeter, Walter, Bishop of Rochester, with Richard de Luci and his brother Walter, Abbot of Battle, went to Canterbury, and summoned the prior and the monks in the king's name to meet the bishops and clergy of England at Westminster, and proceed to the election of an archbishop. Vibert, the prior, and the senior monks accordingly went to Westminster, where the bishops, abbots, priors, earls, and other nobles of the realm were assembled. And when they were all present, Richard de Luci made a speech, in which he told them how zealous the king was in everything which concerned the service of God, and how devoutly attached he was to the Holy Church, and more especially to the Church of Canterbury, which he regarded as his own mother in the Lord; and therefore he left to their free choice the election of an archbishop, provided only they chose a person worthy of such an honour and able to bear its burden. Vibert and the monks, with whom the election lay, retired to another room to consult together; but, though De Luci had told them they were free to choose whom they would, they knew the king so well that they soon came back and declared they could not proceed till they knew what were the king's wishes. Then Richard de Luci recommended S. Thomas to them. The monks still hesitated. Some feared that S. Thomas's great intimacy with the king might destroy their independence of the civil power; others thought it would promote harmony between the Church and the State; while others, again, calling to mind that their Church had been governed by a religious ever since its foundation by S. Augustine, suggested that discipline might suffer under the rule of one so accustomed to a worldly life as the chancellor. But at last, considering the many virtues and graces which shone in S. Thomas's character, their fears and scruples gave way, and they elected him unanimously. Vibert announced to the assembled bishops, peers, and ecclesiastics the election they had made, and the announcement was received by all with the warmest approbation. Some, it is true, noticed that Gilbert Foliot, Bishop of Hereford, a Cistercian monk of high reputation for his ascetic virtues, who was supposed to have himself aspired to the see, was at first not well pleased, but when he found that his was the only dissentient voice, he quickly changed his tone, and became the loudest in praise of the election.

The bishops and peers then went to announce the election to Prince Henry, for the king had written to say that he would hold himself bound by whatever was done by his son. And after the prince had given his full assent, Henry, Bishop of Winchester, demanded that as the archbishop elect had so long governed the realm for the king, he should now be given to the Church free and absolved "from every obligation of the court, from every complaint and calumny, and from all claims," so that henceforth he should be at liberty to attend only to the things of God. To this Prince Henry consented joyfully, and he set S. Thomas free from all secular obligations, so that he could not hereafter be called to account for anything he had done as chancellor.

It has been seen that S. Thomas was very unwilling to accept this sacred dignity, but his reluctance had been overcome by Cardinal Henry of Pisa, the Pope's legate in France. As soon as his election was completed, he left London for Canterbury. Already the heavy responsibility that he was about to take on himself seems to have pressed on his mind; for during this journey he told Herbert de Bosham, one of his most familiar friends, that the preceding night in a dream a venerable person had stood beside him and given him ten talents. He also bade Herbert always tell him in confidence what others said of him, and point out to him whatever he might think wrong in his conduct, "for," added he, "four eyes see more clearly than two;" and Herbert thought that he gave the same charge to some others of his friends. One of the most beautiful traits in S. Thomas's character is the familiar terms on which he lived with his dependents, and the liberty of reproving him which he allowed them, and which they often used rather roughly; but his single aim was the service of God, and self-will and self-opinion were not permitted to have the least influence over him, though his clear intellect and enthusiastic temperament would naturally have made him liable to these failings.

On Saturday in Whitsun-week S. Thomas was ordained priest in Canterbury Cathedral by his old friend Walter, Bishop of Rochester, and on the following day, Trinity Sunday, the 3rd of June, 1162, he was consecrated bishop by Henry of Blois, Bishop of Winchester, to whom this honour was conceded on account of his age and great virtues, as well as his high birth, for he was brother to the late King Stephen, and grandson to the Conqueror.

On this solemn occasion Prince Henry and a great many bishops, abbots, and religious of all ranks, were present. And when S. Thomas came to the cathedral attended by a suitable retinue of clerics and persons of rank, the bishops, monks, and clergy went in procession to meet him, and an immense multitude accompanied them, anxious to do him honour, and rending the air with joyful acclamations. But S. Thomas, heeding not these demonstrations of joy and respect, advanced on foot with an air of great humility and contrition, and tears in his eyes, thinking less of the honour than of the burden that he was about to take on himself. At the close of the consecration, as the new archbishop knelt for the blessing of his consecrator, Henry of

Winchester said to him, "Dearest brother, I give you the choice of two things: beyond a doubt you must lose the favour of the earthly or the heavenly king." And the future martyr, raising his hands and looks to heaven, answered with a fervour which brought the tears to the eyes of both, "By God's help and strength I now make my choice, and never for the love and favour of an earthly king will I forego the grace of the King of Heaven."

S. Thomas was still only archbishop elect, and though he had been duly consecrated, he could not exercise his episcopal functions, for he had not yet received jurisdiction in his see. The Church, in obedience to S. Paul's words, "How shall they preach unless they be sent?" has not only been careful to transmit the apostolic grace to her ministers in their several grades, but she has also required that no man shall assume to himself the apostolic work in any locality, till he is sent or authorized by his immediate superior to do it, the priest by his bishop, the bishop by his metropolitan, and the metropolitan by the successor of S. Peter, from whom, as being the vicar of Christ and the rock on which the Church is built, all mission and jurisdiction flow. The symbol of the metropolitan authority is the pallium, which is said to be sent "from the body of blessed Peter," because it has been blessed by the Pope on the eve of SS. Peter and Paul, and deposited on the shrine of S. Peter.

Accordingly, as soon as S. Thomas was consecrated he sent John of Salisbury and five other messengers to announce his election to Pope Alexander, and ask for the pallium. When the messengers returned bearing the pallium, S. Thomas went out barefoot to meet them. "This mystic government and badge of an archbishop" was then placed on the high altar of the cathedral of Canterbury, and on the feast of S. Lawrence, August 10th, S. Thomas, in full pontifical robes, after swearing obedience in the usual form to the Holy Father, advanced and took it thence. He now for the first time sat on his throne, and had the archiepiscopal cross borne before him, and thus the solemn ceremony was completed.

CHAPTER VII. THE ARCHBISHOP AT HOME.

A NEW life now opened on S. Thomas. He was now admitted to that marvellous familiarity with our Blessed Lord which none but a priest can know. He was, moreover, set to rule over his Lord's house, and would be called to account for the treasured souls committed to his charge. With his characteristic simplicity, he took no heed at first to change his exterior, his dress, his table, or his establishment; but his daily life and his interior were completely transformed.

Each night he rose to say matins and lauds in choir with his monks. When these were finished, he would privately wash the feet of thirteen poor men, to whom he would afterwards serve up a good meal, and give four pieces of money to each before dismissing them. At daybreak he would take a short sleep; but soon arousing himself, would apply to the study of the Holy Scriptures, in which he was assisted by Herbert de Bosham, whom he had selected for this intimate intercourse. Then would succeed his private prayer, which he generally made with "tears in wonderful abundance" at the altar of the Blessed Trinity, where he had said his first Mass, and during which he allowed no one to interrupt him. At nine o'clock he returned to the church either to say Mass or to assist at it. When he said Mass, he generally said only one collect, and scarcely ever more than three, being careful to make his Mass short, "for fear of distractions and suggestions by evil angels," and also because he verified in the august sacrifice of the Gospel the words spoken of its type, "Ye shall eat in haste; for it is the Phase, that is, the Passover of the Lord." While the choir sang he would read some devotional work, often selecting a little prayer-book by his predecessor, S. Anselm; and when he came to the consecration, his tears, his sighs, his reverence, and his devotion were so great that "he seemed in very presence in the flesh to see the passion of our Lord," and his "very handling of the divine sacraments strengthened the faith and fervour of all who witnessed it."

He dined almost in public, occupying the centre of the table on the raised dais at the end of the hall. On his right sat his intimate friends and the learned men whose society he cultivated, and on the left his monks. He would not allow music during the meal, as was then the custom, but had some religious book read aloud; and from time to time he would interrupt the reading to discuss the points of interest which it suggested. But as the reading might weary his soldiers and retainers, he considerately let them dine at another table, a number of places being reserved for the poor whom he daily invited. His guests, too, unless they were persons of known piety, dined apart, for it might not always be desirable that what was said at his table should be overheard by them. His quick eye traversed the hall to see that all were properly served, and if anyone was placed below his rank or seemed to be neglected, he would send him a portion from his own table. The meal was abundantly provided, so that at its close a plentiful supply remained for distribution to the crowds of poor who lived on his alms. In consequence of his weak digestion and the habits of his past life, he could not eat course food; but he partook most sparingly of any delicacy that was served to him, living chiefly on bread, merely tasting the wine-cup as politeness required, before he passed it round, and drinking only water in which fennel or hay had been boiled. One day a person who was dining with him, remarked contemptuously on the delicacy of his food, whereupon S. Thomas answered, "Certes, brother, if I am not mistaken, you take your beans with greater eagerness than I the pheasant before me." And Herbert adds, "This person lived with us for a while, and though he did not care for delicacies, for he was not used to them, he was truly a glutton of coarser food." After dinner S. Thomas would retire with his friends to his private room, where he would discuss some spiritual subject with them; and occasionally, if he found it necessary, he would take a short sleep.

He was as careful as he had formerly been in the administration of justice, resisting boldly the oppression and insolence of the great, and even the commands of the king, and giving judgment in all cases with strict impartiality. He refused presents from suitors, and forbade all his officials to receive them; not allowing even the ordinary fees for paper, wax, seal, &c., to be exacted. It is related that on one occasion an abbot who had a suite in his court, went from one official to another, offering them money to secure their help, and at last, after gaining his cause he went home with his money in his pocket, saying, "I have found a court which not only does not go after gold, but refuses it, despises it, and tramples on it."

When the business of the day was over, he would often be seen sitting in the cloisters, as was the habit of the monks, reading some spiritual book; and afterwards he would go to the infirmary and wait on the sick monks; for he always treated religious with great reverence and affection. No beggar was ever refused alms at his gate. Besides the thirteen poor men whom he daily served in person, twelve others received the same hospitality from a guest-master, excepting only the alms in money; and each morning at nine o'clock an abundant repast was served to one hundred "prebendaries," as the poor pensioners were then called. Moreover, gifts of money and provisions were frequently sent by his order to poor colleges and hospitals; the sick in the neighbourhood were daily visited and provided for; poor wanderers found shelter in his palace; and at the approach of winter warm clothing was distributed to those who needed it. Theobald had doubled the alms given by his predecessor; but S. Thomas doubled those of Theobald, setting aside all his tithes for this purpose.

His chief devotion, however, was to prayer, which maintained his soul in close union with his Lord, and to the study of the Holy Scriptures, which taught him how to follow in His footsteps. To these he gave all his leisure time. Like S. Cecilia he always carried some portion of the Gospels in the large loose sleeves of his dress; and when he went out on horseback, he would call to his side one of the clerics who rode behind him, and would confer with him on the subject of his study; for his great humility ever led him to prefer the opinions of others to his own. So long as he was in his own province, his stole, "that delightful yoke which bound him to Christ," was day and night round his neck. As he rode through the country, he would dismount from his horse and give confirmation to those who came and asked him for it; and in aftertimes crosses were erected, and miracles often were worked, on the spots on which he had thus administered this sacrament.

He held an ordination in Ember week of the September after his consecration, when he took extraordinary pains to ascertain the qualifications of the candidates, so as not to admit any unsuitable person to holy orders. He would often say to his friends, that nothing should ever induce him to consecrate as bishop anyone unfitted for the office. Then he would mourn over his own unworthiness in consequence of his former life; and if his friends would try to console him by the example of others with similar antecedents, who had made good bishops, he would answer humbly, "But they were miracles of divine grace."

It has already been said that on his consecration he had made no violent change in his outward life. This naturally led to much remark, and often to misapprehension of his true character and springs of action, which however vanished on closer observation. The Archdeacon of Poictiers, one of his bitterest enemies, afterwards wrote thus about him:—"We were much deceived in that man by his dress and his noble bearing exteriorly, but interiorly he was far different, as has since appeared, and is now daily evident." But at this time strangers and some of those around him, especially his monks, were much scandalized by his continuing to wear the same coloured secular dress, of costly material and trimmed with variegated foreign furs, which he used to wear as chancellor. At length one of the monks, taking advantage of the freedom which he allowed his dependents, told him that he had had a dream, in which a venerable person had appeared to him and said, "Go, tell the *chancellor* to change his dress without delay, and if he refuse to do so, I will oppose him all the days of his life." S. Thomas's only answer was a flood of tears; but the worldly dress was laid aside. It was, however, only his outer dress which had now to be changed, for his inner garments had already been conformed to his altered spirit. At his consecration he had begun to wear constantly, not only a hair shirt, but a pair of hair breeches down to his knees, and after his death it appeared that he had made this penance even more severe, by changing them so seldom that they were full of vermin. Over the dress of hair he wore a monk's gown, as a token of the religious spirit to which he had secretly bound himself, but this he probably did not adopt till a few years later at Pontigny. His outer garb was a black cappa of very common stuff trimmed with lamb's-wool instead of fur, and a surplice of fine linen over it, this being the dress of the Black Canons Regular of Merton, which he had doubtless worn as a boy in their convent, and which was associated with his earliest aspirations after the love and service of God. This dress he renewed frequently, giving the cast-off one to the poor.

CHAPTER VIII. THE ARCHBISHOP IN HIS PROVINCE.

VERY soon after his consecration, S. Thomas sent the great seal, with his resignation of the chancellorship, to the king. Henry was disappointed, for in spite of the warning from S. Thomas, he seems to have cherished the hope that both offices would be held by his favourite, and that thus he himself should have full command of the Church. In his irritation he called on S. Thomas to resign also the Archdeaconry of Canterbury. But the saint deferred doing so for some little time, probably in order to show the king that this office was independent of him, and Henry never pardoned the delay.

Another matter, also, which could not have been quite pleasing to Henry, was the alacrity with which S. Thomas set to work to recover Church lands, which had been illegally alienated in the time of his predecessors. In some cases, the persons whom he dispossessed had great influence, and they carried their complaints to Normandy, where Henry then was, giving also exaggerated accounts of the change that had come over the archbishop since his consecration, so as to create a strong feeling against him at the court. It is true that S. Thomas had had the prudence to obtain the king's sanction for the steps he was taking about these lands; but still there is no doubt that this zeal in defence of the Church's rights could not have been satisfactory to Henry.

These things, however, had not yet made so deep an impression on the king as to cool his friendship for the archbishop. A few days before Christmas A.D. 1162, he crossed over to England, landing at Southampton, where he was met by S. Thomas and Prince Henry. Taking no notice of his son, he threw himself into the arms of his favourite, and gave expression to the greatest joy on meeting his much-loved friend. His vanity, too, was flattered by hearing on all sides the warm praises of him whom he had selected for the primacy.

The next day they rode together to London, conversing privately with each other during the whole journey. On Christmas day S. Thomas said Mass in S. Paul's, the see of London being then vacant; and for some days after he remained with the king, with whom his influence seemed quite unimpaired, so that none of the courtiers dared to say a word against him.

On Palm Sunday, which fell that year on the 17th of March, the king came to Canterbury and took part in the procession, on which occasion a violent storm arose and blew down the canopies which were erected in the streets to protect the procession as it passed along.

After Easter the king and the archbishop went together to London; and S. Thomas took this opportunity to give up the charge of Prince Henry, who had continued till then under his guardianship.

During this time S. Thomas had been availing himself of his favour with the king to get the vacant sees filled by men of piety and learning. On the 28th April he had the satisfaction of seeing Gilbert Foliot translated from the see of Hereford, and enthroned at S. Paul's as Bishop of London. Gilbert Foliot was a Benedictine monk of the celebrated order of Clugny. He was successively Prior of Clugny and of Abbeville, and Abbot of S. Peter's at Gloucester; and in A.D. 1147 he was consecrated Bishop of Hereford at S. Omer's. He was in high repute for his talents, and still more for his ascetic life, his austerities being so great that the Pope wrote to him, desiring him to mitigate them for the sake of his health, which was valuable to the Church. In the high offices he had held, he had often come into collision with those who encroached on the rights of the Church, and had always stood up fearlessly in their defence. On one occasion, he had placed the Church of Hereford under an interdict on account of the earl's contumacy. On another, he threatened to excommunicate a lay official for summoning the Dean of Hereford to appear before his tribunal. In writing to the Empress Matilda he had said, "In all things in which we can and ought, we are prepared to obey your commands. But if in anything Church authority is offended, we have a full excuse when that is exacted from us which we ought not to do." And to the Pope he wrote, "We know that not to obey your commands is to apostatize, and that it is truly like a sacrilege to oppose your will." S. Thomas must, therefore, have rejoiced at seeing the first see in his province filled by one who seemed to be so imbued with love for the Church, and so alive to the duty of preserving her sacred rights. Gilbert had, it is true, seemed displeased at his election to the archbishopric; but S. Thomas was too noble-minded to be influenced by personal considerations, besides which, his humility would have made him acquiesce in Gilbert's opinion of his unworthiness. Accordingly, he looked to him as a valuable coadjutor in the approaching struggle, and when writing to urge him to consent to the translation, he said affectionately, "that thus he who is united to us by sincere love, may by neighbourhood be conveniently at hand for our wants and those of the Church of God." It will soon be seen how sadly this hope was disappointed.

Early in May, S. Thomas, accompanied by Gilbert and a splendid suite, embarked at Romney on the coast of Kent, to attend a council which Pope Alexander had summoned to meet at Tours. On his landing at Gravelines, he was received with great respect by Philip, Earl of Flanders, and his journey thence to Tours was a constant ovation, the nobles placing their houses and all their possessions at his disposal, and the people flocking to get his blessing. When he reached Tours, the whole city, filled as it then was with great personages, turned out to meet him, and even the cardinals laid aside their dignity to do him honour. He went at once to the Pope, and the crowd who followed him was so great, that the Holy Father was obliged to go into one of the large halls to receive him. The next day all the great dignitaries visited him, and during his stay at Tours he was considered the most distinguished person present. He obtained from the Pope the renewal of many privileges formerly granted to the Church of Canterbury. He was also authorized to take the preliminary steps in the process of canonization of S. Anselm, to whom he had a great devotion.

On S. Thomas's return to England, two interesting ceremonies claimed his care. The first was the consecration of Reading Abbey, a glorious structure which Henry I. had founded, chiefly in expiation of his father's sins against the English. Here he deposited the hand of S. James the Greater, which his daughter, the Empress Matilda, brought to England, and here it remained till the destruction of the abbey at the Protestant Reformation, when it disappeared. Here, too, he himself was afterwards buried.

The other ceremony was the translation of S. Edward the Confessor, who had been canonized on the 7th of February, 1161. When the day for the translation had been fixed, Lawrence, the Abbot of Westminster, thought it desirable to open the tomb in preparation for the function. He several times resolved to do this, but each time his heart failed him through reverence for the precious relics. At length, one early morning after matins, it being still dark, he, the prior, and some chosen monks remained in the choir while the others retired as usual. They had already prepared themselves for their holy task by fasting; and now, after reciting certain litanies and psalms, the abbot, the prior, and two of the monks, all barefoot and vested in albs, went to the tomb, the rest remaining in prayer before the High Altar. When the tomb was opened, the body of the saint was found to be quite uncorrupt. It was clad in a robe of cloth of gold, with purple shoes, a crown of wrought gold on his head, and his signet ring on his finger. His fine, white beard was slightly curling, as it used to be in life; his long, thin fingers looked longer and more transparent than ever; and his countenance wore a venerable air of wonderful calm and majesty. When the monks had recovered from the awe with which this sight inspired them, they wrapped the saint in a costly silk, and laid him, as they had found him, in a new chest, except that Abbot Lawrence took the ring from his finger.

On the 13th of October, a splendid ceremony was performed in the presence of the king, fourteen bishops from England and Normandy, and a crowd of nobles and ecclesiastics. The body was first exposed for the veneration of all present, after which it was carried in procession through the cloisters on the shoulders of the king and nobles, and then placed by S. Thomas in the shrine prepared for it before the High Altar. When the abbey was enlarged and almost rebuilt by Henry III., the body of S. Edward was removed, with a magnificent ceremonial, to the newly erected Chapel of the Kings behind the High Altar, and deposited in the shrine in which it lies uncorrupt, as is generally believed, till the present day, a striking sign to a faithless and sacrilegious nation. Deep and fervent must have been the prayers with which S. Thomas invoked aid in the coming contest from the saintly king, whose name was identified by a loving people with the cherished liberties of their Church and nation.

About this time, S. Thomas had the happiness of filling the two vacant sees with pious and excellent men. On the 26th of August, he consecrated Roger, son of the Earl of Gloucester, Bishop of Worcester; on the 22nd December, he consecrated Robert de Melun, Bishop of Hereford. They were like his parting gift to his province, and with the consecration of Robert, the brief season of peace came to a close.

CHAPTER IX. GATHERING OF THE STORM—THE COUNCIL OF WESTMINSTER.

It has been already said that Henry had not been well pleased with S. Thomas's resignation of the chancellorship, and his zeal in reclaiming Church lands. New causes of displeasure were soon added. S. Thomas preached before the king a sermon, in which he pointed out the difference between the spiritual and temporal powers, and the superiority of the former—a Christian doctrine far from palatable to a Plantagenet.

Also S. Thomas had excommunicated William, lord of the manor of Eynesford, for using violence to the servants of Lawrence, a cleric, to whom he had given the church of Eynesford; and when the king wrote and ordered him to absolve William, he answered, that a king was not competent to say who should be absolved or excommunicated. Still, with his usual charity he absolved William; but, notwithstanding, the king was so angry at his answer that he said to his courtiers, "Now he no longer has my favour."

Another cause of irritation was S. Thomas's opposition to the illegal taxation of the people. It was then the custom for the lords to pay the sheriffs two shillings on every hyde of land, on condition that their tenants and lands were protected from false accusations and violence. At a council at Woodstock, the king proposed that this money should be paid into his treasury. Every one saw how unjust it would be to turn this voluntary offering to the sheriffs into a forced payment to the king; but S. Thomas alone dared to oppose it, pointing out that the payment was made only so long as the sheriffs performed certain services, and there was no law which could make it compulsory. The king got into one of his usual fits of rage, and exclaimed, "By God's Eyes it shall be enrolled." S. Thomas answered, "By the reverence of those Eyes by which thou hast sworn, my lord king, not a penny shall be paid from my lands, nor from the rights of the Church." The firmness of the archbishop saved the nation from this illegal tax.

In revenge for S. Thomas's opposition to his sovereign will, Henry encouraged Clarembald, Abbot of S. Augustine's at Canterbury, to refuse to take the usual oath of canonical obedience to the archbishop. He also allowed Roger, Archbishop of York, S. Thomas's former enemy, to revive the old claim to have his cross borne before him in the province of Canterbury.

Matters had now come to a crisis, and the contest between the Church and the State could no longer be deferred. This contest was not one of those which spring from a mere difference of opinion, which can be attributed to hot temper or indiscreet zeal, or which might have been averted by forbearing charity or skilful management. A deep principle was at stake. Both Henry and S. Thomas were fully alive to this; both had shown by their past conduct, that they would yield points which did not compromise this fundamental principle, but neither would go one hair's-breadth further. Both therefore knew that this must be a combat *à outrance*, and both entered the lists with a corresponding spirit.

The principle at stake involved the very existence of the Church of England. The great question was, Whether the Church should continue under the form of government which our Lord had ordained for the transmission of spiritual life and grace to all the members of His Body, or whether she should henceforth be under the supremacy of a lay sovereign? Was she to be, as hitherto, the channel of grace and the guardian of the keys of heaven and hell? Were her pastors to derive their supernatural mission and jurisdiction, their authority to govern the flock of Christ, to judge the guilty, to bind and to loose, from the rock of S. Peter on which our Lord had built His Church? Or were her mission and jurisdiction henceforth to proceed from the supremacy of a lay sovereign, so that the stream being cut off from the fountain-head, the life-giving waters would cease to flow within her channels, her supernatural powers would be lost, and all her operations would be conducted on merely natural principles, in obedience to the will of lay governors and legislators? The Pagan emperor had said, that he would as soon see a rival Caesar on the throne as a bishop in Rome. Henry Plantagenet practically repeated his words; and this sentiment, so expressive of the undying opposition between grace and nature, has been echoed again and again by the world even to the present day.

The supremacy of the Pope, as the vicar of Christ, was so universally acknowledged in that age, that neither Henry Plantagenet nor his predecessors dared to deny it; but they attacked it indirectly by disputing the exercise of the functions which necessarily belonged to it, and to the clergy as deriving authority from the Pope. The contest was carried on chiefly on three points, namely, the jurisdiction of the Church, the appointment or mission of its ministers, and the guardianship of its property.

From the earliest Christian times the clergy, as teachers and pastors of our Lord's flock, not only held councils and synods for the regulation of matters of faith, morals, and discipline, but, in accordance with the apostolic injunction, they gave judgment in both spiritual and civil causes. In course of time civil causes were taken out of their jurisdiction, but they continued to hold synods, to pronounce public censures, to give judgment in all cases of public scandal, marriages, wills, perjury, breach of contract, tithes, and benefices; and the clergy retained the privilege of being tried by their peers in the ecclesiastical courts a privilege which was also extended to widows and orphans, whom the Church took under her special guardianship. This was the common law and practice of Christendom, and in England it was guaranteed by the ancient laws of the realm, and by formal grants from the Conqueror and his successors.

The rights of the ecclesiastical courts was not a mere question of clerical dignity, but involved, especially in England, many substantial benefits. For in the ecclesiastical courts judgment was given according to fixed laws, which were based on the principles of pure morality, and adopted throughout Europe; and these laws were administered by men of talent and education, whose independent position enabled them to do justice to all, rich and poor, noble and serf, without distinction of persons a final appeal being allowed to the Pope, as the sure refuge of the oppressed, and the heir of S. Peter's infallibility. But in the secular courts of England the jurisprudence was confused and uncertain, partly Saxon and partly Norman, professing to be based on precedents handed down by tradition, but practically overruled by the will and violence of the sovereign and his barons. Moreover, in punishing offenders, the Church followed, even then, the milder practice which is now gradually becoming prevalent, and fines, imprisonment, public censures, suspension from Church communion, and degradation in the case of clerics, were the usual penalties; whereas in the Norman courts, the most sanguinary and cruel punishments, not only death, but barbarous tortures, mutilations, and loss of limb and sight, were arbitrarily inflicted; and even in the imposition of fines, no fixed rule was adopted, as in Saxon times, in proportion to the enormity of the offence, but in almost every case the delinquent was subjected to an *amerciament*, that is to say, his entire personal estate was placed the *mercy* of his lord.

The jurisdiction of the Church was, in fact, the struggle and triumph of spiritual force over physical. It was, therefore, intolerable to the proud Norman kings and barons, who, invincible by all else, felt themselves powerless before the small still voice of God and of conscience. Up to the Conquest the bishops had sat in the courts of the hundred; but the Normans, who looked upon the secular courts as an engine for gratifying their cupidity or wreaking their vengeance, could not brook the presence of the only order of men who dared to oppose their violence. The Conqueror, therefore, removed the bishops from the courts of the hundred; he and his successors laboured incessantly to hinder and paralyze their jurisdiction in their own courts, by making it dependent on the sovereign's arbitrary will; and Henry Plantagenet resolved to crush them effectually, by substituting for the common law of Christendom, a written code based on the tyrannical customs of his race.

The question as to the appointment and mission of the Church's ministers was a very simple one. The practice of the Church was, that vacancies in ecclesiastical benefices and dignities were filled up, in some cases by election, in others by appointment; but in all it was indispensable that the election or appointment should be confirmed by the immediate spiritual superior, through whom mission was transmitted from the Pope as the Vicar of Christ. The Norman kings contended against this practice, and wished to make use of Church patronage to strengthen their own power, to replenish their coffers, or to recompense their servile favourites, without any regard for the interests of religion and the spiritual wants of the people.

The question of Church property was even more simple. The Church held in trust for the people, and especially for the poor, a very large amount of property, with which it built churches and ministered to the wants, both spiritual and temporal, of all classes. It taught the ignorant, fed the hungry, clothed the naked, lodged the stranger, released the captive, comforted the sick and afflicted; in a word, it took heed that, so far as was possible, none should suffer from absolute want or neglect. Such a mode of distributing wealth is not pleasing to the world and its rulers; and hence the property of the poor and the Church has not only been too often coveted by the State, but has been appropriated by it whenever a nation has unhappily severed itself from the centre of Christian unity, and has thus ceased to receive those supernatural graces, which alone can produce the heroic charity of the Catholic Church.

In order to understand the wide interest which was felt throughout England in the contest that was soon to begin, it should be borne in mind that in those days the clerical body included not only bishops and priests, but also the monks and nuns, and a vast number of persons of lower grades, who were employed in carrying on the services of the Church, in the administration of justice, in the management of Church property, education, charity, and all matters requiring superior intelligence and learning. Also, as the Catholic clergy and the religious orders have always been recruited from all ranks of society, not excepting the very lowest, the Church's position was the opposite to that of a hereditary order, and its interests were inseparably connected with those of the laity. The people, too, fully appreciated the superiority of the Church over the king and his barons, whether as judge, landlord, protector, or benefactor. Hence it came to pass, that while Henry was supported only by the nobles who emulated his tyranny, and by such of the clergy as were actuated by fear or personal ambition, S. Thomas's cause was warmly espoused by the mass of the nation, both clergy and laity, who identified it with their own.

The case which led immediately to the contest was that of Philip de Brois, a canon of Bedford, who, having been accused in the time of Theobald of the murder of a soldier, had been tried in the diocesan court and acquitted. Simon Fitz-Peter, one of the king's itinerant justiciaries, now endeavoured to bring him before his own court, whereupon Philip lost his temper and insulted Simon. Simon laid the case before the king who fell into one of his usual fits of rage at the insult to his official, and ordered that Philip should be tried by Simon. But S. Thomas, objecting to the trial of a cleric by a lay court, offered to try Philip in his own court at Canterbury, to which the king reluctantly consented, deputing several bishops and barons to be the archbishop's assessors. Philip pleaded that he had already been tried for the murder and acquitted; but he confessed the insult to the king's official. The court held his plea good as regarded the murder, but found him guilty of the insult, and sentenced him to be deprived for two years of the revenues of his stall, and to make satisfaction to the justice in the usual humiliating form. The king thought the sentence too lenient, but the bishops declared that, for peace and the king's honour, they had punished Philip beyond his due. Henry using his favourite Norman oath, exclaimed, "Par les Oilz Deu, you shall swear that you have not spared him because he was a cleric." They were ready to take the oath; but Henry was not satisfied, and summoned a council of bishops to meet at Westminster.

The council met at Westminster on the 1st of October A.D. 1163. The king opened the proceedings by complaining of the exactions of the archdeacons, who, he said, made money by people's sins; wherefore he demanded that no archdeacon should try any man without the knowledge of the royal official. He went on to require that all clerics who were guilty of any crime should be degraded, and then given over to the king's officers to receive corporal punishment. These demands were not only illegal, but doubly unjust; for not only had the clergy an undoubted right to benefit by the milder and more equitable jurisdiction of the ecclesiastical courts, but the crime would have been twice punished.

As Henry insisted on having an answer the same day, the bishops retired for consultation. All the bishops, except S. Thomas, were disposed to yield; but he said that it was unjust to condemn a man twice for the same fault, and that the liberty of the Church was in danger, for which a bishop ought to be prepared to give his life. To this the bishops answered, "Let the liberty of the Church perish, lest we perish ourselves. Much must be yielded to the malice of the times." Whereupon S. Thomas exclaimed, "Who hath bewitched you, foolish bishops! Much must be yielded to the malice of the times, I grant; but are we to add sin to sin? It is when the Church is in trouble, and not merely in times of peace, that a bishop should dare to do his duty. It was not more meritorious for bishops of old to give their blood for the Church, than it is now to die in defence of her liberty. I declare, God be my witness, that it is not safe for us to leave that form which we have received from our fathers. Nor can we expose anyone to death, for we are not allowed to take any part in a trial of life and death."

When the king found that, owing to S. Thomas's firmness, he could not carry his point, he demanded that he and the bishops should promise to obey the royal customs in all things. After consultation with the others, S. Thomas answered in the name of all, that they would do so "saving their order." This reservation enraged the king, who put the question to all the bishops singly, when all gave the answer agreed on, except

Hilary of Chichester, who, frightened by the king's anger, said that he would do so "in good faith;" but he gained nothing by this change, for the king turned on him and insulted him. Henry then insisted on having an absolute and unconditional promise. In vain did S. Thomas plead, that in his oath of fealty he had sworn to give him "earthly honour *saving his order*," the royal customs being included in "earthly honour;" and that the condition *saving his order* being universal throughout Christendom, he could not depart from it. The discussion was prolonged till late at night, when the king left the room without saluting the bishops. S. Thomas then rebuked Hilary severely for changing the form of his answer without consulting him and the other bishops, after which they all retired to their lodgings.

Early the next morning the king sent to order S. Thomas to resign the posts and honours of which he had had charge since his chancellorship, and the demand was immediately complied with. The king then left London without informing the bishops of his departure.

At this time there happened to be at the court of Henry a prelate of great reputation, Arnulph de Lisieux, uncle to the Earl of Flanders. He had distinguished himself by his zeal in the service of Pope Alexander, and his talents gave him great weight. But in this affair he seems never to have grasped the principle at issue, and being of a timeserving disposition, he tried to keep on good terms with both parties, and did much mischief. He now suggested to Henry that it was only S. Thomas who made a firm stand against his will, and that he would carry his point more readily by detaching the bishops from their metropolitan. Unhappily, Henry found no difficulty in acting on this fatal advice; for three of the bishops, terrified at having incurred his anger, had followed him when he left London, and these were readily gained to his side. These three deserters from their order were Roger of York, Gilbert of London, and Hilary of Chichester. Hilary was probably influenced by fear, and Roger, by ambition and personal jealously; but it is hard to account for Gilbert's sudden fall. He had already done much for our Lord by his zeal for the Church and his mortification of the flesh; but, like the young man in the Gospel, he wanted singleness of heart, and would not obey the call to part with worldly honour and wealth, or, it might be, even life itself. A few years before, the ascetic Gilbert seemed much further advanced on the road to sanctity than the brilliant chancellor. But in that race, too often, in accordance with our Lord's words, the first is last, and the last first; and thus it came to pass that, while Gilbert appears henceforth as the enemy of the Church, and the king's chief adviser and supporter in all that is evil, the single-hearted Thomas wins the martyr's glorious palm and crown.

Before very long Henry summoned S. Thomas to meet him at Northampton, in the hope that he might gain more by personal influence in a private conference. As S. Thomas was approaching Northampton, the king sent him word to wait for him where he was, because the large retinues of both could not easily be accommodated in the town. S. Thomas accordingly turned aside into a field; and when before long Henry arrived, he was careful to be the first to make his salutation. Their horses began to kick and neigh, which prevented their meeting till they had changed them. Then they withdrew apart, and Henry began by reminding S. Thomas of all the favour he had shown him, asking him how he could so suddenly forget all the proofs of his affection, so as to be not only ungrateful, but his opponent in everything. "Far be it from me, my lord," answered S. Thomas; "I am not ungrateful for the favours I have received, not from yourself alone, but from God through you; therefore, far be it from me to resist your will so long as it agrees with the will of God. You are my lord, but God is your Lord and mine; and it would be good for neither of us that I should leave His will for yours; for in the awful judgment we shall both be judged as the servants of our Lord, and one will not be able to answer for the other. We must obey our temporal lords, but not against God; for, S. Peter says, we must obey God rather than man." "I do not want you to preach me a sermon just now," said the king. "Are you not the son of one of my rustics?" S. Thomas replied, "In truth, I am not sprung of royal race; no more was blessed Peter, the prince of the apostles, to whom our Lord deigned to give the keys of heaven and the headship of the universal Church." "True," rejoined the king, "but he died for his Lord." S. Thomas answered, "I, too, will die for my Lord when the time comes." "You trust too much to your elevation," retorted the king. "I trust in the Lord," replied S. Thomas, "for cursed is he that putteth his trust in man." Henry then urged him to give up the obnoxious clause, but all in vain; and at length finding that S. Thomas was inflexible, he broke up the conference.

Both parties appealed to the Pope, who was then at Sens. Arnulph de Lisieux crossed the Channel six times in three months on embassies to the Holy Father, in order to place the royal customs before him in a favourable light. In France, Henry was hated and feared, while S. Thomas's cause excited the deepest interest, and his messengers met with the warmest reception. The Earl of Flanders expressed to them his sympathy, and offered assistance in case their master should be driven from England. The Earl of Soissons promised solemnly to consign all the revenues of his earldom to his use. The King of France "pledged himself on the word of a king to receive him not as a bishop nor an archbishop, but as a brother sovereign;" while bishops and abbots professed their readiness to make every sacrifice to help him. As for the Pope, he was in great difficulties; for the Emperor of Germany and the Antipope had forced him to fly from Italy, and take refuge in France, and he feared lest he should drive Henry into schism by opposing his will. But notwithstanding, he received S. Thomas's messengers most honourably, sighing deeply at the news they brought, extolling his courage, and "praising God without ceasing for vouchsafing to the Church such a shepherd."

Meanwhile S. Thomas had to resist the entreaties of Hilary of Chichester, Robert of Hereford, and many of his friends, who trembled at the king's fiery wrath. They made, however, no impression on him, and his resolution seemed to be immovable. At length there came to him Philip, Abbot of Aumône in the diocese of Blois, bearing letters from the Pope, who recommended great moderation and submission, in the hope that prudence might avert the impending troubles. Philip also brought letters from the cardinals, who said that Henry had assured them, that he required submission to his demand only for the sake of his dignity, and he would not take advantage of it to the Church's prejudice. Philip urged S. Thomas to yield on the ground that the Pope wished it, and that the responsibility now rested with the Holy Father. Obedience to the Pope was a plea that S. Thomas could not resist; his own gentle nature, too, disinclined him to unnecessary contention; and therefore, without inquiring closely into Philip's trustworthiness, he gave ready faith to his assurances, and agreed to follow his advice.

S. Thomas now hastened to Woodstock, where the king then was, and promised in general terms, omitting the obnoxious reservation, to observe the royal customs. Henry somewhat mollified by his submission, received him graciously, though not with his former affection. At the same time he said, that as the opposition to his demand had been public, the unconditional promise to observe the royal customs should be equally so; and for this purpose he should summon the bishops and nobles to a council at Clarendon.

CHAPTER X THE COUNCIL OF CLARENDON.

ON the 29th of January, 1164, the Council of Clarendon met. S. Thomas had meanwhile begun to doubt, whether he had not acted imprudently in trusting to the Abbot of Aumône's assurances. He knew Henry well, and could not believe that he would really abstain from taking advantage of any promise, which he might make to the detriment of the Church. He, therefore, resolved not to repeat his unconditional promise, but he wished to keep his intention secret till the time for action should arrive. Notwithstanding, it came to the knowledge of Henry, who was very angry and prepared to carry his point by force. The council, chamber was filled with armed men; all who should dare to oppose the king were openly threatened; good men trembled, and S. Thomas alone was unmoved.

Two bishops, Joceline of Salisbury and Roger of Worcester, were the first who came to S. Thomas, and with tears besought him to have pity on them, for they had incurred the king's displeasure by their bold reproofs, and their lives were in danger if he were not obeyed. S. Thomas tried to inspire them with courage, but refused to yield.

Next came the Earl of Leicester and the Earl of Cornwall, the king's uncle, and entreated him to save them and their royal master from the disgrace of the violent course he was prepared to pursue. But S. Thomas answered calmly, "It would not be a new nor an unheard-of thing if we did die for the Church, since a countless host of saints have so taught us by word and example; God's will be done."

Then came Richard of Hastings, grand-master of the English Templars, and Hostes of Boulogne, also a Templar, and pressed him with the same arguments, which the Abbot of Aumône had so successfully employed; solemnly pledging themselves that if the king's dignity were satisfied by a public submission, he would not attempt to injure the Church, nor would more be heard of the matter.

Once more S. Thomas's firmness yielded to this argument, not from any vacillation of purpose, but because he loved peace, and his charity disposed him to hope all things of Henry, even against his own past experience. Therefore, after consulting the other bishops, he went to the king and said, "My lord king, if the controversy between us had been about my personal rights, then I would never have opposed your will; but you must not be surprised if I am more scrupulous in the cause of God. With a lively hope in your prudence and moderation, I assent to what is required of me, and in good faith promise to observe the customs," adding, "in the word of truth," which was considered equal to an oath.

Scarcely had he uttered the words than the king cried out in a loud voice, "You have all heard what the archbishop has promised me on his own part; it now only remains that, at his bidding, the other bishops shall do the same." "I will," replied S. Thomas, "that they satisfy your honour as I have done." Then all the bishops rose and made the promise, except Joceline of Salisbury, who, as if seized by a sudden misgiving, asked the archbishop if he ought to make the promise, and on being told that he ought, he did so; whereupon the king shook his head at him, and said that he was always in opposition to him.

After all had spoken, the king said, "Every one has heard the promise that the archbishop and bishops have made, that the laws and customs of my kingdom shall be better kept and observed. In order that there may be in future no contention on the subject, let my grandfather Henry's laws be committed to writing." This proposal opened the archbishop's eyes, for it was unusual to put into writing customs which were not included in the law of the realm, and were often contrary to it. In order to gain time he observed, that being one of the youngest present, he could not be expected to know what these laws were; and as the matter was of great importance, and it was getting late, it would be better to adjourn till the next day. This was accordingly done.

The next day Richard de Luci and Joceline de Baillol drew up the code, which has ever since been famous under the name of the Constitutions of Clarendon. So far from containing the ancient customs and prerogatives of the crown of England, it was only a compendium of the tyrannical acts of the Norman kings. As the constitutions were read aloud, S. Thomas, after consulting Herbert and the other divines, objected separately to each. To the first constitution, which declared that all causes of advowsons and presentations to livings should be tried in the king's court, he objected that such causes were purely spiritual and ecclesiastical, and that clerics would be summoned before a civil tribunal.

When he heard the third constitution, that clerics were to be tried on all accusations by the king's justiciary, he exclaimed, "By this wicked canon clerics are brought before a secular judgment seat. Christ is judged anew before Pilate."

As to the fourth constitution, which forbade all persons to leave the kingdom without the king's leave, he said that it would put a stop to pious pilgrimages, and make the kingdom a spacious prison; and that if the Pope were to summon a council, and the king were to forbid the prelates to attend, must they not obey Christ's Vicar in spite of the prohibition?

On hearing the seventh constitution, which forbade that anyone who held in chief of the king, or any of his household, should be excommunicated or an interdict placed on their lands without his leave, he remarked, that by this the Church was simply degraded, and the power of binding and loosing even kings, which God had given her, was taken from her.

To the eighth constitution, which prohibited appeals to the Pope without the king's leave, he answered, that the archbishop who should consent to this would be guilty of perjury; for when he received the pallium he took an express oath not to hinder appeals to the Pope; adding, that it would be a sad day when the refuge of the oppressed was taken from them, and they were not able to have free recourse to the mother of all Churches, the Church of Rome.

To the twelfth constitution, which ordered that the revenues of all vacant bishoprics and religious houses should be paid to the king, he objected, on the ground that the king's treasury was not the place for the property of the poor, and that though this practice had sometimes prevailed, yet that the Church must always expostulate and never consent to it.

This twelfth constitution further declared, that when an appointment to a church was about to be filled, the king should summon the principal persons of that church, and the election should be held in the Chapel Royal. On which S. Thomas remarked, that to sanction such a diversity from the rest of Christendom, would be to start a schism, as well as to overpower the freedom of election by the king's authority. It is worth noticing that though these constitutions had been drawn up with the express object of enslaving the Church, yet it was said in this last of them, that the newly-elected dignitary should swear allegiance to the king, *"saving his order,"* thus tacitly sanctioning the reservation for which S. Thomas was contending.

But though S. Thomas had protested against each article as it was read aloud, his words had fallen on unheeding ears. As soon as the reading was concluded the king called on the archbishop and the bishops to sign and seal these constitutions. But S. Thomas instantly replied, "By the Lord Almighty, during my lifetime seal of mine shall never touch them." This bold reply threw the assembly into confusion. The king reminded S. Thomas of his promise to observe the royal customs; the terrified bishops bade him beware of perjury; the nobles and courtiers stormed and threatened; while the saint in vain protested, that these were not the true royal customs sanctioned by the laws of the realm. At length S. Thomas, wishing not to exasperate the king, asked for delay, as the matter was of such importance that he and the bishops could decide better after deliberation. Three copies of the code had been prepared on one sheet. One of these S. Thomas tore off and took away;

the Archbishop of York took a second; and the third was deposited in the royal archives. Some of the bishops are said to have signed and sealed, but who they were, or how many, is unknown; their signatures were invalid without that of their archbishop, and even his would have required the Pope's confirmation.

Quitting this stormy scene, S. Thomas mounted his horse and rode towards Winchester. Contrary to his usual custom, he rode alone. Solemn thoughts pressed on him. This had been an eventful day, a great crisis for his Church. How had he done his part? Had not he, by his weak compliance, given a fatal wound to the Spouse of Christ, whom he loved better than his life? Was this the end of all his fervent aspirations?—of all his vows to die for her? And how could he, whom all called perjured, hope to strengthen his still weaker brethren, and to erect a bulwark against the raging flood of iniquity which was sweeping the land? Oppressed by such self-communings, he rode along in silence. His suite rode behind, and discussed in subdued tones the events of the day. Some said that their master had done all that was necessary, while others were indignant that he should have so endangered the liberties of the Church. At length Alexander Llewellyn, the cross bearer, raising his voice in the heat of discussion, exclaimed, "Iniquity rages against Christ. The synagogue of Satan profanes God's sanctuary. No one is safe who loves the truth. This tempest has overthrown the columns of the Church, and during the shepherd's folly the sheep are scattered before the wolf. Now that the chief has fallen, who will stand? Who will triumph in the battle?"

The excited tone caught the archbishop's ear, and turning, he asked, "To whom do your words apply, my son?"

"To you, who have to-day betrayed your conscience and your fame," answered the impetuous Welshman; "to you, who have left an example to posterity which is hateful to God and contrary to justice. You have stretched out your consecrated hands to observe impious constitutions. You have joined with the wicked ministers of Satan to overthrow the liberty of the Church."

The saint groaned, his heart was well-nigh broken, and meekly bowing to the hasty reproof, he cried, "By my sins I have brought into slavery the Church which my predecessors ruled so wisely in dangers as great as these. And no wonder, since I was not taken, as they were, from the cloister but from the court, not from the school of Christ, but from Caesar's service. I, a proud, vain man, a feeder of birds, to be made the shepherd of the sheep! Of old the favourer of actors and the follower of hounds, and now the pastor of so many souls! I plainly see that I am deserted of God, and fit only to be cast out of the holy see which I fill." Then a flood of tears broke forth, and in bitterness of sorrow he sobbed aloud.

Herbert rode up and tried to console him. "One thing only remains," said he; "if, as you say, you have fallen basely, rise the more bravely. Be cautious, strong, and valiant. And know for a certainty that the Lord will be with you, as He was with David, who had been an adulterer and a murderer; as He was with S. Peter, who had apostatized; with blessed Magdalen, who had been a sinner; with S. Paul, who had persecuted the Church. You, too, have been a Saul, now you desire to be a Paul. The scales have fallen from your eyes, and your Jesus will show Himself to you openly, and teach you what great things you must bear for His name."

Somewhat consoled by these words, the saint turned all his thoughts to making reparation for his fault. His tender conscience exaggerated it, and not content with increasing his penances and forming good resolutions for the future, he would not say Mass for above forty days, till he should receive absolution from the Pope. The Holy Father wrote to him from Sens on the first of April, and reminded him of the difference between sins of deliberation and those of ignorance and frailty; adding, "If, then, you have committed anything for which you have now remorse of conscience, we counsel you to confess it, whatever it be, in penance to a discreet and prudent priest; and after this the merciful Lord, who looks more to the heart than the actions, will, with His usual pity, forgive you." Then, giving him the apostolic absolution, he bade him no longer abstain from Mass. The Bishop of Poictiers, too, wrote to him, saying, "I give God endless thanks that, as I know from the excellent testimony of others, and now from your own, you never did absolutely promise to observe, as their author boasts, nor did you sign as others did, those detestable and profane customs which have made their appearance in our days." Thus in the school of weakness and contempt, of penance and contrition, was the martyr trained for the future combat.

CHAPTER XI. THE COUNCIL OF NORTHAMPTON.

But though S. Thomas so bewailed his conduct at Clarendon, Henry felt that he had gained nothing beyond the petty triumph of having humiliated his adversary. He showed his vexation in many small ways. John of Salisbury, S. Thomas's most trusted counsellor, was banished the kingdom. Not only were Roger of York and Abbot Clarembald encouraged in their pretensions, but Gilbert of London, also, was allowed to claim independence of the archbishop, on the ground of some ancient British or Roman custom.

Henry further sent to the Pope to ask that Roger of York should be legate in England instead of S. Thomas. The Pope answered, "York has ever been subject to Canterbury, and shall be as long as I live." Henry scarcely listened to the answer, but despatched anew Geoffrey Ridel, Archdeacon of Canterbury, and John of Oxford to press his suit. These two messengers were afterwards notorious for their unprincipled advocacy of their master's cause, and John received the name of "the swearer," on account of the false oaths he was ever ready to take to answer the purpose of the hour. On this occasion they told the Pope, on their knees, that S. Thomas's life was in danger if Henry were further irritated, and the Holy Father believing them, gave them letters which transferred the office of legate to Roger, but with the condition that they were not to be delivered without S. Thomas's consent. This condition of course made them null; but they in some measure answered Henry's purpose, for he showed them about publicly, to prove that the Pope had given him power over the archbishop. Before long he returned them to the Pope, and pressed for ampler powers; but though he was well supported by some of the cardinals, he was unsuccessful.

Meanwhile, S. Thomas made every effort to bring about a reconciliation, and he seems, from time to time, to have cherished the hope that it was within his reach. Louis, King of France, alarmed at Henry's boasts and threats, offered the saint an asylum in his dominions; but he gratefully declined it, because, he said, there was hope of peace; and he begged of Louis to act as mediator, and, if he had the opportunity, to reprove Henry "for ever thinking evil of a man, who had served him so much and so faithfully, who had ever loved him with a true love, and upon whom he had conferred so many honours." Soon after, it appeared to him that the chief obstacle to peace was a report, that he had denounced Henry to the Pope and the King of France as a persecutor and oppressor of the Church, and he therefore wrote again to Louis, and begged him to bear witness that this was untrue.

At another time, the Bishop of Evreux having told him that Henry had said, that peace would be obtained by the archbishop's obtaining from the Pope the confirmation of the royal customs, S. Thomas, only too gald to shelter himself behind the rock of Peter, actually asked the Pope to confirm them. Of course his request was refused. Shortly after the Pope wrote to S. Thomas and his suffragans, that though they ought to act with great moderation and to avoid offending the king needlessly, yet he forbade them "in virtue of obedience "to bind themselves to anything against the liberty of the Church, and especially against the Roman Church, or to take any other form of oath than that which bishops were accustomed to take to kings. He also wrote to the monks of Citeaux, Clairvaux, and Pontigny, then celebrated for sanctity, desiring them to pray fervently for S. Thomas and the Church in England.

S. Thomas spared no effort to conciliate the king. But all in vain—peace still eluded his grasp. As a last resource he determined to try what he could do by personal influence; and going to Woodstock where Henry was staying, he asked for an interview. But admission was denied him. Then, indeed, his heart sank within him; and, chafed and wounded by failures, to which he was so unaccustomed, he resolved to visit the Holy Father in spite of the king's illegal prohibition. Twice he made the attempt to embark at night, and cross from Romnel, now Romney, and twice he was driven back, either by the contrary wind, or by the fears of the sailors, who dreaded the king's anger if they should help his escape. On the last occasion his attendants, believing him to be really gone, became alarmed for their own safety, and took to flight. One cleric alone remained, and, on the following evening he retired to the archbishop's room, where he sat musing on his master's sad fate. At length, when it was very late, he said to a boy, who was with him, "Go, shut the outer door of the hall, that we may sleep more safely." The boy went with a light, but soon returned in terror, declaring that he had seen the archbishop sitting alone in a corner, and he thought it was his ghost. The cleric would not believe him, but, going out, saw that it was indeed his master. He brought him some refreshment; and then S. Thomas sent for a few of the monks, and told them how all had come about, how he had tried to escape, but God had barred his way. The next morning the king's officers arrived to seize his property; but when they saw him, they were greatly surprised, and not a little confused. As for Henry, he was rejoiced to hear the archbishop was not gone; for he feared that should he have an interview with the Pope, the kingdom would be placed under an interdict.

Soon after, S. Thomas went again to Woodstock, and this time he succeeded in obtaining an audience. Henry received him courteously, and made a joke of his attempted flight, saying, "So, my lord, you wish to leave my kingdom. I suppose it is not large enough to hold both you and me." But, though nothing particular was said, the king's manner gave S. Thomas the impression that a crisis was near; and he told his friends that the time was come when he must either yield disgracefully or fight bravely to extremities; and it soon appeared that he was right.

Thus eight months passed, and Henry found that he made no progress in overcoming S. Thomas's passive resistance. His patience was exhausted, and he determined to crush him by one great act of despotic power. Little did he know what strength was in that heart, inflamed by the pure love of God; nor did he dream that the very acts of violence and contumely by which he had been wounding the sensitive and chivalrous

Thomas, had served only to drive out self-love, and to render him proof against future trials.

A case was soon trumped up to serve the king's purpose. One John the marshal laid claim to a part of the archiepiscopal manor of Pagham, and the cause being decided against him in the Archbishop's Court, he appealed to the King's Court, as a recent law allowed, on the ground that justice had been denied him by the archbishop; but instead of taking an oath on the Gospels, as the law required, he had produced a book of songs from under his cloak, and, in spite of the remonstrances of the judges, had sworn on it. Notwithstanding, he had obtained a summons for the archbishop to appear in the King's Court, on the feast of the Exaltation of the Holy Cross, the 14th of September; when the archbishop, being himself ill, had sent four of his knights to answer for him, and to produce his attestation and that of the sheriff as to the invalidity of the appeal. The king, however, was very angry that the archbishop did not appear in person, and, on this frivolous ground, a charge of contempt of the King's Court was got up against him.

A council was ordered to meet at Northampton, on Tuesday the 6th of October, A.D. 1164; but S. Thomas, instead of being summoned as usual, was peremptorily commanded by the sheriff to appear as a culprit, to answer the above charge. He set out for Northampton on the appointed day, and as he approached the town word was brought him, that the king had allowed his lodgings to be occupied. He therefore refused to go further unless this was put right. Henry gave the necessary order, and S. Thomas took up his abode in the monastery of S. Andrew. The king was out hawking when he arrived, so they did not meet that day.

The next day, Wednesday, S. Thomas went after Mass to the castle, and was kept waiting in the ante-room while the king was hearing Mass. When Henry came out, S. Thomas rose to receive him, and showed himself ready to give the usual kiss if the king should offer it, but he did not do so. S. Thomas then asked leave to visit the Pope, and was refused. No business was transacted that day, but the king told him that his cause would be tried on the morrow.

On Thursday, the council met for business. All the English bishops, except the Bishop of Rochester and another who had not yet arrived, were present, and also several Norman bishops, and all the earls and barons. The archbishop was accused of contempt of the King's Court. He pleaded illness, and that he had sent his knights in the usual form to answer for him. But his plea was not listened to, and by the king's command he was condemned to the confiscation of all his movable property, which seems to have been considered equivalent to a fine of £500. Then there arose a contention between the bishops and the barons as to who should pronounce the sentence; the barons saying that as laymen they could not pass sentence on a bishop, and the bishops answering, "This is not an ecclesiastical, but a secular court; we sit here as barons and not as bishops. If you pay respect to our ordination now, you should have done so before to the archbishop; for if you cannot pass the sentence, still less can we pass it on one who is our archbishop and our lord." At length the king became angry, and ordered Henry, Bishop of Winchester, to pronounce the sentence, which he accordingly did. S. Thomas received it in silence, and all the bishops, except Gilbert of London, gave security for his submitting to it. He said, however, privately to those near him, "Though I hold my tongue, all posterity will speak for me and exclaim against this iniquitous sentence."

When this matter had been disposed of, a demand was made on him for £300, which he had received from the wardenship of the castles of Eye and Berkhamsted. He replied that he was not bound to answer this demand, as it had not been included in his summons; but of his own free will he would observe, that he had spent that sum, and much more out of his own pocket, in repairing these castles and the Palace of London, as anyone might see. The king objected that these repairs had been done without his sanction, and demanded judgment to be given against S. Thomas; whereupon S. Thomas with his usual magnanimity exclaimed, that money should never stand between him and his sovereign, and he would, therefore, immediately give security for the payment of the £300. His sureties were the Earl of Gloucester and two of his own men, one of whom was William of Eynesford.

On Friday a further demand was made for 500 marks, which the king had lent him during the war of Toulouse, and 500 more advanced by a Jew, for which the king had been surety. "I do not deny," answered S. Thomas, "that I received 500 marks from the king; but I assert that it was a gift and not a loan, and it is unworthy of his highness now to require payment. It would be more gracious of him to remember the many services which I rendered him at that time when I was chancellor." The king, however, turned a deaf ear to this plea, and insisted on sentence being given against S. Thomas; whereupon the court decided, that as the archbishop admitted that he had received the money, and could not prove that it was a gift, he must find security for the repayment. S. Thomas objected that as he had property in the kingdom far superior in value to the sum required, it was unbecoming the king's majesty, and indecorous to himself, to ask for surety. But the peers reminded him with bitterness, that all his personal property had been confiscated the first day of their sitting, and that he must therefore either find bail or remain a prisoner; the king meanwhile not only approving of this shameful proceeding, but urging it on with indecent haste, unbecoming the dignity of a king and the generosity of a man. Notwithstanding, five noble spirits, whose names have not descended to posterity, came forward in opposition to the king, and became bail each for 100 marks.

Then a monstrous demand was made on the part of the king, for an account of the proceeds, during vacancies, of the archbishopric and all the bishoprics and abbeys which had been in the keeping of S. Thomas during his chancellorship. S. Thomas answered that he had received no notice whatever on this subject, and had come entirely unprepared; but that at a fitting time and place he would satisfy the king. The consideration of this matter was deferred till the next day. All now saw plainly that Henry was bent on the archbishop's ruin, and from this time forth many of the barons ceased their usual visits to him.

Early on Saturday morning the Bishop of Winchester went to the king, and generously offered him 2,000 marks of his own, if he would abandon the proceedings against the archbishop. But money was not what Henry wanted, and the offer was peremptorily rejected.

When the council met, S. Thomas was called on "to account for the revenues of the vacant bishoprics and abbeys, estimated at from 30,000 to 44,000 marks. It was well known to all, that S. Thomas had spent all the money that came into his hands most magnificently, for the king's service and with his sanction; and, moreover, before his consecration, the king, through his son, had relieved him from all obligations he might have incurred as chancellor, as was the general custom in all similar cases, even when a monk of one abbey was made abbot of another. But right and reason had no weight with Henry. He ordered the gates of the castle to be secured, so that none should go out without his leave; and all now believed that imprisonment, if not death, awaited S. Thomas.

S. Thomas and the bishops retired to a private room to consult, and then it was seen how terror-stricken the bishops were. All those who leant to the king's side urged S. Thomas to resign the see and throw himself on the king's mercy. "Would to God," said Hilary of Chichester, "you were not archbishop, but plain Thomas Becket." "If you would remember, father," said Gilbert of London, "what benefit the king has conferred on you, and the ruin that hangs over the Church if you persist in opposing him, you would resign your see and ten times as much if you could; and perhaps the king would reward your humility by giving you it back again." "It is enough," replied S. Thomas; "your opinion is evident and so are its motives." For all believed that Gilbert hoped to take S. Thomas's place. Bartholomew of Exeter advised a temporizing policy; while Robert of Lincoln, a plain, blunt man, said, "It seems to me that this man will lose his life or his bishopric; what good his bishopric will do him if he lose his life, I do not clearly see." Even good Roger of Worcester, who so often got into disgrace with his cousin the king, by standing up for S. Thomas, was now afraid to give his opinion. "For," said he, "if I say that we have received the cure of souls to resign it at the king's bidding, I shall speak against my conscience; but if I advise resistance to the king's will, there are plenty who will carry my words to the king, and I shall be treated like a public enemy." Only the venerable Henry of Winchester spoke out fearlessly and said, "We ought to blush for shame at this discussion. For if our archbishop shall set us the example of resigning at the beck and nod of a temporal sovereign, the cure of souls committed to him by God, what will become of the whole Church which is endangered in his person? He is therefore bound to resist these oppressions; and he has no cause to fear, for his enemies cannot accuse him of a single crime or dishonourable act."

After all had given their opinion they sat for some time in silence. Then they wished to adjourn; but the door had been locked on them, and they could not get out. Two earls came quickly from the king and opened the door, for they supposed that S. Thomas was going to make his submission. But he told them that he wished to consult certain persons who were more learned than himself, and he therefore asked leave to adjourn, promising that at the next meeting he would give his answer. The bishops of London and Rochester were chosen to carry this message to Henry; but Gilbert, instead of giving it faithfully, said that the archbishop wished for a little delay, in order to make preparations for obeying the king. When S. Thomas heard what Gilbert had said he was very angry, and declared that he would give for answer, not necessarily what the king willed, but whatever should be dictated to him from heaven. Notwithstanding, they were then allowed to adjourn.

Henceforth, the numerous knights and others who had adhered to S. Thomas and dined in his hall, were afraid to go near him, and his table was almost empty. Whereupon he sent out his servants to call in the poor, the lame, and the blind, saying that they would be a more powerful aid to him in his adversity than the retainers who had deserted him.

The next day was Sunday, and this day of rest was spent by the saint in prayer and consultation with holy men, in whose fervour and wisdom he could find support.

Early on Monday morning he was seized with an acute pain, to which he was subject, and which confined him to his bed. "When the king heard it he was very angry, thinking it was a trick to gain time; and he sent the Earls of Leicester and Cornwall to ascertain the truth. They found S. Thomas in bed and unable to move; but he said to them, "Do not suppose this is a device on my part, for to-morrow I will go at all hazards, even if I be carried in a litter." In the course of the day, however, the pain abated.

For many months past, all who loved the Church had had their eyes fixed anxiously on S. Thomas. Prayer had been made for him at Citeaux, at Clairvaux, at Pontigny, and many other monasteries in France; and scattered over fair England, there were many communities of holy monks and nuns, and many saints—S. Godric, S. Gilbert, S. Ælred, and others—who looked up to him as their father, and ceased not day nor night to plead for him before God's mercy-seat. This Monday night there came to him an unknown monk, who bade him say on the morrow the Mass of S. Stephen, the protomartyr, and promised that he should thus be delivered from his enemies.

At length came Tuesday, the 13th of October, a notable day in many ways. To our saint it brought a sweet and encouraging memory, for it was the first anniversary of that joyous festival when he had been allowed the happiness of translating the honoured relics of S. Edward, the guardian of England's Church and liberty.

Rumours were afloat that violent hands would be laid on S. Thomas in the course of the day; and early in the morning the bishops went to him, and tried to persuade him to resign his see; assuring him that he would certainly be condemned for high treason, and asking what good there would be in his archbishopric when he had incurred the king's hatred? But S. Thomas answered them with unshaken firmness: "Brethren," said he, in accents of touching sadness, "you see how the world opposes me; but I mourn still more that the children of my Mother should fight against me. For even were I to hold my peace, after ages would tell how you have left me alone in the contest, and how twice in these two days you have judged me, who, sinner though I be, am your archbishop and father. And now I gather from your words that you are ready to assist in passing against me not a civil sentence merely, but a criminal one. But I command you all, in virtue of your obedience and under peril of your order, not to be present in any judgment against my person; and lest you should do so, I appeal to our Mother, the Church of Rome, the refuge of all the oppressed. If, as the rumour runs, secular hands are to be laid on me, I order you, in virtue of obedience, to use ecclesiastical censure in behalf of your father and archbishop. For be assured, that though the world should roar, the enemy rise up, or the body tremble (for the flesh is weak), yet, by God's help, I will not be base enough to give way, nor to desert the flock intrusted to me."

Gilbert of London immediately appealed to the Holy See against S. Thomas's command to use censures in case violence was done him; after which the bishops went away; Henry of Winchester and Joceline of Salisbury only remaining behind to comfort and encourage the saint.

When they were all gone, S. Thomas prepared himself for the battle. In obedience to the unknown monk, he said the Mass of S. Stephen at his own altar; and as he celebrated the Holy Sacrifice and offered up himself in union with the Immaculate Lamb and with the protomartyr, his eyes were so blinded with tears that he was often compelled to stop in the middle of the prayers. His selection of this Mass made a great impression on those who were present, for the Introit begins with the words, "For the princes sat and spake against me;" and it was also noticed that, though it was not a festival, he celebrated with his pallium.

When Mass was over he placed the Blessed Sacrament in his breast, as was often done in those days on trying emergencies: and he was about to set oat for the court on foot, vested as he was and carrying his cross. But his clerics and some Templars who were friendly to him, persuaded him to lay aside his mitre and pallium, to throw his black cappa over the sacred vestments, and to go on horseback. On the way to the castle however, he said to Alexander Llewellyn, "I wish I had come as I first proposed, in my vestments and with the weapons most suitable to a bishop, that the court might see who it is they have twice judged."

On arriving at the castle, S. Thomas dismounted, and taking the cross from Llewellyn, was about to enter the hall, where several of the bishops were waiting. Then Robert of Hereford ran up to him, and asked leave to carry his cross; but S. Thomas answered, "No, my son, suffer me to retain it as the banner under which I fight." Gilbert of London was standing under the gateway, and Hugh de Nunant, Archdeacon of Lisieux, who had come in the archbishop's train, said to him, "My Lord, why do you suffer him to carry his own cross?" But Gilbert answered, "My good friend, he always was a fool, and always will be." Then all made way for the primate as he passed through the hall to the council-chamber.

Meanwhile the king, hearing in what guise the archbishop was approaching, was awe-struck, and not daring to face him, retired to an inner room, whither the barons followed him. Then S. Thomas sat down in his usual place in the council-chamber, still holding his cross, and the bishops stood around. At length Gilbert of London, who stood next him, tried to take the cross from him, saying, "You carry your cross. Now, if the king were to draw his sword, what hope would there be of peace?" But S. Thomas answered, "If it could be so, I should wish always to carry it; but I know what I am now doing. My cross is a sign of peace, and I would preserve God's peace for myself and the Church in England. If the king were to draw his sword, it would be a bad token of peace." After a time the bishops were summoned to the king in the inner room. Roger of York purposely went in after the others; and, as an insult to S. Thomas, he had his cross carried before him, notwithstanding that the Pope had recently forbidden him to do so in the province of Canterbury, a prohibition which he had set aside for a time by a fresh appeal.

S. Thomas was now left alone in the council-chamber with his clerics. There he sat in calm dignity, his majestic figure according well with the solemn grandeur of his garb and the emblem of salvation which he bore. Herbert sat at his feet, FitzStephen stood near; and the others were at no great distance. Then Herbert said in a low voice, "My lord, if they lay violent hands on you, you can excommunicate them all." But FitzStephen overhearing it, replied, "Far be it from our lord to do so; not so did the holy apostles and martyrs of the Lord when they were taken. Rather let him pray for them, and forgive them, and possess his soul in patience. If he should suffer for justice sake and for the liberty of the Church, then, by God's grace, his soul would be at rest, and his memory in benediction." At these words John Planeta and Ralph de Diceto, Archdeacon and afterwards Dean of S. Paul's, and the others who were by, were affected to tears. FitzStephen was about to speak again, but one of the king's marshals tapped him on the shoulder and forbade him to speak to the archbishop. Whereupon he made signs to his master by way of reminding him to look at the crucifix he was bearing, and to occupy himself in prayer, for in these must be his sole confidence. And when in after years they met in a foreign land, S. Thomas thanked his faithful attendant for the consolation that these signs had afforded him.

From time to time there issued from the inner room the noise of fierce, stormy words, and angry threats, so that danger seemed imminent, and S. Thomas and his companions crossed themselves devoutly. And presently there came forth some of the ushers, who, glaring fiercely at S. Thomas, shook their wands threateningly at him. Again they crossed themselves and prayed: and S. Thomas, stooping down, said tenderly to Herbert, "I am afraid for you; but do not fear for yourself, for you shall share my crown." And Herbert answered bravely, "We must neither of us fear; for you have raised a noble standard, by which not only the powers of the earth, but those of the air are overthrown. Remember that once you were the standard-bearer of the King of the Angles, and were never overcome; it would, indeed, be a disgrace to be overcome now that you are the standard-bearer of the King of the Angels." Thus did this heroic little band mutually keep up their courage, each thinking of others rather than himself; the clerics fearing only for their master, and he trembling only for them.

Meanwhile there had been a stormy scene in the inner room. As soon as the bishops went in, the king began to complain that the archbishop should have come to him cross in hand, as if he were not a Christian king. Then the courtiers chimed in, some saying that his conduct was an insult to the whole kingdom, others calling him proud and vain; others, again, declaring that he was perjured and a traitor; and all adding somewhat fresh to the storm of abuse. The bishops, too, told what he had done that morning; how he had reproved them for joining in the two previous judgments; how he had forbidden them to take part in any future proceedings against him; and how he had appealed to the Pope. Then Henry, in a great rage, sent several barons to inquire of S. Thomas, whether he had really said what the bishops alleged; and whether he was prepared to give bail that he would abide by the sentence of the court about the money he had spent as chancellor.

S. Thomas answered with great dignity, "In all devout and due subjection I obey the king for God's sake in all things, saving God's obedience, the Church's dignity, and the honour of a bishop in my person. I am not bound to give any account of my chancellorship, because I was summoned only for the cause of John the marshal; and, moreover, when I was chosen archbishop, before my consecration I was delivered over by the king to the Church of Canterbury free from all secular claims. You and most ecclesiastics in the kingdom know this well, and I therefore call on you to testify this truth to the king; for it would not be safe, though it is according to law, to bring witnesses against him, neither need I do it, for I am not now pleading my cause. I can give no sureties for the accounts, because the bishops and my friends have already been bound; nor ought I to be required to find bail in a cause which has not been adjudged against me. As to the prohibition I have placed upon the bishops, I acknowledge that I told them they had condemned me too severely for a single absence, which was not contumacious; and therefore I appealed against them, forbidding them, during this appeal, to judge me for a secular cause committed before I was archbishop. And I again appeal, and place my person and the Church of Canterbury under the protection of God and my lord the Pope."

Struck by the truth and dignity of this answer the barons withdrew in silence to the king. But some of the king's partisans said to each other within S. Thomas's hearing, "King William who conquered England, knew how to tame his clerics. He imprisoned his own brother Odo, Bishop of Bayeux, for rebellion against him. He cast Stigand, Archbishop of Canterbury, into a dark dungeon, where he died. And Geoffrey, Earl of Anjou, our king's father, caused Arnulf, Bishop-elect of Seez, and many of his clerics, to be mutilated, because he considered himself elected bishop without his leave."

The king, on receiving S. Thomas's answer, was in a very great fury. He decreed that all who took the archbishop's part should be accounted guilty of treason. He threatened to mutilate on the spot Joceline of Salisbury and William of Norwich for having sided with him; and he tried to compel the bishops to join in the sentence against him, in spite of the archbishop's prohibition, which, he said, had no force against the express provisions of Clarendon. But in that age of faith, though men might evade the Church's commands, and from wickedness or timidity would often take part in crime and injustice, yet they did not dare, by a direct act of disobedience, to throw off the Church's authority and defy her supernatural powers. All the bishops, therefore, were thrown into consternation at the idea of disobeying their primate's recent prohibition, and they represented strongly to the king, that it would be better, even for his cause, that they should not place themselves in the primate's power by disobedience, promising at the same time to appeal to the Pope against his prohibition. With much difficulty the king was induced to consent, and they withdrew to the council-chamber.

While this discussion was going on, Roger of York had taken on himself to leave the room, and, passing through the council-chamber, called out to two of his clerics, Master Robert le Grand and Osbert de Arundel, "Let us go, for we ought not to see what will soon be done with my lord of Canterbury." "No," replied Master Robert, "I will not go till I see what God wills in his regard; for if he should lose his life for God and His justice, he could not have a finer or better end." For all the lower clergy, who did not look for advancement from the king, were on the side of S. Thomas.

Then the bishops came into the council-chamber and took their places near S. Thomas. Robert of Lincoln was weeping, and the others could scarcely restrain their tears. Bartholomew of Exeter, a timid but well-disposed man, fell at S. Thomas's feet, and said, "My father, have pity on yourself; have pity, too, on us, for the hatred against you is our ruin." Joceline of Salisbury and William of Norwich also pleaded with him for their own safety. But S. Thomas replied gently to Bartholomew, "Flee hence, my brother, for you savour not the things that be of God." Hilary of Chichester reproached him bitterly for having "placed his bishops between the hammer and the anvil" by his late prohibition, forcing them to go against the royal dignities which they had pledged themselves at Clarendon to observe in good faith, without deceit, and lawfully. To which S. Thomas answered, "Whatever is against the Church or the laws of God, cannot be kept *in good faith and lawfully*; nor can a Christian king have a dignity which is the destruction of the Church's liberty, to which he has sworn. Besides, the king sent these very royal dignities to the Pope for confirmation, and he returned them condemned; thus teaching us what to do: for we are ready to receive what he receives, and to reject what he rejects. Furthermore, if we fell at Clarendon (for the flesh is weak), we must take courage and contend now with our foe in the strength of the Holy Ghost; and if we then swore to what was unjust, you know that an unlawful oath is not binding."

Meanwhile the barons were with the king, consulting about the sentence that was to be passed on S. Thomas; and presently they came out in a body, with the Earls of Leicester and Cornwall at their head, and advanced towards him, while the bishops removed to some distance so as to take no part in what was being done. When the barons entered, S. Thomas was about to rise to them, but Herbert whispered to him to receive them sitting, as better befitting his position as their father, and the cross which he bore. So he sat calm and dignified, without the least sign of fear.

Then the Earl of Leicester said, "The king commands you to render up your accounts as you promised to do. Otherwise hear your sentence." "Sentence," said the archbishop, rising, "Lord earl, my son, hear me first. You know, my son, how intimate I was with our lord the king, and how faithfully I served him. It, therefore, pleased him that I should be advanced to the Archbishop of Canterbury. God knows, I willed it not, for I knew my own weakness; and rather for the love of him than of God I gave way, which to-day is clear enough, when God and the king have both deserted me. Still, in my promotion, when I was elected before Henry, the king's son and heir, who was appointed for that purpose, the question was asked, 'How did they give me to the Church of Canterbury?' And the answer was, 'Free from all secular obligations.' I therefore am not bound, nor will I plead respecting them." "This is different," answered the earl, "from what the Bishop of London told the king. But how will you avoid his judgment? You are his subject, and have many castles and lands in fief and barony." "I have nothing in fief or barony," replied S. Thomas; "for whatever kings have given to the Church, they have given as a free alms, and the king himself has declared and confirmed the same. Wherefore, by the authority and office which God's ordinance and the law of Christendom give me, I forbid you to pass judgment on me." The earl replied, "Far be it from me to transgress your command to my soul's detriment. I now hold my peace, and so far as I am concerned, I leave you free." Then turning to the Earl of Cornwall, he added, "You hear that the archbishop in God's name has imposed silence on me; do you, therefore, say what the king has ordered." But the Earl of Cornwall answered, "I will not venture upon what was not ordered me." The Earl of Leicester rejoined, "I beseech you, my lord, to wait till your answer is brought you." "Am I, then, a prisoner?" inquired S. Thomas. "No, by S. Lazarus, my lord," replied the earl. The barons were retiring when S. Thomas added, "Son and earl, yet listen. By as much as the soul is more worthy than the body, by so much are you bound to obey God and me rather than your earthly king. Neither law nor reason permits children to judge their father. Wherefore I decline the judgment of the king or anyone else; and before you all I here appeal to the Pope, placing the Church of Canterbury, my order, and my dignity under God's protection and his. And you, my brethren and fellow-bishops, who have served man rather than God, I summon to the presence of the Pope; and so, guarded by the authority of the Catholic Church and of the Holy See, I go hence."

With these words S. Thomas moved down the council-chamber, and as he passed along with a majestic air, wearing the sacred vestments, carrying his cross, and followed by Herbert alone, though some called out "perjured" and "traitor," yet all made way for him, and none dared lay a finger on him. In the middle of the hall was a heap of firewood, in passing which, he caught his foot on one of the logs, and stumbled. Then some of the motley multitude assembled there began to insult him, throwing straws and other small things at him. Randolph de Broc and Hamelin, the king's illegitimate brother, also cried out, "There goes the traitor." Whereupon, looking severely at them, he said, "If I were a soldier, my own hands should prove you false."

On reaching the court he mounted his horse, when it appeared that the gate was locked, and he could not get out. But Peter de Mortorio, one of his followers, saw a bunch of keys hanging on a nail in the wall, and happily the first key that he tried, unlocked the gate; and thus they passed into the street, where an immense crowd was collected.

When the king heard how S. Thomas had quitted the council, he was frightened lest some injury should be done him, and an interdict should fall on his kingdom. So he sent a herald to proclaim through the town that no one must molest the archbishop. But in truth there was no need for this precaution, for the multitude outside, who had watched through the livelong day in fear and trembling lest he should have been killed, raised a joyful shout on seeing him, crying out, "Blessed be God, Who has saved His servant from the face of his enemies." And they pressed round him, kneeling to him, and asking his blessing, so that he could scarcely get his horse through the crowd. Then turning to Herbert, whom, having been unable to find his horse, he had taken up behind him, he said, "What a glorious procession escorts me home! These are the poor of whom Christ spake, partakers of my distress. Let them come in that we may feast together." The doors of the refectory were accordingly thrown open, and all who would, came in and sat down at his table.

CHAPTER XII. THE FLIGHT.

ON entering the monastery of S. Andrews, S. Thomas went at once to the chapel, and placed his cross on our Lady's altar. He remained for some time in private prayer, and afterwards sang None and vespers, the usual hour for which was already past. Then he went to the refectory, when it appeared that of forty retainers who had come in his train to Northampton, only six remained faithful to him.; but the poor whom he loved and had invited to his table, happily filled the places of the deserters. During the meal, Gilbert of London and Hilary of Chichester came in; and pretending to wish for a reconciliation, they craftily proposed that, as the dispute was only a money question, S. Thomas should place his manors of Otford and Mundeham for a time in the king's hands, adding, that they were sure the latter would not retain them, but would waive all further claims on S. Thomas, and receive him back into favour. The saint at once perceived that this concession would really be a tacit acquiescence in the king's unjust claims and illegal pretensions; and therefore he answered, "The manor of Heccham, I am told, once belonged to the church of Canterbury, but it is now in the king's possession. There is no hope at present of recovering it; but I would rather expose this head of mine to danger, than resign the claim even to that manor," at the same time placing his hand on the crown of his head, a gesture which was recalled after his martyrdom as having had a peculiar significance. The two bishops returned to Henry, and widened the breach by repeating S. Thomas's answer.

While they sat at table, FitzStephen said, "This has been a sad day;" but S. Thomas answered, "The last day will be sadder." After a time he added, "Dwell in silence and in peace. Let no sharp word proceed from your mouth. If anyone speak against you, do not answer him, but suffer him to speak evil of you. The evil is not spoken against me, but against him who, when evil is spoken, recognises it in himself." The book that was read that evening, according to the usual custom, was the Tripartite History on the persecution of Liberius; and the text, "When they persecute you in one city flee to another," being quoted, S. Thomas raised his eyes, and, meeting those of Herbert, both understood that he would obey our Lord's injunction. He sat at table till nightfall, when, after grace had been said, he sent his three friends, the Bishops of Worcester, Hereford, and Rochester, to the king to request permission for him to go away the next day, and also that he should be given a safe-conduct to visit the Pope. Henry was in high spirits, but refused to give an answer till the morrow,—a reply which, they thought, foreboded danger; and secret messages from some of the privy councillors confirmed these fears.

Before S. Thomas left the table, he ordered his bed to be placed behind the high altar. He had spent one of the preceding nights in the church with his clerics, taking the discipline, repeating the Litanies, and genuflecting at the invocation of each saint; and some of his clerics, supposing that he was going to do so again, asked leave to keep vigil with him. But he answered, "No; I would not have you troubled." Osbern, his chamberlain, kept every one away from the part of the church where his bed was laid, saying that the archbishop was very tired, and must not be disturbed; and the monks, believing him to be asleep behind the altar, sang compline in a low voice.

Meanwhile, the saint ordered one of his most faithful servants, Roger de Brai, and two Gilbertine lay-brothers, Robert de Cave and Scailman, in whom he confided, to get four strong horses, though not out of his own stables, for fear of exciting suspicion, and to place them at the monastery gate as if they were waiting for some visitor. Then the Litanies were said, with a genuflexion at the name of each saint; and after they were finished, S. Thomas took a tender and sorrowful leave of his devoted Herbert, whom he directed to go with all speed to Canterbury to collect what money and valuables he could, and then to cross the sea and await him at the Monastery of S. Bertin, near S. Omer. And as he expected that, as soon as his flight should be known, the king would give his property to be pillaged, he recommended Herbert to take special care of a favourite book, which he valued far above the rich paraphernalia belonging to his dignity.

Finally, when all his preparations were completed, he laid aside his stole for the first time since his consecration: and then, wearing his usual black cappa, and his hair-shirt by way of hidden armour, and taking with him only his pallium and his archiepiscopal seal, he set out alone. At the monastery gate he found Roger de Brai and the Gilbertine brothers, with the horses. The night was dark and very rainy; no one was out; and as they rode along in silence, they passed unobserved through the streets till they reached the north gate of the town, which was nearest the monastery, and which happened fortunately to be the only one at which guards had not been placed. The rain poured down so heavily that S. Thomas's cappa was soaked, and twice through the night he had to cut off a piece to lighten its weight. Notwithstanding, before morning they rode twenty-five miles to Grantham, a village half-way to Lincoln. Here they rested for a little time, and the saint had a short sleep which enabled them to push on to Lincoln, where they found shelter in the house of a fuller, called Jacob. S. Thomas now changed his dress for that of a lay-brother, and henceforth he went by the name of Brother Christian. At Lincoln he took a boat, and accompanied by Robert de Cave alone, his two other companions having gone by land to Sempringham, he went for forty miles by water till he reached an island, on which stood a convent called the Hermitage, belonging to the Canonesses of S. Gilbert of Sempringham. He was now in comparative safety, for this fen country, which he had happily reached, was inhabited, like the Theban desert of old, by few except the holy men and women who, under the direction of S. Gilbert, had erected houses for prayer and penance in the most secluded spots. Being in great want of rest, he remained at the Hermitage for three days, enjoying the peace which reigned in this abode of saintly women, and partaking of the poor fare of the house with such simplicity and cheerfulness, that the brother who was his companion, seeing him sitting alone at a meal of a few herbs, and remembering his high dignity, was so overcome as to be obliged to leave the room lest his tears should distress the saint.

From the Hermitage he took his way through the fens to S. Botolf's, ten miles off, now called Boston, and thence to Haversholme, and to Chickesande in Bedfordshire, passing from one Gilbertine house to another, travelling by night when he was in a neighbourhood where he might be known, till at length he arrived safely at Eastry, a village belonging to his see, close to Sandwich, and only eight miles from Canterbury. Here he lay hid in the priest's house; and there being a little window which opened into the church, he had the consolation of assisting at Mass, unknown to the people, and even to the priest who officiated. A cleric, who was in the secret, would bring him the kiss of peace from the altar; and before the congregation had dispersed, he could give his farewell blessing to his much-loved flock, quite unconscious of his presence, from whom he was about to tear himself.

Meanwhile, on that memorable Tuesday night, one of S. Thomas's attendants at Northampton, who was not aware of his flight, had a dream in which he heard a voice saying, "Our soul has escaped like a sparrow from the snare of the fowlers; our snare is broken, and we are delivered." And lo! the next morning he found it was true.

Early on Wednesday morning, Henry of Winchester came to see S. Thomas; and having asked Osbern, the chamberlain, how the archbishop was, Osbern answered, "He is well, for he left us last night, and is gone we know not whither." "And may God's blessing go with him," replied the venerable prelate, with a deep sigh and tears in his eyes.

When the king heard the news, he was at first speechless with anger, but at length he said, "We have not yet done with him." Henry was no common foe to deal with, for the violence of his passions was equalled by his deep and clever cunning. He perceived at once how great an advantage S. Thomas had gained on him by flight, since he could now lay his cause at the Pope's feet and make Europe ring with the tale of his wrongs; and he therefore resolved to turn the tables on him by assuming a policy of forbearance and moderation. With this view he restrained his passions, and instead of pillaging the saint's property and persecuting his friends, as would have been his natural course, he merely ordered his goods to be placed in safe custody, while the appeal which the bishops had made to the Pope was pending. He obliged the bishops to start with the least possible delay, selecting as his envoys, not only Roger of York, Gilbert of London, and Hilary of Chichester, but also Roger of Worcester and Bartholomew of Exeter, who were known to be personal friends of S. Thomas, and he associated with them several ecclesiastics and laymen of good station, in order to give an air of respectability to the party. By them he also sent letters to the King of France and the Earl of Flanders, begging them not to receive a traitor, Thomas, *late* Archbishop of Canterbury, who had fled from England without any just cause.

On Monday, the 2nd of November, the bishops and their party embarked at Dover. The weather was tempestuous, the sea was rough, and before long the ship was in such danger, that Gilbert of London, throwing off his cowl and cappa, made ready to swim for his life; and it was with great difficulty that they regained the port from which they had sailed. On the same day, a little before daybreak, S. Thomas and his three faithful companions left Sandwich in an open boat, which was the best vessel that the priest in whose house he was concealed, could venture to hire for him. But though the waves ran mountains high, the little boat which carried God's saint and his fortunes, rode safely over the stormy billows, and before evening landed him at low water on the sands at Oie, about a league from Gravelines. But he was not yet out of danger, since he was now in the territories of Matthew, Earl of Boulogne, who bore S. Thomas ill-will, because, as chancellor, he had opposed a sacrilegious marriage between Matthew and Mary, Abbess of Romsey and daughter of King Stephen. They, therefore, found it necessary to avoid the towns, and to travel on foot as befitted poor lay-brothers.

The rough voyage had exhausted S. Thomas, and the heavy shoes and dress of a lay-brother, which he still wore, wearied him greatly, so that he trudged on with difficulty; and at last he was so worn out that he sat down on the roadside, and declared that he could not walk another step, and they must either carry him or get him a beast to ride on. With some difficulty they found a boy, whom they sent to the next village to hire a horse, but he was so long away that they became alarmed lest he should have betrayed them. At length, however, he returned with a sorry ass, without a saddle, and with a halter of straw. On this they threw a cloak, and S. Thomas mounted and rode a couple of miles; but the rough paces of the creature tired him, and, finding it easier to walk, he dismounted. He now dragged on his weary -way on foot with such evident difficulty, that a poor woman, struck with his noble air and his languid gait, ran into her house to fetch him a walking-stick. The only stick she could find had been used as a spit, and was covered with grease; but notwithstanding, the simple soul offered it to him, and he accepted it with the warmest thanks.

Soon after they came up to a party of young men, one of whom had a hawk on his wrist. S. Thomas, forgetting for the moment his present troubles, looked with such interest at the bird which reminded him of happier days, that one of the party exclaimed, "If I am not mistaken, that is the Archbishop of Canterbury." For it was already rumoured that he had landed on that coast. But Brother Scailman, with ready presence of mind, retorted, "Simpleton! did you ever see the Archbishop of Canterbury travel in that guise?" Happily they were allowed to pass unmolested, but the incident showed them what caution was needed.

That Monday night they stopped at a grange belonging to the monks of Clairmarais, and Brother Christian occupied the lowest place at the table. Notwithstanding the fright he had so lately had, he could not throw off his old habits, and as he ate he gave the best portions off his plate to the children and others of the family. His host remarked this well-known peculiarity of the archbishop's and then observing the unusual height, the broad calm brow, and the beautiful long hands of his guest, he called his wife and told her his suspicions, that the humble brother was no other than the fugitive archbishop. She ran at once to look at him, and returning to her husband, cried, "Certainly, good man, it is he;" then joyfully fetching all the best luxuries of her simple store—apples, and nuts, and cheese—she placed them before Brother Christian. When supper was over, the host came in with a beaming smile of welcome; and when Brother Christian asked him to sit down beside him, he would only sit at his feet, saying, "My lord, I thank God you have come under my roof." "Why," answered Brother Christian, "who am I? Am I not only a poor lay-brother, called Christian?" But the man replied, "I know not what you are called, but I know you are a great man and Archbishop of Canterbury." Then S. Thomas, seeing that he was known, no longer denied who he was. But the next day, fearing the man might talk to others about him, he took him on with him to Clairmarais, a Cistercian monastery near S. Omer, about twelve miles from Oie, which was to be his next stage.

Meanwhile, Herbert had executed the commission which his master had given him before leaving Northampton. Thanks to the policy which Henry had thought it prudent to adopt, he had been able to collect one hundred marks and a few silver vessels; and the ports being still open, he had made the best of his way to the monastery of S. Bertin, near S. Omer, where for four or five days he and some of S. Thomas's other retainers had awaited his arrival. The very night the saint reached Clairmarais, Herbert came from S. Bertin to see him. The meeting was a very joyful one. But when the saint narrated the various incidents of his journey, his fatigues, his perils, his hairbreadth escapes, Herbert was much affected at the change in his beloved master's fortunes; whereupon S. Thomas said, "If we have received good from the hand of the Lord, why should we not receive evil?" Then Herbert thought of the text, "The just man will never be sorrowful, let what may happen to him."

As Henry's messengers had arrived that day at S. Omer, and it was generally known that S. Thomas was expected at Clairmarais, it was thought prudent that he should not remain there. Accordingly, that night after matins he and his party went in a boat through the marshes to a solitary hermitage, called Eldeminster, which had once been the abode of S. Bertin. As they went along, towards morning one of the party said, "My lord, you are weary with travelling, and we are going to most hospitable people, who will rejoice at your escape; do them the favour on your arrival of allowing them to break the abstinence." "No," answered S. Thomas; "to-day is Wednesday, and we must abstain." "But, my lord," replied the other, "we must not put them to much trouble, and perhaps they may have no supply of fish." "That is for God to provide," rejoined S. Thomas; and as he spoke, a large fish, called a brenna, leapt into his lap, as if in answer to his faith. They remained three days at the hermitage of Eldeminster, and on the fourth, at the pressing invitation of Godeschal, the abbot of S. Berlin's, they went on to his monastery.

While S. Thomas was at his monastery, he had a visit from Richard de Luci, who had been sent with Henry's letter to Philip, Earl of Flanders. Richard tried to persuade him to return to England with him, and, finding entreaties useless, had recourse to threats. But S. Thomas checked him, saying, "You are my man, and ought not to speak to me thus." Richard retorted, "I give you back my homage." To which S. Thomas replied, "You never borrowed it from me."

In the early part of this year, when John of Salisbury was banished, Philip, Earl of Flanders, had received him courteously, and had sent a message through him to S. Thomas, offering him assistance and protection if he should be compelled to leave England. Notwithstanding, it was thought prudent to ascertain whether Henry's letter had made any change in his sentiments; and with this view, S. Thomas sent two abbots to him to ask for a safe-conduct and free passage through his territory. Philip replied that he would consider the matter, and that he had power enough to keep an archbishop within his dominions. As this answer foreboded danger, S. Thomas consulted with Milo, Bishop of Terouenne, who happened to be visiting him, as to his safest course.

The bishop purposely delayed his departure till it was quite dark, and when he was going away, S. Thomas, with attendants carrying torches, escorted him to the door. S. Thomas then bade the attendants go away, as if he had a few last confidential words to say to the bishop; and as soon as they were gone he mounted a horse, which the bishop had prepared for him, and they rode that night to Terouenne. The next day he went on to Soissons, where his attendants rejoined him. And now he was safe, for he was in the dominions of Louis, King of France.

CHAPTER XIII. RECEPTION IN FRANCE.

But though S. Thomas was now secure from all personal danger, he was still very anxious as to the reception he should meet with from the Pope and the King of France. He knew that Henry's ambassadors would have no lack of rich presents wherewith to win their way, and that fair and crafty words would not be spared to conceal the truth, and make the worse appear the better cause; while he, poor and friendless, had only truth and justice on his side. He therefore despatched Herbert and another of his suite from S. Bertin's, bidding them follow Henry's messengers at the distance of a day's journey, and bring him word how they were received.

Henry's messengers found Louis at Compiegne, and presented him their master's letter. Louis read it in their presence, and when he came to the words, "Thomas, late Archbishop of Canterbury," he asked repeatedly who had deposed him; and they being too confused to answer, he added, "Truly I am as much a king as the King of England; yet I could not depose the very least of the clerics in my kingdom. I know the archbishop well; he is a noble-minded man, and if I knew where to find him, I and my whole court would go out to meet him." "But," interposed the Earl of Arundel, "he did much harm to France at the head of the English army." "That was no more than his duty," rejoined Louis, "and it makes me admire him the more. If he had been my servant he would have done as much for me." They urged Louis to write to the Pope on their behalf; but so far from doing so, he called Franco, the Pope's almoner, and gave him a message to the Holy Father in S. Thomas's favour. Seeing there was no chance of success in this quarter, they soon took their leave, and went on to Sens, where the Pope was then residing.

They found in the course of their journey, that it was not in England only that popular feeling was on S. Thomas's side, for wherever they passed the warmest sympathy was expressed for his cause. Nor was this surprising, since One Spirit breathes through the whole Catholic Church, and one pulse thrills through all its members. After leaving Compiegne, fearing popular violence, they thought it prudent to conceal who they were; and accordingly, they put the Earl of Arundel at their head, and the bishops with the rest of the party rode behind him, as if they were only his household and retainers.

The day after the departure of Henry's messengers, Herbert and his companions arrived at Compiegne. As soon as they said that they came from the Archbishop of Canterbury, they were admitted to an audience; and when Louis heard that they belonged to S. Thomas's household, he kissed them, and received them most graciously. He listened with great interest to their narration of S. Thomas's sufferings, for he had not forgotten the friendship which had sprung up between them when S. Thomas was chancellor, and he told them about the embassy he had received from Henry, and the answer he had returned; adding, "Before King Henry so hardly treated a friend of his, and a person of such station as the archbishop, he ought to have remembered the verse, 'Be ye angry and sin not.' " "He would perhaps, my lord, have remembered it," answered Herbert's companion, "if he heard it as often as we clerics do in the office,"—a reply which amused Louis. The next morning, after consulting his ministers, Louis promised his protection to the saint, adding, in reference to Henry's pretensions, "It is one of the *royal dignities* of France to protect fugitives, especially ecclesiastics, and to defend them from their persecutors." Then Herbert and his companions took their leave, and they, too, went on to Sens.

They reached Sens the day after Henrys ambassadors, and though their poor appearance commanded little respect from the cardinals and the retainers of the Papal court, they were admitted that very evening to an audience of the Holy Father. They told him humbly and simply what their master had suffered; and he was so touched at the recital, that he said with tears, "Your lord is yet alive, you tell me; he can, then, while still in the flesh, claim the privilege of martyrdom." As they were very tired he soon dismissed them with the apostolic blessing.

The next day the Pope held a consistory of cardinals, to give public audience to the King of England's ambassadors, Herbert and his companions being present. Gilbert, Bishop of London, opened the business of the embassy by a plausible speech, which placed the late occurrences in a false light most favourable to his master. "Father," said he, "the care of the Catholic Church is yours: those who are wise, your prudence directs and strengthens; those who are unwise, your apostolic authority corrects. Not long since a difference arose between the State and the priesthood; the occasion was unimportant, and a little moderation would have set all right. But my lord of Canterbury, trusting to his own private opinion and neglecting our counsel, has urged matters unnecessarily far, and has thus entangled himself and his brethren. But when we withheld our assent, as we were bound to do, he tried to cast reproach upon the king and ourselves; and, as if to heap infamy upon us, without any violence having been shown to him, or a threat used against him, he fled, even as it is written, 'The wicked man fleeth when no man pursueth.'" "Spare, brother," cried the Pope. "Shall I spare him, my lord?" asked Gilbert. "Brother, I did not say spare him, but spare yourself," replied the Holy Father. Gilbert was so abashed at this reproof, that he could not say another word.

Hilary of Chichester spoke next. "My lord and father, your blessedness is ever careful to restore to a state of peace and concord whatever has been done amiss to the injury of many, lest one man's presumption should destroy many, and create a schism in the Church. To this point my lord of Canterbury has been inattentive, and has brought trouble and anxiety upon himself and his followers, the king and the kingdom, the clergy and the people. Such conduct comports ill with his high position; in fact it never comported, nor in any case could have comported—"He spoke in Latin, and having made a grammatical error in the use of the verb *oportuebat*, he kept on repeating the word, at which there was a general laugh, and one of those present said, "You have come to a bad *port*." Whereupon Hilary stopped short, and sat down.

Roger of York spoke more cautiously. He contented himself with accusing the archbishop of excessive and habitual obstinacy, to which he attributed the present difficulty; adding, "The only remedy for this is, that your discretion should lay a heavy hand upon him." Bartholomew of Exeter said only a few words requesting the Pope to send legates to England to judge the cause, which could not be decided in the absence of the archbishop.

Finally, the Earl of Arundel asked for a hearing; and as he was not learned, he spoke in Norm an- French, and not knowing anything about law and the rights of the case, he made such a speech as might be looked for from a blunt, kindhearted, and loyal Englishman first praising the king for his devotion to the Holy Father, then praising the archbishop still more highly, "though," said he, "some people think him too sharp," and finally, begging the Pope to remove the dissension between "so good a king and so excellent a prelate." This moderate speech made a more favourable impression than the preceding ones, the mendacious character of which was evident to all the assembly.

While the bishops were speaking against S. Thomas, Herbert, who was of an impetuous nature, rose twice to contradict them; but the Pope, gently checking him, said, "Peace, my friend, forbear to defend your bishop: there is no charge against him."

The ambassadors were very urgent that a legate should be sent to England, with full powers to judge the cause and give final sentence. Henry made a great point of this; because, in the first place it would compel the archbishop to return to England, when he would have him in his power; and in the next, he made sure of being able, by dint of bribes, threats, and crafty devices, to induce the legate to give sentence in his favour. The Pope, however, saw through his motives; and so far from granting his request, he proposed that the ambassadors should wait till the archbishop, who was at no great distance, should arrive at

Sens, when he could himself hear both parties, and pass sentence without delay. But the bishops knew too well the badness of their cause to consent to this straightforward course, and they therefore excused themselves on the ground, that their master had bound them to leave Sens in three days. Still they pressed their suit most earnestly; and it is said that they even promised an increased payment of Peter's pence for the future. But Christ's Vicar cannot be bribed. He stood firm; the most he would grant being, that he would send a legate after he should have seen S. Thomas; nor would he consent to order the saint to return to England. As the ambassadors were retiring, the Bishop of London came back, and asked with what powers the legate would be invested. "With all that are requisite," answered the Pope. "That is," said the crafty Gilbert, "with full powers to decide the question without appeal?" "Not so, brother," rejoined His Holiness; "to hear appeals is my glory, which I will not give to another." At the end of three days, the ambassadors left Sens, and returned to report to Henry the failure of their mission both with the Pope and the King of France.

It has been already told how S. Thomas made his way from the monastery of S. Bertin to Soissons. The day after his arrival at Soissons, Louis happened to come to the town; and hearing that S. Thomas was there, he went at once to visit him. In his early youth, about five and twenty years before, Louis had acted as Henry was now doing, and had tried to force the clergy of Bourges to elect a favourite of his own for their archbishop, thereby drawing down an interdict on his dominions. He had, however, soon seen his error and had submitted to the Church's laws; and through the rest of his life he proved the sincerity of his repentance by his devotion to the Holy See. It was therefore natural that, apart from his personal friendship for S. Thomas, he should take the warmest interest in his cause. Accordingly, he now received him most honourably, expressed deep sympathy for his sufferings, and offered to supply all his wants—a generous offer which the saint declined for the present, though the time might come, he said, when he should require the proffered aid.

Many of the most distinguished personages of the realm, and among them Henry, Archbishop of Rheims, brother to the king, called on S. Thomas, and when, a few days after, he set out for Sens they joined his party by way of doing him honour; so that the saint who so lately had been wandering in disguise, footsore, and in fear of his very life, now rode along with a splendid cavalcade of more than three hundred horseman. It happened that, as he travelled along the bank of a river, Henry's envoys, on their return from Sens, passed down the opposite bank, dreading not only some sudden outbreak of popular indignation, but hastening on with as little ostentation as possible, in order to elude some knights who, they had been warned, were preparing to attack and plunder them. Struck with the painful contrast between their own discomfiture and the honour done to their adversary, they sent Guy Rufus, Dean of Waltham, back to Sens, to see and report on the saint's reception by the Pope.

As S. Thomas and his brilliant retinue approached Sens, many of the cardinals came out to meet him, while others hung back and looked coldly on him. The Pope received him with great affection, and even reverence, giving him the place of honour at his right hand, and bidding him keep his seat when he was rising to address the assembled court. At a meeting of the cardinals in the Pope's own room, he related all that had occurred at Clarendon, confessing his fault in having promised, even in general terms, to observe the royal customs; and then, as he spread out the copy of the constitutions which he had carried off from the council, he said, "These, Holy Father, are the laws which the Church of God is called on to receive." The Pope ordered that they should be read aloud, and the perusal created a great sensation; for as the Pope seems not to have heard them previously, it is evident that, when Henry had professed to send them for the Pope's confirmation, he had either sent some garbled version, or submitted only their general purport to him. When the reading was concluded, the Pope passed sentence upon them, saying, "That though there were some among them which the Church might tolerate, others were of such a character that nothing could save them from condemnation." Then turning to S. Thomas, he added, "But though your fault, brother, has been great, yet you have done your best to atone for it. You have fallen, it is true; but you have risen stronger than before, and the sufferings you have undergone are sufficient to obliterate your offence."

There was still another matter which weighed on S. Thomas's conscience, and he sought relief for it by pouring out the sorrowful thoughts which had pressed upon him ever since his fall at Clarendon, and to which he had already more than once given utterance. "The truth must be told, holy fathers," said he, "before God and you. I say it with sobbing and groaning, these evils have fallen on the Church on my account. I went up into Christ's fold, not through the strait gate of canonical election, but I was thrust in by the king's influence. It was sorely against my will; but, nevertheless, it was the handiwork of men, and not of God. "What wonder, then, if it has ended in misfortune! Yet if I had resigned my charge to the king, as my fellow-bishops urged, it would have been a pernicious precedent of yielding to the will of princes; and I therefore forbore to do so until I should come into this holy presence. I now acknowledge my uncanonical election; and for fear of still worse results, lest I should lead my flock to perdition, I resign into your hands, Holy Father, the burden of the Archbishopric of Canterbury, which I have no longer strength to bear." With these words he took the archiepiscopal ring from his finger, and placed it in the Pope's hands.

This touching act of self-humiliation took every one by surprise. Some of the cardinals were disposed to seize this opportunity to conciliate Henry by removing S. Thomas to another see. But the Pope perceived that such a concession to the king would imperil the Church's liberties, and he therefore answered, "My brother, your zeal in the Church's cause has atoned for your informal election: receive now the see afresh from my hands, free from the defects of your former title. We shall maintain you in your cause, because it is the cause of the Church."

When S. Thomas had been some little time at Sens, he became anxious to retire to some place, where he could live in the seclusion befitting his poverty and altered position. He therefore applied to the Pope, who, sending for the abbot of the Cistercian monastery of Pontigny in Burgundy, committed the saint and his followers to his charge. At the parting interview, the Holy Father said to S. Thomas, "Whereas, my brother, you have as yet spent your life in luxury and a high estate, and know not what privation is, we wish you to learn, in company with some of Christ's humblest servants, how to subdue the flesh to the spirit, living as a simple monk, and an exile in the cause of Christ. Be of good courage, my brother, resist the enemy, and wait with patience till the day of peace and consolation from on high shall visit you."

CHAPTER XIV. PONTIGNY.

S. THOMAS and his friends took up their abode at Pontigny on the feast of S. Andrew, A.D. 1164. The monks received them joyfully, and treated them with the hospitality for which their order has ever been famous. A number of cells close to each other were set apart for their use, and a brother, called Roger, was appointed to wait on them. This Roger afterwards wrote an interesting biography of the saint, by whom he was ordained priest.

S. Thomas had now entered on a new phase of life. Popularity, magnificence, and brilliant success had characterized his past career; but all these had now passed away, and as the Holy Father had said, though still in the flesh, his martyrdom had begun. From the time when, at his consecration, he had made his choice between the love and favour of an earthly king and the grace of the King of Heaven, the thought of martyrdom seems never to have quitted him. At Westminster, he had openly declared his readiness to "die for his Lord;" at Northampton, he had laid his life on the altar, and offered it up with the Precious Blood of that Lord; and henceforth, his days were only a succession of humiliations, protracted hopes, and ever-recurring disappointments, which, like a purifying fire, consumed all natural high-mindedness, impetuosity, and human infirmity, and made the saintly offering like unto the fine gold of the sanctuary, of which his glorious crown was to be woven.

When S. Thomas had been three or four days at Pontigny he entered the chapter-house, and explaining fully to the monks the cause for which he was suffering, commended it and himself to their prayers. He then began the course of mortification and penance which the Holy Father had recommended to him, living as a simple monk, and conforming himself, so far as he possibly could, to the rule of the holy community with whom he dwelt. He not only assisted at the offices in the choir, as he had been accustomed to do at Canterbury, but he joined the monks in the hay-field and at harvest-time, and took his share in all the outdoor labours which form a part of the Cistercian rule, but which, from his previous habits and his age, for he was now near fifty, must have been most irksome and painful to him.

The monks supplied him with meat and many luxuries which were forbidden to themselves, but he wished to restrict himself to their diet. He therefore bade Roger bring him the ordinary fare of the house among the dishes provided for him; and he ate at a table by himself, so that no one might perceive that he partook only of herbs. Before long, however, his delicate constitution gave way, and he became seriously unwell. When Herbert asked him what was the cause of his illness, he tried to change the conversation; but his attached friend would not be repelled, and at last he was obliged to confess its real origin. Herbert induced him to return to his usual fare, and his health was at once restored.

He also wished to wear the dress of the order, and asked the Pope to supply him with a habit. The Holy Father blessed one of thick, rough cloth, and sent it to him with a message, that he sent such a one as he had and not such as he wished; and the Abbot of Pontigny clothed him privately with it. The hood happened to be disproportionately small, whereupon Alexander Llewellyn, who was standing by, said in his dry way, "It is serious enough, but whether it is regular or not I am sure I do not know. It is plain that my lord, the Pope, has not fitted over well the hood to the cowl." S. Thomas answered with a laugh, "It was done on purpose, lest you should mock me again as you did the other day." "How and when was that, my lord?" asked the cross-bearer. "The day before yesterday," replied S. Thomas, "when I was vesting for Mass and had put on the girdle, you asked what stuck out so behind. Now you would call me humpbacked, I suppose, if my hood were over large. So, you see I am only protected against your gibes." Such was the playfulness with which the saint tried to conceal his austerities; for though his face was full, his body was very thin, and it was his long, stiff hair-shirt, reaching from his neck to his knees, which caused the bulky appearance that had excited his cross-bearer's mirth.

When S. Thomas was chancellor he had often longed to have more time for study, and after his consecration he would frequently say to Herbert, "Oh that I could lay aside the cares of the world, and in peace and quietness attend to sacred studies! How carefully I would atone for the time I have lost!" The coveted leisure was now at his disposal, and he turned it to good account. He first studied canon law, under Lombard of Piacenza, in order to qualify himself to defend the cause of the Church. But before long, John of Salisbury, who seems to have kept a sharp look out on the saint, and to have acted the part of a faithful monitor, wrote to him, reproving him for his course of study, which seemed to him unsuitable in the present circumstances. "Wherefore," continued this judicious adviser, "my counsel and the height of my wishes is, that you should turn to the Lord with all your mind, and to the help of prayer. Put off meanwhile, as much as you can, all other occupations; for though they may seem very necessary, what I now recommend is to be preferred as more necessary. . . . Do you not remember how it is written, that in the trouble of the people the ministers of the Lord shall weep between the porch and the altar, saying, 'Spare, O Lord, spare Thy people!' 'I was exercised,' says the prophet, 'and I swept my spirit, searching with my hands for God in the day of tribulation.' Who ever rose with a feeling of compunction from the study of law and the canons? I say more than this: the exercises of the schools sometimes increase knowledge till a man is puffed up, but seldom, if ever, inflame devotion. I would rather that you meditated on the Psalms, or read the moral books of S. Gregory, than that you philosophized in scholastic fashion. It is good to confer on moral matters with some spiritual man, by whose example you may be inflamed, rather than to study and discuss the disputatious articles of secular learning. God knows in what sense, with what devotion, I propose these things. Take them as you please. But if you do them, God will be your helper, and you need not fear, what man may scheme. He knows that we have no mortal to trust to, as I think, in our present trouble." The saint took his friend's advice, which no doubt agreed with his own experience. He resumed his study of the Holy Scriptures with Herbert, and found such consolation in it, that after the office in the choir, he would constantly be seen with some book of Scripture in his hands, the Psalter and the Epistles being his favourite studies.

Such was the daily life by which the saint strove to bring the flesh into subjection to the spirit. As if to quicken his zeal and courage, our Lord was pleased at this time to reveal to him the great trial that awaited him. One day, as he was making his thanksgiving after Mass at the altar of S. Stephen, he heard a voice calling, "Thomas! Thomas!" Whereupon he asked, "Who art thou, Lord?" And our Lord answered, "I am Jesus Christ, thy Lord and thy Brother; My Church shall be glorified in thy blood, and thou shalt be glorified in Me." S. Thomas thought he was alone, but the abbot was waiting for him behind one of the columns, and heard what was said. The saint however, bound him to silence till the promise should be fulfilled.

Had it been possible for S. Thomas to lay aside the responsibilities of his sacred office, and to think only of himself, he might have found happiness in the peace and seclusion of Pontigny. But troubles from without soon came to disturb him.

When Henry's ambassadors arrived in England, they found the king at Marlborough, where he gave them audience on Christmas Eve. When he heard that the Pope would not send a legate with full powers to try S. Thomas in England, his anger knew no bounds. The next day, notwithstanding its being Christmas Day, he issued a decree confiscating all the property of the Archbishop and Church of Canterbury, and banishing all S. Thomas's relatives and household, and all the relatives of his followers, from all of whom an oath was to be exacted that they would go without delay to S. Thomas, wherever he might be. Moreover, the execution of this cruel decree was committed to the ferocious Randolph de Broc, who carried it out with merciless severity. All who were in any way connected with the saint, even those who had given him a night's lodging, or shown him any kindness in his wanderings, clerics and laymen, old men, delicate women, young children, and even infants, to the number of four hundred, were transported to the coast of Flanders, and left there in the depth of winter, without any means of support, to find their way as they best could to Pontigny. Only a few escaped banishment, but they had to wander about the forests, shunned by their friends, for it was a crime to speak to them or harbour them. William of Salisbury, a priest, was captured and imprisoned in Corfe Castle for six months; and others, who were in wealthy circumstances, got off by the payment of heavy fines. William Fitz Stephen, afterwards the saint's biographer, was the only one who was unmolested,—a piece of good fortune which he owed to his wit in writing a rhyming prayer, which he presented in the chapel at Bruhull to the king, who took a fancy to it and pardoned its author.

As for the poor outcasts in Flanders, death soon released the more delicate and infirm, and Catholic charity came to the rescue of the survivors. Henry's cruelty had called forth a general burst of indignation, and Catholics from far and near, strangers equally with friends, vied with each other in succouring these confessors for the Church. The king, nobility, and clergy of France were foremost in this work of charity; the Empress Matilda and the Earl of Flanders contributed their aid; religious houses opened their doors to them, while many, among whom was a nephew of S. Thomas, were hospitably received by the King and Queen of Sicily, and the Sicilian clergy. The Pope had at once dispensed them from their oath to go to S. Thomas; but, notwithstanding, as time passed on, these unhappy exiles made their way to his cell, and during the whole six years of his exile they were an unceasing burden and sorrow to him.

Besides all this, he had the grief of knowing that his church was suffering on his account. Many of the bishops in whose dioceses he had benefices, took possession of them and turned out his clerics, who did not dare to resist. The rest of his benefices were given in charge to the Bishop of London, whose official, Robert Uscarl, made the most out of them for his master's benefit, oppressing the tenants, depriving the clerics of their revenues, wasting the property, letting the churches go to ruin, and fining and imprisoning those who complained. One insult touched Thomas to the quick, which was, that the king forbade his name to be publicly mentioned, as usual, in the prayers of the Church. But what made all this persecution the more bitter, was, as he wrote to the Pope, that "the more he had loved the king, the more he had opposed his injustice, until his highness's brow fell lowering upon him," and then in the hour of trial he was "deserted in the quarter where he had looked for support," "the bishops siding with the court," not perceiving that "in attacking him they were attacking their own privileges," and were "accelerating their own perpetual servitude by lending the king's arrogance wings to fly." And therefore, moved by the urgency of the case, he besought the Holy Father to "put forth his severity, and coerce those who had stirred up this persecution;" adding, with a touch of lingering affection for Henry, "but lay it not at the king's door: he is the instrument and the agent, not the author of these machinations."

Amid these sorrows, the noble conduct of S. Gilbert of Sempringham must have afforded S. Thomas some little consolation. It was well known that S. Thomas had escaped from Northampton, by the help of S. Gilbert and the order with which he had peopled the fen country; but, so great was the veneration in which he was held, that no one had dared to touch him. The king, however, wishing to starve out S. Thomas by exhausting the generosity of his foreign friends, now issued a decree making it treason to send him money from England, under the usual sanguinary penalities of loss of eyes and limbs, burning, &c. S. Gilbert being accused of having sent money to him, he and his priors were summoned to Westminster to answer the charge. The judges, out of respect for his gray hairs and his sanctity, were disposed to be lenient, and only required him to take an oath declaring his innocence. But, though he could easily have done this, for he had not sent money to S. Thomas; yet he refused to swear, lest the world should suppose that he thought it wrong to help the confessor for the Church. The judges threatened him with exile; his priors reminded him of the ruin he would bring on his order, and remonstrated with him for running such risks on account of what they deemed a mere point of honour. But S. Gilbert caring more for the Church than for home or order, thanked God for now giving him the opportunity in his old age, after a life of peace, to bear the reproach of Christ, and suffer for His Church; and while the priors sat round him in Westminster Hall, with blank and gloomy faces, he laughed, and joked, and bought trinkets of a hawker-boy by way of diverting their anxiety. The judges were puzzled what to do, and, not wishing to proceed to extremities, they sent to the king, who was in Normandy, to enquire his pleasure. Meanwhile, S. Gilbert and his priors were detained in London; and though he was unusually gay, they were in dismay, and it was as much as he could do to prevent their taking the oath, and returning to their convents. At length, when all had made up their minds to die in a foreign land, there came an order for their dismissal; for Henry, in spite of his violent passions, was not incapable of generosity, and probably he was touched by the heroism of the aged saint. Then, when all danger was past, S. Gilbert told the judge, but without an oath, that he had not sent money to S. Thomas; and he and his priors returned to Sempringham, thanking God for their deliverance.

S. Thomas's strong and impetuous character would naturally have disposed him to take at once such steps as would have put a stop to this oppression; but long-suffering forbearance, in imitation of her Divine Head, has ever been the practice of the Church. In the present case it was especially necessary, because Henry, in the first burst of pride and passion, had written to Reginald, Archbishop of Cologne, one of the chief supporters of the Anti-Pope, saying, "I have long wished for an opportunity to recede from Pope Alexander and his cardinals, who dare to uphold against me that traitor Thomas, once Archbishop of Canterbury." He had also sent John of Oxford and Richard of Ilchester to the emperor, pledging his word to bring fifty bishops to obey the Anti-

Pope; and though he had not yet carried out his intentions, it was to be feared that any hasty or severe step might drive him into open schism.

Accordingly, the Pope recommended S. Thomas to act in a conciliatory spirit, in all possible ways consistent with the liberties of the Church and the dignity of his office, and to forbear all proceedings against Henry's person or kingdom till Easter 1166: "after which time," he added, in a prophetic spirit, "God will vouchsafe to us better times, and you, as well as ourself, may adopt more rigorous measures with safety." Meanwhile, in order to leave no doubt as to his own opinion he wrote to Gilbert, Bishop of London, reproving him and his fellow-bishops for their conduct, and bidding him use his influence with the king to induce him to restore to S. Thomas his favour and all his property. Later he ordered him and the Bishop of Hereford to go to the king, and warn him to desist from his evil practices, and to make satisfaction for all that he had done amiss. The only effect of these letters was, that Gilbert no longer dared to hold S. Thomas's benefices, but transferred them to the royal treasury; and after going, as directed, with the Bishop of Hereford to the king, he wrote the Pope a plausible reply, in which he placed his master's conduct in the most favourable light, representing S. Thomas's exile as voluntary and uncalled for, and the royal customs as affecting only civil cases, hinting significantly that England might be driven by persecution to join the Anti-Pope, when there would be no lack of priests to receive the pall of Canterbury from him, and to fill the suffragan sees in obedience to him.

The Empress Matilda also exerted herself to promote peace. Soon after S. Thomas's flight Henry sent John of Oxford to misrepresent the case to her, and as she inherited the tyrannical temper of her race, she was easily exasperated against the saint. But a few days later, a messenger arriving with a letter from him which opened her eyes to the true state of the matter, she expressed great interest in his cause; and when, subsequently, the constitutions of Clarendon were read to her, she found fault with the greatest number; and what offended her most, was their being reduced to writing, and a promise being demanded from the bishops for their observance, "for this," she said, "was without precedent." She therefore spared no effort to turn her son from the wicked course on which he had entered; but all in vain.

The king, as well as the principal nobles and ecclesiastics of France, did all in their power to effect a reconciliation, but with equal want of success. Henry would not even consent to have an interview with the Pope if S. Thomas were to be present, and the Holy Father, in ordinary justice and prudence, would not judge the cause except in the presence of both parties.

Nor was S. Thomas himself remiss in his efforts for peace. For a while he did nothing, hoping that time would cool down the king's passion, and trusting chiefly to the effect of prayer to touch his heart. But when months had passed away and Easter of the following year was come and Henry still continued obdurate, he resolved to try what he could do. He, therefore, wrote to him in a solemn, but gentle tone, and he sent his letter by Urban, a Cistercian abbot, who was remarkable for his winning manners. In this letter he excused himself on the ground of the solemn charge committed to him, and then went on to say, "My lord, the daughter of Sion is held captive in your kingdom. The spouse of the Great King is oppressed by her enemies, afflicted by those who ought most to honour her, and especially by you. Oh, remember what great things God has done for you, release her, reinstate her in her kingdom, and take away the reproach from your generation. . . If it be that you hear my words and prove yourself from this day forward God's faithful soldier, then He will bless you greatly, and give glory to your sons and your sons' sons. But if not, then truly I dread (may God avert it!) that 'the sword shall not depart from your house' till the Most High has made clean vengeance for His people."

Urban soon returned, and reported that he had had no success with Henry. S. Thomas then wrote a second letter in a more tender and affectionate strain. In the superscription he styled himself, "his own once in the flesh, and now much more in the Spirit"; and he went on to say, "Waiting I have waited for the day when God should turn your

Majesty from crooked ways and evil counsels; silently and anxiously have I waited for the tidings of my son and lord the King of England, who was once seduced by the enemies of the Church, being by the Grace of God restored to it in abundant humility; and though I wait in vain, still I weary not, but pray for your Majesty day by day."

This letter having proved as ineffectual as the former one, S. Thomas wrote a third letter of affectionate warning, which he sent by Gerard, surnamed the Discalced, a monk who was celebrated for his austerities, his boldness of speech, and the gift of reconciling those who were at variance. In this letter he said, "I have very earnestly desired to meet your Majesty in person, and to converse with you. . . . I hoped that the sight of me might recall to your mind the zealous and faithful services which I have before now rendered you according to the best of my conscience (so help me God, at the last day when we shall all stand before his throne to receive according to the deeds we have done in the body!) I hoped that when you saw me, who am now forced to beg my bread among strangers, you might at least be touched by some feeling of kindness. . . . . But for your Majesty's sake I was much more anxious. You are my liege lord, and as such I owe you my counsels: you are my son in the Spirit, and I am bound to chasten and correct you. . . . . Let my lord, therefore, if it please him, listen to the counsels of his subject, to the warnings of his bishop, and to the chastisements of his father. And, first, let him for the future abstain from all communion with schismatics. It is known almost to the whole world with what devotion your Majesty formerly received our Lord the Pope, and what attachment you showed to the See of Rome; and also, what respect and deference were shown you in return. Forbear then, my Lord, as you value your soul, to withdraw from that see its just rights. Remember moreover, the profession which you made to my predecessor at your coronation, and which you deposited in writing upon the altar at Westminster, respecting the rights and liberties of the Church in England. Be pleased also to restore to the See of Canterbury, from which you received your consecration, the rank which it held in the time of your predecessors and mine, together with all its possessions, its villages, castles, and farms, and whatever else has been taken by violence either from myself or my dependents, lay as well as clerical. And further, to allow us to return in peace and quietness to the free discharge of our duties. Should your Majesty be pleased to act in this manner, you will find me prepared to serve you as a beloved lord and king, faithfully and devotedly, with all my might, in whatsoever I am able—saving the honour of God and of the Roman Church, and saving my order. *But otherwise, know for certain that you shall feel the vengeance of God."*

To this letter Henry returned a sharp answer. S. Thomas's letters had, however, terrified him, for he saw that the next step would be the excommunication of himself and an interdict on his dominions. Passionate and obstinate as he was, he had faith enough to make him quail before the thunders of the Church, and he shrank from the indignation of his subjects when the churches should be closed, the sacraments denied them, the merry bells silent, feast and holiday banished, and fair England looking like a heathen land. To increase his difficulties, even the resource of schism was lost: for the Anti-Pope was dead, the Italian cities had revolted from the emperor, Alexander had returned in triumph to Rome on the 23rd of November, 1165, and thus the convenient time for Henry's excommunication, which the Pope had foretold, had arrived. Had the bishops now done their duty, Henry might yet have been reclaimed. But he had thrown off his only true friend, who loved both his body and his soul, and had replaced him by Gilbert of London and Roger of York, worldly, selfish men, who cared not to help him into a path which would withdraw him from their own influence, while other courtly bishops were at hand to smooth his downward course.

Perplexed and harassed, seeing before him an inextricable labyrinth, he held at Chinon a conference with such of his friends as were "most notorious for their skill in evil, conjuring them with promises and threats to assist him, and complaining with sighs and groans of the conduct of the archbishop, who, he said, would take from him both body and soul; and, in conclusion, he called them all a set of traitors, who had not zeal nor courage enough to rid him from the molestations of one man." At these words, which some years later acquired such fatal significance, the Archbishop of Rouen, rebuked him warmly, but gently, as was his way, and not with the sternness which the occasion called for.

Then the courtly Arnold of Lisieux suggested that the sentence might be warded off by an appeal to the Pope; for it was the law of the Church that an accused person might defer his sentence for a period short of a year, by giving notice to his judge before sentence was passed that he appealed to the Pope. Henry caught gladly at this proposal, and the Bishops of Lisieux and Seez were despatched in haste to give notice of the appeal to S. Thomas, and thus to defer the sentence till Low Sunday, 1167; and the Archbishop of Rouen accompanied them, not to take part in the appeal, as he protested, but to try to mediate a reconciliation. People did not fail to remark on the strange coincidence, that Henry, while contending for the royal customs which did away with the right of appeal, should be himself compelled to have recourse to it.

Henry also sent John of Oxford to the Pope, charged with fair words to his Holiness, and rich presents to all who had influence with him. No envoy could have been more suitable; for John's readiness to swear whatever was to his interest, had won him the nickname of the "Swearer." Moreover, he had been Henry's envoy to the schismatic emperor, and had accepted the deanery of Salisbury in defiance of the Pope's prohibition.

CHAPTER XV. VEZELAY.

THE Pope's prediction was fulfilled. Better times were vouchsafed to the Church, and His Holiness was in a position to take decided steps in favour of S. Thomas.

In anticipation of Easter, when S. Thomas would be free to act against Henry, the Pope wrote to him ordering him to do justice on all who, after due warning, should retain the property of the Church, except only the king, about whom he gave no special order. He wrote also to the English bishops to the same effect. S. Thomas forwarded these letters to Gilbert and the other bishops, and ordered them to restore, and compel their subjects to restore, within forty days all property belonging to his clergy, under pain of excommunication. Gilbert wrote to the king, asking leave to obey, but without success.

In order to strengthen S. Thomas's authority the Pope, on April 8th, 1166, issued a bull, granting S. Thomas and his successors the primacy of England, and he wrote to Roger, Archbishop of York, announcing the appointment and forbidding them to encroach on the ancient rights of his office, especially with regard to the coronation of the king. Further, on Easter Day, April 24th, he appointed S. Thomas his legate over all England, except the diocese of York, and he ordered the English clergy to obey him as his own representative. Again, on May 3rd he wrote to Gilbert and directed him to enforce the restitution of Church property under pain of excommunication without appeal.

S. Thomas sent one copy of the Pope's letters appointing him legate to the bishops of Hereford and Worcester, and another to Gilbert, Bishop of London, ordering them to show them to the other bishops, and warning them of the danger they incurred by not obeying the Pope more zealously.

After taking these preliminary steps, S. Thomas proceeded to action. With this view he made a journey to Soissons, where were three famous shrines, one dedicated to our Blessed Lady, another to S. Gregory,

Apostle of England, whose relics are there, and a third to S. Drausius, whose aid men used to invoke before a combat. Before these three shrines he watched for three nights, and then, on the 3rd of June, the day after the Ascension, he hastened to Vezelay, on the borders of Burgundy and Nivernois, intending to pass sentence on Henry and his party on the following Sunday. But the same day Louis sent him word that Henry was seriously ill, and on this account he deferred the sentence against him.

On Whit Sunday, the 12th of June, he celebrated High Mass in the old church of Vezelay, in the presence of a concourse of people of different nations who had flocked thither for the festival. After the Gospel, he mounted the pulpit and preached an energetic sermon, at the close of which, to the surprise of all present, and even of his own followers, who were not aware of his intention, he explained the real causes at issue between him and the King of England, and his own efforts at reconciliation; and then, with the deepest emotion, he invited Henry publicly to the fruits of penance, and warned him of the sentence hanging over him, unless he should speedily repent and atone for his outrages against the Church. After this he proceeded to excommunicate John of Oxford for schism in communicating with the emperor and Reginald of Cologne, and for usurping the deanery of Salisbury against the commands of the Pope; and also, for various just causes, Richard of Ilchester, Richard de Luci, Joceline de Baillol, Randolph de Broc, Hugh de S. Clare, Thomas FitzBernard, and all who should put forth their hands against the property of the church of Canterbury, or ill-use those to whom it rightfully belonged. He also suspended Joceline, Bishop of Salisbury, for having conferred the deanery of Salisbury on John of Oxford at the king's command, though he had been warned that the Pope had forbidden him to give it to anyone till the Canons of Salisbury, who were in exile with S. Thomas, could return and make a canonical election. Finally, he published the Pope's condemnation of the Constitutions of Clarendon, excommunicating all who observed them and absolving the bishops from their unlawful promise to do so.

When S. Thomas returned to Pontigny, he found awaiting him the notice of Henry's appeal, which the Bishops of Lisieux and Seez and the Archbishop of Rouen had left in his absence; and though it was informal, because the prelates had not waited to deliver it in person, and many of his followers advised him to disregard it, he determined, as was his custom, to abide by the Pope's decision concerning it. Before very long the Bishop of Salisbury and all the persons who had been excommunicated, appealed to the Pope, and fixed the second Sunday after Easter, 1167, for the term of their appeal. The English bishops, too, at the instigation of Gilbert of London, appealed to the Pope against any sentence which S. Thomas might hereafter pronounce against them.

S. Thomas's letter to the Bishop of London announcing his appointment as legate did not reach him till the end of June. In it S. Thomas ordered him and all the English bishops to restore, and compel their clergy to restore within two months his property, and that of his clergy, given them by the king. This letter was placed by a stranger on the altar of S. Paul's Cathedral, while the bishop was celebrating Mass there on the feast of the Commemoration of S. Paul, the 30th June, 1166. It produced a startling effect on the bishop. He wrote at once to Henry, beseeching him to allow him and the other bishops to obey this apostolic mandate, by the authority of which they were overwhelmed; but Henry was too well trained by his bishops in contempt for ecclesiastical authority to heed episcopal scruples. Then Gilbert's only resource was to write to the Pope, complaining, in piteous and abject terms, that "while matters are in this state between the king and his Lordship of Canterbury, it is impossible for me, or any other bishop in this kingdom, to obey the commands of the one and avoid the insupportable anger of the other."

The abject, selfish spirit of Gilbert, as contrasted with the courage and unworldliness of S. Thomas, is strikingly exhibited in a letter, which Gilbert wrote to his friend Cardinal William of Pavia on the following occasion. A nobleman had encouraged one of his retainers to take possession of a small religious house in the diocese of London; whereupon the Pope, being appealed to, ordered Gilbert to obtain restitution, or to excommunicate the nobleman and his retainer. Gilbert could not get leave from the king to excommunicate the nobleman, and the Constitutions of Clarendon forbidding him to do so without his permission, he now found himself in the terrible dilemma of being compelled to disobey either the Pope or the king. He therefore wrote to his friend, "And truly rather would I have been without my bishopric than incur either of these calamities. Either of the swords is heavy; one of which kills the soul, the other the body; the former indeed heavier, but the latter is by no means light. And what profit will there be in my blood to my dearest lord the Pope, if I should go down to the pit stigmatized as a traitor to my king; or if (which God forbid) I retain my life at the price of disobedience? If I obey not my lord the Pope's commands, woe is me; yet if I do obey, nothing remains for me but to fly a kingdom whose laws I have violated. If, indeed, the cause were one in which death or exile could be worthily undergone, gladly would I face either in compliance with my lord's wishes. But surely six miserable monks dwelling together in Panteney, without any rule or order, are not of such importance, that to obtain for them a few acres of land, the Chief Priest of Christendom should interrupt his friendly relations with the King of England."

Gilbert is said to have written to S. Thomas at this time a violent letter, upbraiding him with too great subserviency to the king. The genuineness has been doubted, among other reasons because it is not noticed in any of the numerous letters on both sides that still exist. Besides, the notorious falsehood of the charge would have greatly damaged Gilbert's own cause.

All these lesser appeals were eventually unsuccessful. The Pope confirmed the sentences pronounced by S. Thomas at Vezelay, for he had already ordered him to condemn all who had usurped Church property, and he had warned the bishops he would uphold all such sentences.

But still, the appeals answered Henry's purpose, which was, to gain time for acts of violence and to weary out his opponent by delays. S. Thomas, out of obedience to the Pope, had been passive for eighteen months, and now, when the moment for action was come, his long-deferred hopes were postponed for another year; for another year he had to eat the bread of charity in a foreign land; for another year he had to endure the pain of keeping his friends in exile, pining for the ties of family and home; and, above all, of knowing that his beloved Church was a prey to the spoiler. But this was only the first of those disappointments which made his life a protracted martyrdom.

As soon as Henry heard what had occurred at Vezelay, he ordered all the English ports to be strictly guarded, so as to prevent the delivery of the archbishop's letters. He also assembled the bishops and nobles, and made them swear not to assist the archbishop, nor to receive letters from him or the Pope, nor to appeal to anyone but himself. Notwithstanding, the archbishop's cause was so identified with the national liberties, that hundreds of persons of all classes, and especially from among the white monks, as the Cistercians, Carthusians, and Gilbertines were called from the colour of their habit, were ready to run every risk in his service, and in spite of opposition his letters and mandates were duly delivered. Many clerics and laymen were in consequence thrown into prison, churches were plundered, and such illegal outrages were committed, that even Hilary of Chichester remonstrated and told Henry that he was the best supporter the archbishop had, "for," said he, "you put him in the right by your violent proceedings, and you provide him with the counsel and assistance of the best clerics in your dominions by driving them into exile with him." This reproof touched Henry, and made him sigh, but his passions overcame his prudence. His bursts of rage used often to lead to scenes most derogatory to his dignity, whether as a man or a king. On one occasion, when he was at Caen transacting business concerning the King of Scotland, Richard de Humez said something which seemed like favouring the {Scotch; whereupon Henry "broke into violent abuse, calling him a traitor, and in his fit of passion he flung down his cap, undid his belt, threw from him his pall and robes, tore the silk covering off his couch, and sitting down on the floor, began to chew stalks of straw," like a petulant, sulking child. A letter written to S. Thomas at this time, presents a curious picture of Henry's conduct when he was in one of his usual fits of rage. "You know, I conclude, in what a strait the messenger was who delivered the letter to the king. His fingers were thrust into his eyes, as if to tear them out, till the blood flowed; and hot water was forced down his throat, till he confessed that the letter came from Master Herbert. He is not yet released from prison, though the king has received an order to that effect from his mother."

But Henry's master-stroke was a petty act of revenge against S. Thomas himself. The Cistercians held their general chapter as usual at Citeaux on Holy Cross Day, the 14th of September, 1166, when Henry wrote to warn them that if they attached any value to their possessions in his dominions, they would no longer harbour his personal enemy, the Archbishop of Canterbury, in one of the houses of their order. After the close of the chapter, Gilbert Abbot of Citeaux, Bishop of Pavia, who had been a Cistercian monk, and several other abbots, went to Pontigny, and read Henry's letter to the monks. Then turning to S. Thomas, who was present, they said, "My lord, the chapter does not drive you out of their house in consequence of such a letter as this; they merely lay the letter before you, that you may consider and decide what is to be done. The chapter and all present know well that your regard for the Cistercian order is too great to allow a heavy calamity to befall it." This plain hint left S. Thomas no choice, and after exchanging a few words with his clerics, he said that he would quit the hospitable roof under which he had received so much kindness, adding cheerfully, "The Lord who feeds the birds of the air and clothes the lilies will provide for me and my fellow-exiles." The assembly was moved to tears by his faith and generosity, and the abbot and monks of Pontigny refused to part with him. But he stood firm to his declaration that he would go, and the other abbots did not care to risk their earthly possessions, even for the

Church's cause; and therefore the monks of Pontigny were obliged to submit to the loss of their saintly guest.

The exiles had now to consider whither they should turn in search of an asylum. But their consultation was carried on in a cheerful spirit. One of the party said merrily, "that as they could not go where they would they must go where they could." And when Herbert reminded S. Thomas of the offers of the King of France two years before at Soissons, the saint bantered him, saying, "It would seem, my brother, that you are looking out for the pleasures of a king's court, which hardly suit our bonds in the Gospel." But the King of France was now their only resource, and so Herbert was sent to inform him of their plight.

Louis was travelling when Herbert fell in with him. When he heard why S. Thomas was quitting Pontigny, he exclaimed, "O religion, O religion, where art thou? Those whom we believed to be dead to the world, fear its threats; and professing to despise the things that perish, for their sake turn back from the work of God which they had taken in hand, and drive God's exile from them." Then, turning to Herbert, he said, "Salute your lord the archbishop, and promise him in my name, that though the world and those who are dead to the world desert him, I will not do so. Let him tell us what city, or castle, or other place in our dominions he would prefer, and he shall find it prepared for him." S. Thomas selected the royal Abbey of S. Columba, near Sens; and here he lived for nearly four years at the King of France's expense, from the feast of S. Martin, the 11th of November, 1166, till the close of his exile.

The day S. Thomas quitted Pontigny was a sorrowful one to the community, who had felt the charm of his saintliness and were much attached to him. The abbot to whose charge he had been committed two years before by the Pope, had been made Archbishop of Lyons, and his successor was Guarine de Galardim, who was now so reluctant to part with the exiles. He and some of his monks accompanied them on their way to Sens; and as they went along, S. Thomas rode apart in silence, and it was noticed that he was shedding tears. Then the good abbot began to upbraid him for his effeminacy in being so attached to the house he was leaving, and added, by way of consoling him, "Why do you mourn? Do you want money for your necessities, or a more splendid equipage? Is there ought that we can do for you?" "It is not that," replied S. Thomas, "but I feel that my days are numbered. God revealed to me last night that I shall die by the sword. Yet I am not so sorrowful for the revelation, for which I rather give the Most High all the thanks in my power; but I grieve for those who have followed me and have borne so much for me, for I know for certainty that when I am struck down the sheep ill have no shepherd." The good Guarine, with prejudices of an ascetic monk, smiled and said, "So you are going to be martyred. What has a man that eats and drinks to do with martyrdom?" With saintly humility S. Thomas replied, "I know that I am too fond of worldly pleasures; but the Lord is good, who justifies the wicked, and He has deigned to reveal this to me, who am all unworthy." He then told the abbot, that in the vision of the light before he seemed to be in a church, he knew lot where, defending his cause before the Pope and cardinals, the Pope being on his side, and the cardinals against him, when four soldiers rushed in and cut off that part of his head which was anointed at his consecration; and by this he understood that he should glorify God by a hard but precious death. S. Thomas told this vision also another abbot, under a promise of secrecy till the event should verify it, and after his death both abbots made it known.

As S. Thomas was quitting Pontigny, he told the monks that one of his successors would repay them for hospitality to him. This promise was in part fulfilled, when the tithes of Romney were settled on them by Stephen Langton, S. Edmund, and Blessed Boniface, his successors in the See of Canterbury, and the two first, like himself, exiles for God's cause, and guests at Pontigny. But the monks understood that its true fulfilment took place when, on the 16th of November, 1240, the relics of S. Edmund were brought to their church, where they are still preserved. This was also asserted by Pope Innocent IV. in the bull of S. Edmund's canonization. The first miracle which was worked at S. Edmund's tomb was the cure of a cripple, whom the monks called Thomas, out of gratitude to the saintly guest, who, they considered, had repaid their hospitality by the gift of the venerated body of his saintly successor.

CHAPTER XVI. JOHN OF OXFORD.

THE favourable turn in S. Thomas's affairs was of short duration. John of Oxford had gone to the Pope in a defiant spirit, utterly ignoring S. Thomas's sentence. Happening to meet in the Pope's ante-room Hubert Lombard, a great friend of S. Thomas's, and afterwards Pope as Urban III., he offered him a kiss. But Lombard refused to kiss him, and asking aloud whether he was not excommunicated, he looked very foolish. The presence of this unprincipled man at the Papal Court, caused S. Thomas grave anxiety, but his only resource was to dispatch messengers to oppose him.

Towards the close of the year 1166, these messengers returned with the news that John and the other excommunicates had been absolved, that John had been confirmed as Dean of Salisbury, and that he had obtained the appointment of William of Pavia, Cardinal Priest of S. Peter's Chains, a warm partisan of the king's, as legate a *latere* with full power to decide the cause without appeal, in return for which he had abjured the Constitutions of Clarendon in the king's name.

On the Feast of the Purification, John Cumin and Raoul de Tamworth, two of his colleagues, arrived at Tours on their way home. They confirmed the report of S. Thomas's messengers, and added that John had ingratiated himself with the Pope by suggesting that peace might be restored between S. Thomas and the king, if anyone could be found to negotiate it faithfully, which he had offered himself to do. For this they openly called him a traitor to the king, because he had promised for his own ends to do what the king considered impossible. It was, however, said that William of Pavia was to have for a colleague Otho, Cardinal Deacon of S. Nicholas in the Tullian prison, and it was hoped his influence might temper the malignity of Cardinal William.

John of Oxford soon returned to England and removed all doubts as to the success of his mission. He. went about boasting, not only of his confirmation as Dean of Salisbury, but that he was exempted from the jurisdiction of the archbishop and every other bishop, and subject only to the Pope; that legates were coming at the king's request to decide without appeal whatever his Majesty should think fit to propose against S. Thomas; and that, so high was he in the Pope's favour, that he had obtained for the king what no king was ever able to obtain for himself, namely, his Holiness's consent to a marriage in the third degree of affinity between Henry's son Geoffrey and the daughter of the Earl of Bretagne.

On landing in England, he found the Bishop of Hereford waiting for a fair wind to cross the sea privately in answer to the archbishop's summons to all the English bishops to come to him within forty days. He at once forbade him to go, first in the king's name, and then in the Pope's. The bishop inquired whether he had any letters to that effect. John asserted that he had, and that the Pope forbade all the bishops to obey the archbishop in anything till the arrival of the legates, who were appointed at the king's request to decide the cause finally. The letters could not then be seen, as they were with his baggage at Winchester; but the bishop sent one of his clerics to Winchester, where they were shown to him and the Bishop of London, who also was waiting to cross the Channel. Then there seemed to be no doubt about the matter, for the Pope's letters, both to the king and the bishops, said plainly that the legates were "persons *de latere nostro*," and that he had "committed to them the fulfilment of his own office in all things." When the Bishop of London saw these letters, he exclaimed, as if unable to contain himself for joy, "Then Thomas shall be no more archbishop of mine." As for the Bishop of Hereford, who was much attached to S. Thomas and had done his best to obey him, he returned home and took the matter so much to heart, that he fell ill and died shortly after, on the 27th of February, 1168.

When the news of John of Oxford's boasted success spread through France, it produced universal consternation. For Cardinal William of Pavia was known to be fond of money, and also a great personal friend of Gilbert's; and it was reported that the Archbishopric of Canterbury was to be given him if he would rid the king of its present occupant, and that he had promised to decide the cause in the king's favour. The minds of good Catholics were greatly disturbed; it was feared that the Church in England was crushed, and England rent from Catholic unity; and even the Pope's good name was called in question. The King of France took it as a personal matter; for, said he, "Is not my dishonour attempted in this crafty design upon the life of an innocent man and an exile for justice and the Church's liberty, who is thus impiously delivered up to those that hate and persecute him, while I have determined, as long as his exile lasts, to cherish him, as it were, in my bosom; as indeed I am now doing?" He would have forbidden the legates to enter his kingdom, if S. Thomas had not dissuaded him from this strong step, the odium of which would have recoiled on the saint.

As to S. Thomas, he was greatly perplexed. The Pope's letter to himself, it was true, spoke of the legates as being only mediators between him and the king, and bade him give way for a time in everything that would promote concord, promising, if this means failed, to authorise him hereafter to exercise his powers freely. But there seemed to be no doubt that stronger letters, declaring that the legates had full and final jurisdiction, had been sent to the king and the English bishops. Great as was the trial to his faith, his hope did not fail, nor did he falter in his obedience. He wrote to his envoy at Rome, "If this be true, then without doubt his lordship the Pope has suffocated and strangled, not only our own person, but himself and every ecclesiastic of both kingdoms, yea, both Churches together, the French and the English. For what will not the kings of the earth dare against the clergy under cover of this most wretched precedent?" He wrote also to the Pope, saying, "May it please your Holiness not to expose our innocence to peril at the hands of my Lord William of Pavia, through whom our persecutors boast that they will cause us to be deposed. Whether he is to come with such powers we know not; but this we know, that unless compelled by your Holiness, we shall never trust ourselves to any judge except your Holiness. Far be it from the Church of God that such things should be accomplished, as a priest, who is one of the clerics of our above-named friend and lord, but just now has promised to the King of England, that as legate he will determine the cause at issue between us to the king's liking."

To the cardinals, many of whom were generally believed to have been bought over by Henry's gifts, he addressed a letter well calculated to stir up within them the love of justice and the fear of God, which were the source of the lofty courage which animated himself. He wrote as follows: "The Lord hath said, 'Love *justice*, ye that are judges of the earth.' This it is that you must love, this that you must observe; this it is that brings about *peace* and preserves it. Whence Isaias says, 'The effect of *righteousness* shall be *peace*'; and David, '*Righteousness* and *peace* have kissed one another.' These twain are so leagued, that he who does justice finds peace, and none other Beware, my lords, beware lest ye treasure up for yourselves wrath against the day of wrath; rather lay up for yourselves treasures in heaven, resisting the oppressors and relieving the oppressed. Otherwise, let God judge between you and me and my fellows in exile the fatherless, and widow, and helpless infant that God with whom there is no acceptance. The blood of my slain at your hands, let Him avenge. ... I write these things not to anger, but to caution you, God knoweth, He who searcheth the heart; lest the day of the Lord come to you like a thief in the night, the day of fierce anger which spareth no one. Trust, then, to me, my beloved lords, . . . resume your strength, gird yourselves with the word of the Most High as with a sword, unsheathe the sword of the blessed Peter, avenge the injury of Christ and of His flock; let your eye spare not, make haste to do judgment and justice for all that suffer wrongfully. This is the royal way; this is the way that leadeth to life; this is the way that you must walk in if ye would follow the footsteps of Jesus Christ, and the footsteps of His apostles, whose vicars ye are. It is not by craft, it is not by wise schemes that the Church is to be governed, but by justice and truth. Who follows these need fear no danger." All these letters, as well as many more that he wrote to such of his friends as could help his cause, give touching evidence of the keenness of his feelings, of his ardent love for the Church, of the chafing of his noble spirit at the baseness and cruelty of his enemies, and of his heroic courage, in contrast with the cowardly and mercenary spirit of many of the chief persons at the English and Papal Courts.

Gradually, however, it came out that matters were not so bad as they seemed to be. It was true that John of Oxford and all the excommunicates had been absolved, but only in case they should be at the hour of death, and on the condition that they made restitution of all Church property, failing to do which, the absolution became void. John of Oxford's own absolution depended further on the truth of his oath, that he had not communicated with the Anti-Pope's followers, and every one believed that he had perjured himself in taking this oath. And as to the unlimited legatine commission and the appointment of Cardinal William, in order to obtain these concessions John had sworn in the king's name that the Constitutions of Clarendon would be given up, and he had been so submissive to the Pope, that even his own colleagues in the embassy called him a traitor to the king. But now it came out that the whole affair was a dishonest trick, that the unscrupulous "Swearer" had pledged his master without authority, and that his master did not consider himself bound by his envoy's fake swearing.

As soon as this treachery came to the Pope's knowledge, he withdrew the extraordinary powers of the legates, and he wrote to them desiring them to make it their first business to console the archbishop, and on no account to enter Henry's dominions without his consent, or to take any decided step till *he should be reconciled to the king*, thus reducing them to mediators, and, in fact, making it dependent on S. Thomas's will whether they should have any authority or not.

But, notwithstanding, John of Oxford had done good service to Henry. A few months before the bishops, intimidated by S. Thomas's legatine authority, were becoming anxious to be reconciled to him, and Henry was beginning to fear that if he were deserted by them, he should be compelled to give peace and liberty to the Church. But John's perjury and boasts had not only gained time, but had turned the tide of feeling and inspired his party with fresh courage, so that, as S. Thomas complained, neither bishop, nor abbot, nor any of the clergy treated him with respect or obedience, as if his deposition were certain. Moreover, some of the great men of France, despairing of his cause, and weary of the charge of keeping the exiles, had sent away those whom their charity had hitherto supported, and these unfortunate persons must either perish of cold and hunger, or be provided for by the more onerous spirits, who were already over-burdened with the charge of their fellow-exiles.

CHAPTER XVII. THE CARDINAL LEGATES.

THE year 1167, the third of S. Thomas's exile, was drawing to its close when the legates arrived in France. They had run many risks on their journey, for the emperor had regained ground, the Pope had quitted Rome, Italy was overrun by hostile armies, and thus they had been obliged to travel in disguise to Venice.

On their arrival in France, Cardinal William of Pavia addressed to S. Thomas a letter which made him uneasy, because its tone was that of a judge rather than of a mediator. S. Thomas wrote an answer which, with his usual humility, he submitted to the approval of John of Salisbury, his constant monitor. John said that the style was deficient in humility and moderation, and the letter was conceived in a spirit of bitterness very foreign to the sincerity of Christian love. This severe reproof from an inferior was received with perfect meekness, and the archbishop sat down, like a little child, to write another letter, which he again submitted for approval. But John was bard to please, and wrote back: "Your second letter suits my taste as little as the first; it is too full of suspicions, and immoderately seasoned with sarcasms; and I fear temerity on our part will give our enemies a handle against us." So this letter also was rejected, and a third attempt was made; but, unfortunately, the letter which was actually sent, has not been preserved.

At length the legates arrived, and paid their first visit to S. Thomas at Sens. They explained to him that the object of their coming was to make peace between him and the king, to the honour of God and saving the liberties of the Church an intimation which was quite satisfactory. They then went on to Normandy where Henry was. Here they remained for some time, and had repeated audiences of the king; but they could make no progress; for though Henry professed to desire a reconciliation, he was only trying to gain time and to protract the negotiations. Wishing to avoid the appearance of having come on a fruitless errand, they at length summoned S. Thomas to meet them in ten days at Les Planches on the borders of France, between Gisors and Trie. S. Thomas had but three horses for himself and his suite; it would be difficult on so short a notice to raise funds for the expenses of the journey; and, moreover, he wished to be assisted by the advice of some of his fellow-exiles, who were dispersed in various directions. He was therefore obliged to ask for another week's delay, at which Henry pretended to take offence. But at length the exiles with difficulty reached the place of conference, where they were all magnificently entertained at the King of France's expense.

The meeting took place on the 18th of November. The night before, the archbishop dreamt that some one offered him poison in a golden cup; and the next day his followers saw the fulfilment of this dream in the smooth and insidious words of William of Pavia, which seemed to breathe only love and peace, but were really fraught with secret danger to the Church. The legates began by saying a good deal about Henry's love for the Roman Church, his power, his inflexibility of character, the great favours he had conferred on the saint and his many just causes of complaint; and then passing on to the badness of the times, with many exhortations to humility and moderation, they proposed that S. Thomas should promise to observe to King Henry, whatever customs his predecessors had observed to former kings. This promise would have been an indirect assent to the Constitutions of Clarendon, which Henry asserted to be ancient customs; and therefore S. Thomas answered, that he could not enter into this engagement because the Pope had condemned these customs in their presence at Sens. They then proposed that he should at least return to his see in peace, without mentioning the customs one way or other. But he answered with the English proverb, "Silence speaks consent." After this they tried insidiously to get him into their power, by proposing that he should submit his cause to their arbitration, intending, if he refused, to throw the blame of their fruitless mission on him. But he, perceiving their aim, answered with great wisdom, that whenever restitution should be made to him and his clerics for all their property which had been seized, he would willingly accept the arbitration of their lordships, or anyone else whom the Pope should appoint; but that meanwhile, being dependent even for their daily bread on the charity of the King of France, they had not the means to enter on any litigation. They then made another attempt to catch him unawares, by asking whether, if the bishops should appeal again, he would consent to the legates giving judgment. But he was aware that the bishops had never been assembled to consider the pretended appeal which was being got up in their names, and that many disapproved of it, while others knew nothing about it; and therefore he answered, that he had received no instructions from the Pope; that when he did so, he would answer accordingly; but that the poverty of himself and his friends prevented their undertaking lawsuits and expensive journeys. During the conference, William of Pavia openly espoused Henry's cause, and tried to throw the blame of the quarrel on S. Thomas. But when at its close the saint, with great humility, asked the legates to advise him as to the line of conduct they considered most for the interest of the Church, they could only express their confidence in his zeal, and declare that his present line of conduct could not be altered for the better. Thus they parted with mutual expressions of goodwill.

The legates now made their way back to Henry. When he heard of their approach, he came out two miles to meet them; and welcoming them cordially, attended each to his house.

The day following, being Monday the 27th of November, early in the morning after Mass, they were invited to attend the king, and entered the council-chamber with the archbishops, bishops, and abbots who had admission. On their reappearance, after a space of about two hours, the king came out as far as the outer door of the chapel, and there said publicly in the hearing of the legates, "I trust my eyes may never light upon another cardinal." In such haste was he to get rid of them, that he would not let them wait for their own horses, but mounted them upon the first that could be found near the chapel. Thus the cardinals took their departure with not more than four attendants.

The archbishops, bishops, and abbots stayed with the king, and re-entered the council-chamber, where they remained till evening. Afterwards they visited the cardinals, all in evident confusion; and after remaining some time they returned to their houses. The day following they were closeted with the king till twelve o'clock; then they visited the cardinals; then they returned to the king, and again to the cardinals, carrying secret messages backwards and forwards. The day after, the vigil of S. Andrew, the king rose at daybreak, and went out to hunt and hawk, so that it was surmised that he absented himself on purpose.

Very early the bishops met at the chapel royal, and adjourned to the council-chamber; here they deliberated in the king's absence, and then withdrew to the church near which the cardinals lodged. Henry had been careful to summon only such persons as were unfriendly to S. Thomas, and consequently the only English bishops now present were the Archbishop of York, and the Bishops of London, Salisbury, Chichester, and Worcester, the last being added for appearance sake. There were present, however, the Archbishop of Rouen, the Bishops of Bayeux and Angouleme, a great many abbots, and a vast multitude of clergy and laity. After the cardinals were seated, the Bishop of London rose and made a long and pointless oration, which evinced the troubled state of his mind; for it was only a rambling recapitulation of all the wrongs to the king and himself of which he accused S. Thomas. The legates answered that they had no powers to act as judges, but only as mediators; whereupon the bishops renewed their appeal, fixing its term for the feast of S. Martin, the 11th of November, 1168.

After all was over, the cardinals sent letters to S. Thomas, prohibiting him, in the Pope's name and their own, from acting in disregard of the appeal till the Pope had been consulted. But S. Thomas wrote back that he well knew, and they could not be ignorant, how far their commands were binding on him; and that by God's grace he should act as he thought most for the interest of the Church. He also sent them a verbal message finding fault with their conduct for various and obvious reasons; and also calling on them to replace the sentences, as the Pope had directed, on all the excommunicates who had not made satisfaction.

The bishops also sent messengers to S. Thomas, but he refused to receive them, because one of those from whom they came was the Bishop of London, whom he looked on as excommunicate; and also because they had held communion with the excommunicates, whose absolution had been fraudulent.

The cardinals took leave of the king on Thursday the 7th of December. On parting, Henry entreated them, most humbly and with tears, to intercede with the Pope to rid him altogether of S. Thomas. William of Pavia, too, seemed to weep, but Cardinal Otho could scarcely help laughing at this piece of acting.

CHAPTER XVIII. THE SUSPENSION.

THE legatine commission was thus brought to a close with no result, except that the legates had thrown the whole matter into greater confusion than before. Overstepping their powers, they had suspended S. Thomas, and thus brought contempt upon his acts, though without in the least impairing their validity. They had also taken on themselves to order the Bishops of Norwich and Chichester to absolve anew all who had been fraudulently absolved on John of Oxford's return from Rome, thus helping by a second invalid absolution to harden those unhappy excommunicates in their impenitence. And when the Pope ordered them to replace the censures, unless the excommunicates would at once restore the Church property which they had usurped, they flatly refused to do so; plainly declaring that as the excommunicates had received the Church property by the king's mandate, it was impossible, so long as they themselves were in his territory, to punish the offenders or even to remonstrate with him, and that neither for the Pope nor for any other mortal would they on any account oppose him.

But though their mission was at an end, the cardinals still lingered in the neighbourhood of Henry's court and continued their work of mischief, by throwing the weight of their high position on the king's side, and openly professing to use their influence to obtain for him the support of the Holy See. Nor were they remiss in fulfilling these promises; for at one time they wrote to the Pope on behalf of the excommunicates; at another they represented that Henry was willing to cede the two most obnoxious of the constitutions, namely, those forbidding appeals and subjecting the clergy to the secular courts; then again they suggested insidiously various plans for arbitration, by persons who would be within the influence of Henry's promises and threats; and, finally, they proposed S. Thomas's translation to another see. This proposal was taken up warmly by many, and even, to S. Thomas's great mortification, by the Bishop of Worcester, who, though much attached to the saint, was being wearied out by the protracted strife. But S. Thomas's answer to the suggestion was as unflinching and heroic as ever, "We wish our lord the Pope and our other friends to know that sooner than suffer ourselves to be torn from our Church of Canterbury, God, the inspector of hearts, knoweth we would consent to be slaughtered. Let them waste no labour on such a prospect, for there is no calamity which we should not prefer to that. You may inform them also, that if every other grievance were removed, yet so long as that man retains the possessions of our own or any other church in his dominions, we would rather die any death than basely live and suffer him to enjoy them with impunity." Well might the Church's champion express himself thus vehemently, for, as S. Thomas wrote to the Pope and the cardinals, at this very time Henry was keeping vacant no less than seven bishoprics in the provinces of Canterbury and Rouen, and appropriating their revenues; and at the same time he was putting forth his hand against the clergy, imprisoning and beheading them, tearing out the eyes of some, forcing others to the trial of single combat and the ordeals of fire and water, and giving them up to be trodden underfoot and spoiled by his satellites. So great was S. Thomas's sorrow, that with touching pathos he wrote, "Our soul sinks under its sufferings; we are worn out and almost ground beneath the weight of our miseries . . . we have endured vexation upon vexation, we have not strength left us to endure the least of their annoyances, and we can scarcely breathe for our anguish."

Messengers from both sides to the Pope were now to be seen going to and fro, all hurry and bustle, some dying on the way, but others succeeding them, and the number ever increasing, so that the threshold of the apostles was said to be worn by them. Both parties were courteously received, though their bearing and appearance were very different. S. Thomas's messengers were taken from his fellow-exiles, whose poor appearance and the tales they could tell of what they had themselves undergone and witnessed, were the best credentials of their veracity, and the most forcible arguments in support of their master's cause. As for the king's envoys, they came with great pomp and ostentation; and when they found that they could not move the Pope by flattery or promises, they had recourse to threats, intimating that Henry would join the Anti-Pope, rather than allow S. Thomas to retain the See of Canterbury. But the Holy Father was as insensible to threats as to flattery; and setting before them the alternative of life and death, he said, that though he could not prevent their choosing the way of those that perish, yet by the grace of God, for his part, he would not recede from the right way. Messengers came also from the legates, but they did not at all agree in their accounts, for whatever one said, the other unsaid. Thus the winter and spring passed away, and summer was drawing nigh, and it was still unknown what would be the Pope's decision. But he wrote to the King of France that he would not fail the Church of God nor his friend of Canterbury, whenever he could uphold him with justice; and his words inspired the exiles and all good Catholics with hope.

It was probably at this time, though it may have been some years earlier, that an attempt was made by the King of France to obtain the pardon of at least some of S. Thomas's clerics, and the restoration of their benefices. Henry consented to see them, and accordingly they came to Angers, where he had been keeping Easter; and on Low Sunday he gave them audience.

John of Salisbury was the first who was brought in, and after saluting the king, he asked to be allowed to return to England and to have his benefices restored, as he had never wilfully offended the king, but was ready to be faithful and loyal to him as his earthly lord, saving his order. On the king's part it was answered, that as he was born in the king's dominions, and had there risen to riches and station, he ought, as the king's subject, to have been faithful to him against the archbishop and everyone else; and then an oath was proposed to him, that he would be faithful to the king in life and limb and in preserving his earthly honour against all men, and especially that he would observe his written customs and royal dignities, let the Pope, or the archbishop, or his own bishop, do what they might. John replied that he had been brought up from his youth by the Church of Canterbury, that he was sworn to the obedience of the Pope and the archbishop, and he could not desert them nor promise to observe the customs; but he was willing to pledge himself to receive whatever the Pope and the archbishop received and to reject what they rejected. This did not satisfy Henry, so he was ordered to withdraw.

Herbert de Bosham was now called for, and as he came in, the king said to those near him, "Now we shall see a specimen of pride." Herbert was tall and striking, and had on a handsome tunic, and a mantle of green cloth of Auxerre hanging over his shoulders, and reaching, after the German fashion, down to his ankles. After the usual salutation he took his seat, and being questioned as John had been, he made for the most part the same answers. Mention being made of loyalty and the archbishop, he said that the archbishop above all men was loyal, for that he had not suffered his Majesty to go astray unwarned. Of the customs he spoke as John had done, adding that he wondered the king had put them in writing; for in other kingdoms likewise there were evil customs against the Church; but they were not written, and for this reason there was hope, by God's grace that they might become disused.

The king wishing to catch him in his words, asked, "And what are the evil customs in the kingdom of our lord the King of France?"

Herbert. "The exaction of toll and passage from the clergy and pilgrims. Again, when a bishop dies, all his movable goods, even the doors and windows of his house, become the king's. So in the realm of the King of the Germans, though these and similar evil customs exist they are not written."

The King. "Why do you not call him by his proper title, the Emperor of Germany?"

Herbert. "His title is King of Germany, and when he styles himself emperor, it is 'Emperor of the Romans, the ever august.' "

The King. "This is abominable. Is this son of a priest to disturb my kingdom and disquiet my peace?"

Herbert. "It is not I who do it; nor am I the son of a priest, as I was born before my father entered orders; nor is he a king's son, whose father was no king when he begat him."

Here Jordan Tarsun, one of the barons sitting by, said, "Whosesoever son he is, I would give my barony he were mine." This made the king angry but he said nothing. After a little, however, he dismissed Herbert, who withdrew.

Philip de Calne or Caune entered next. He was a Londoner, and for two years before S. Thomas's exile, had studied the Holy Scriptures and taught law at Tours. He was a man of great reading and very eloquent; but being in weak health, he had not accompanied the archbishop, nor had he been sent to Rome, nor mixed up in proceedings against the king. He had influential friends, who explained all this to Henry, and reported also how, when he heard that his property had been confiscated on the archbishop's account, he had exclaimed, "Good God, what does our good king want with me?" Henry was anxious not to seem to have granted nothing graciously, so he remitted the oath which had been proposed to the others, and restored Philip to his possessions.

Thus ended the attempt to obtain relief for the poor, needy clerics. John of Salisbury, moreover, complained that the journey had cost him £13 and two good horses, besides interfering with his occupation as a teacher, by which he gained his subsistence, and what was worst, all went for nothing.

At length about the middle of the summer of 1168, the Pope's answer arrived. It fell like a thunderbolt on S. Thomas, and was an unexpected triumph to Henry. The Holy Father actually suspended the archbishop. It seems that when the legates found how completely their mission had failed, they became alarmed for their own safety in the event of S. Thomas excommunicating the king or laying an interdict on the kingdom. William of Pavia consequently wrote to the Pope, beseeching him with tragic earnestness to treat the king less harshly, for otherwise "he and his colleague would be cast into prison, where they would pass a short and wretched life even worse than death;" and in order to pacify

Henry and liberate themselves, they suggested that the archbishop should be suspended, Henry having pledged himself under his own hand and by his envoys, to make peace at once if his honour and dignity were propitiated by this measure. Thus misled by the legates, as well as by Henry's messengers and the persons at the Papal court whom Henry's gifts had seduced, the Holy Father resolved to try whether more might not be gained by appealing to Henry's generosity than in any other way. He therefore wrote to him in a tone of fatherly affection, and after reminding him, that in the things of God and the Church "it is more glorious to be conquered than to conquer," he informed him that, hoping to mitigate his indignation, he had forbidden the archbishop to pronounce any sentence against him, or his nobles, or his kingdom, until, to use the Pope's own words, "you take him back into your favour, and he is reconciled to you." This letter Henry had liberty to show only "if the archbishop should presume to aggrieve" him, his nobles, or his land, and his envoys swore under pain of an anathema to keep it secret. But no sooner did they reach England than they forgot their oath and its penalty, and published it everywhere; so that even Geoffrey, one of William of Pavia's clerics, "openly protested that they had perjured themselves and incurred an anathema."

As for Henry, to rest any hopes on his generosity was like building on the sand washed by the stormy ocean's waves. Now that his demand granted, he was so puffed up that he could not contain himself, and seemed at a loss how to express the full insolence of his triumph. In order to hold up S. Thomas and his followers to general contempt, he caused his suspension to be cried through the streets both in England and Normandy, and had copies made of the Pope's letter, and sent round to all the churches in his dominions. He could not refrain from mentioning the names of the cardinals who had taken his gold, and of the agents who had distributed his gifts; even going so far as to tell the Bishop of Worcester, that he and all the other bishops were exempted from the archbishop's jurisdiction, and need fear no threats, for "he had the Pope and all the cardinals in his purse." Nay, so elated was he that he openly boasted of "having at last obtained the prerogatives of his grandfather, who was, in his own realm, at once apostolic legate, patriarch, and emperor, and whatever else he choose"; thus plainly confessing what were his secret intentions when, on various occasions, he tried to extract from S. Thomas a promise to give him only the privileges enjoyed by his predecessors. Not content with empty words only, he proceeded to alienate many of the lands of the Church of Canterbury, wantonly to destroy the remaining property, and to levy exactions on the whole body of clergy, declaring that, as his immunity from censure was to last till it pleased him to receive the archbishop into his favour, he would put it off till the Greek Kalends—*i.e.*, for ever.

The Pope's letter to S. Thomas differed, however, in one material point from that to Henry, for it promised the saint that if peace were not concluded by the beginning of Lent, he should then receive apostolic letters empowering him to act against Henry. This totally altered the case, and showed how groundless were Henry's mad boastings. But the Pope's letter was written in May, and Lent was yet far distant.

S. Thomas's feelings on this most trying occasion cannot be better described than in his own words, which occur in a most powerful letter to the Pope. "O my father, my soul is in bitterness. The letters by which your Holiness was pleased to suspend me have made myself and my unhappy fellow-exiles a very scorn of men and outcast of the people, and, what grieves me worse, have delivered up God's Church to the will of its enemies. Our persecutor had held out sure hopes to the Earl of Flanders and others of the French nobility, that he meant to make peace with us; but his messengers arrived with new powers from your Holiness, and all was at an end. What could our friends do for us when thus repulsed by your Holiness's act, and smitten down as with the club of Hercules? Would that your Holiness's ear could hear what is said of this matter by the bishops, nobles, and commons of both realms, and that your eye could see the scandal with which it has filled the French court! But your Holiness counsels me to bear with patience the *meanwhile*. And do you not observe, father, what this *meanwhile* may bring about to the injury of the Church, and of your Holiness's reputation? *Meanwhile*, he applies to his own purposes the revenues of the vacant abbeys and bishoprics, and will not suffer pastors to be ordained there; *meanwhile*, he riots in uncontrolled insolence against the parishes, churches, holy places, and the whole sacred order; *meanwhile*, he and the other persecutors of the Church make their will their law; *meanwhile*, who is to take charge of the sheep of Christ, and save them from the jaws of wolves, who no longer prowl around, but have entered the fold, and devour and tear and slay, with none to resist them? For what pastor is there whose voice you have not silenced, and what bishop have you not suspended, in suspending me? . . . And yet I doubt not that this struggle for the Church's liberty would long ago have been brought to a close, unless the king's wilfulness, not to use a harsher term, had found patrons in the Church of Rome. God requite them as is best for His Church and for themselves. The Almighty, All just Lord God judge between them and me. Little should I have needed their patronage, if I had chosen to forsake the Church and yield to his wilfulness myself. I might have flourished in wealth and abundance of delicacies; I might have been feared, courted, honoured; and might have provided for my own in luxury and worldly glory, as I pleased. But because God called me to the government of His Church, an unworthy sinner as I was, and most wretched, though flourishing in the world's goods beyond all my countrymen, through His grace preventing and assisting me I chosed rather to be an outcast from the palace, to be exiled, proscribed, and to finish my life in the last wretchedness, rather than to sell the Church's liberty, and to prefer the iniquitous traditions of men to the law of God. For myself, I know that my own days are few; and that unless I declare to the wicked man his ways, his blood will shortly be required at my hands by One from whom no patronage can protect me. There silver and gold will be profitless, and gifts that blind the eyes of wise ones. We shall soon stand all of us before the tribunal of Christ, and by His majesty and terrible judgment, I conjure your Holiness, as my father and lord, and as the supreme judge on earth, to render justice to His Church and to myself against those who seek my life to take it away."

But touched as the Holy Father must have been by this pathetic appeal, and grieved as he must have been at the perjury and insolence of Henry and his envoys, still he was not to be turned from the long-suffering, but firm policy, which has ever proved the Church's strongest weapon. He resolved still to wait till Lent for Henry's repentance, thus leaving him without excuse, should he prove obdurate, as it was to be feared he would. The cardinal legates were recalled; and after having done as much mischief as they well could, they returned home penitent, and confessing with shame that in too many points they had sacrificed the Church to the king's wishes. At a parting interview, Cardinal Otho strongly urged Henry to be reconciled to S. Thomas, and to make restitution of the Church property. Henry answered that the archbishop might return in peace to his see, but that he would restore nothing, because, as he swore with recondite oaths, he had spent all he had received on the poor, which everyone knew to be false.

During the long *"meanwhile"* till Lent, S. Thomas could only wait and drink in patience the bitter chalice of sorrow and humiliation, which was presented him by the loving Lord who had Himself drained it to its dregs. As he wrote to a friend: "The Church of Canterbury is almost destroyed, and I and my fellow-exiles are afflicted beyond measure. . . . Yet since this matter is beyond help, so long as God sees fit I will make myself bear it manfully—yet not I, but the grace of God which is with me."

The only consolation he had in his affliction, was found in the generous sympathy of the great Catholic-hearted nation whose guest he was. The King and Queen of France, and many other influential persons, wrote to the Pope remonstrating warmly at his suspension; and as for the people, their indignation was unbounded, so that it became a proverb among them, "The princes of the church are faithless companions of thieves, for they authorize the plunder of Christ's patrimony to share in it."

CHAPTER XIX. THE POPE'S ENVOYS—THE CONFERENCE AT MONTMIRAIL.

BUT though the Pope would not allow S. Thomas to take any strong step which might irritate Henry, he thought it was desirable that he himself should give him timely warning of the sentence which would fall on him, should he not fulfil his promises and make peace before the beginning of Lent. He therefore sent him letters of commonition, the bearers of which were Simon Prior of Montdieu, Engelbert Prior of Val de S. Pierre, and Bernard de Corilo, a monk of Grammont. Henry received them with his usual duplicity, and in answer, told the envoys that he wished sincerely for peace, if the archbishop would only make a show of submission. He had a further reason for speaking thus, which was, that he had for some time been at war with France, and having been unsuccessful, he had become really anxious for peace with Louis, and he thought he should obtain better terms if he professed a wish to be reconciled also with S. Thomas. A meeting between the kings had been arranged to take place on the Epiphany, A.D. 1169, in a plain near the castle of Montmirail in the Chartraine. The Pope's envoys believing Henry's professions, thought the occasion favourable for a reconciliation between him and S. Thomas, and they therefore induced Louis to invite the latter to be present. S. Thomas and his friends accordingly went to Montmirail.

The exiles, who had now pined for home during four long years, were naturally filled with hope at the prospect of this meeting. Before the conference began, they gathered round the saint and almost unanimously pressed him to omit all mention of the constitutions, and especially the obnoxious words "saving his order," and to throw himself unconditionally on Henry's mercy and generosity. This advice was seconded by Louis, by the Prior of Montdieu, and the Archbishops of Rheims, Sens, and Rouen, who urged their request the more strongly because Henry had said, that he wanted merely a verbal consent before the King of France for the sake of his own honour, and that he was waiting only to be reconciled to the archbishop before taking up the cross and going to Jerusalem. S. Thomas told them that he was prepared to substitute "saving God's honour," for the obnoxious phrase "saving his order," but he did not think it prudent to go further. This gave great dissatisfaction; and though a few did indeed murmur, that "it was not safe to omit all mention of God's honour and the Church's liberties for the sake of man's favour," yet the general feeling went so much the other way, and S. Thomas was so strongly pressed to concede this point, that he seemed as if he would yield, and he probably would have done so, had it not been for his experience at Clarendon. The discussion was still going on when he was summoned to the presence, and as he went no one knew what he was going to say. Then Herbert pressed through the crowd that was thronging into the presence-chamber, and going close up to the saint, whispered in his ear, "Beware, my lord, and walk carefully. If you omit the words 'saving God's honour,' as you formerly omitted the words 'saving your order,' your sorrow will be renewed, and the more bitterly, because what you have already suffered will not have taught you wisdom." The crowd prevented an answer, but the saint turned and gave his friend a look which quite reassured him.

The kings were sitting together when S. Thomas entered. At the first sight of Henry, S. Thomas rushed forward and threw himself at his majesty's feet, and William Archbishop of Sens, who accompanied him, knelt beside him. Then Henry caught him by the hand, and raised him, whereupon, standing up, he accused himself as an unworthy sinner, of having been the cause of all the troubles that had befallen the English Church; adding, "Have mercy on me, my lord, for I throw myself on God and your majesty to the honour of God and your majesty." But as soon as Henry caught the words "to the honour of God," he flew into a rage, and loaded S. Thomas with abuse and contumely, calling him vain, proud, and ungrateful, casting up against him all the acts of his past life, and even going back to his chancellorship, The saint took all this patiently and without the least sign of perturbation, and he answered the king's abuse with humility and modesty, in terms neither too submissive nor too unbending. Henry, however, would not listen, but turning to the King of France, cried, "My lord, see how foolishly and how proudly this man deserted his Church, for he ran away by night, though neither I nor anyone else drove him out of the kingdom; and now he persuades you that his is the cause of the Church, and that he suffers for justice sake, and thus he has deceived many. Now, my lord the king, and holy men and princes here present, I ask for nothing from the archbishop but that he should keep those customs which his five immediate predecessors (some of whom are saints and famed for miracles) all observed to mine, and to which he has himself formerly assented; let him again, in your presence, as a priest and a bishop, pledge himself to these without any subterfuge."

This speech produced a great effect, and some cried out, "The king humbles himself enough." But S. Thomas remained silent. Then Louis said to him in rather an insulting tone, which greatly pleased Henry and his friends, "My lord archbishop, do you wish to be more than a saint?" S. Thomas answered meekly, "It is true that there have been archbishops before me greater and holier than I, every one of whom extirpated some of the abuses in the Church; but if they had corrected all, I should not now be exposed to this hot and fiery trial. Our fathers have suffered because they would not withhold the name of Christ; and shall I, to recover a man's favour, suppress Christ's honour?" King Henry replied, "This phrase I will never receive, lest the archbishop should seem to wish to save God's honour, and not I, who desire it still more." S. Thomas reminded him that the oath of allegiance contained the words "saving my order"; on which Henry rose in anger and withdrew.

The Pope's envoys followed him, and besought him to obey the Pope's mandate, by taking the archbishop into favour, and restoring him his church in peace; to which he replied, "Perhaps it will be the advice of my friends to restore him to the Church, but I will never take him back into favour; for then I should make void the privilege which the Holy Father has granted me, by which the archbishop's power is suspended till he is taken back into favour." They were then going to give him the second letters of warning from the Pope, which were in a more severe tone than the former ones; but they refrained from doing so, on his saying that he would do, in deference to their advice, what he had refused to do in the conference, lest it should not seem a free act on his part. He then promised that if they could induce the archbishop to swear to the customs, he would correct, according to the advice of religious men whom he would summon, whatever might seem harsh and intolerable in them, boasting at the same time that there was no other Church in the world which had such liberty and peace as that in his dominions.

The envoys now returned to S. Thomas, whom they found surrounded by a number of nobles and bishops, French, English, Normans, Bretons, and Poitevans, all pressing him to give up that little phrase, and accept peace for himself and his followers. "If you had then seen the archbishop," says Herbert, "you would have thought him a victim standing before the executioners, whose tongues were their weapons, all of whom sought to suppress God's honour, yet thinking that in this they were doing Him service." And as he stood, he "turned now to one, and now to another, assuring them that he would do as they wished him, as far as it was consistent with God's honour; but that it did not become a priest and a bishop to submit himself in any other way to the will of men of the world, especially in a question which concerned the liberties of the Church." He also reminded them, that in England he had suppressed the words "saving his order," and that, so far from regaining the king's favour, he had suffered more severely than before. Still, however, they pressed him, saying, "Why should we be better than our fathers?" To which he replied, "The blessed Anselm was the only one who was urged to swear to observe the customs, and rather than do so he was driven into exile."

At length, finding that "he stood firm in the midst of all their solicitations, like a city founded upon a rock," the mediators of peace left him, and going to the kings, told them that he was inflexible, calling his firmness obstinacy. Then, as night was coming on, the kings mounted their horses and rode away, without saluting the archbishop; and as they rode along, Henry boasted that that day he had been avenged of his traitor.

Meanwhile, the nobles insulted the saint, saying within his hearing, that he always was proud, wise in his own eyes, a follower of his own will and opinion; imputing the failure of the negotiation to his arrogance; and adding, that the worst thing that had happened to the Church was the choice of him as a ruler, and that through him she would soon be destroyed altogether, as she now was in part. And one of the counts said, "As he sets himself in opposition to the will of both kingdoms, he is unworthy of the protection of either. He is rejected of England, let him find no countenance or support in France." But the saint put a restraint upon his tongue, and appeared as if he did not hear them. Only when his old and tried friend, the Bishop of Poictiers, an Englishman by birth, reproached him with bringing destruction upon the Church, he answered mildly and humbly, "Nay, brother, take care that the Church is not destroyed by you; for, by God's grace, she will never be destroyed by me."

His followers and fellow-exiles, too, were disappointed at the failure of their hopes of peace. As they rode home, Henry de Hoctune was riding immediately before S. Thomas, and his horse happening to stumble, he cried out, "Come up—saving the honour of God, and of Holy Church, and of my order." S. Thomas was vexed, but remained silent. However, when they drew up to breathe their horses, he said to his clerics, "Beloved companions, who have suffered everything with me, why do you so think and speak against me? Our return and restoration is but a little thing; the liberty of the Church, of which the king says nothing, is of far greater consequence. At length I will accept the best peace I can get, but you never yet saw such short bargaining." Then brave Herbert, riding up to him, said, "God be praised, my lord, that through all the worriment to which you have this day been exposed, our Lord has sustained you; so that you have borne the whole of it without flinching, and without being betrayed into anything subversive of God's honour. No doubt the Most High will honour you yet, in return for the honour you have this day shown Him."

The saint was now indeed drinking to the very dregs the bitter chalice of suffering. The only sweet which it had hitherto contained had now been withdrawn; for the friends, whose love and fidelity had been such a solace to his affectionate nature, had now deserted him. The King of France, his noble and generous protector, had cast him off. Bishops and nobles, eminent for their piety and zeal in God's service, spoke ill of him. And even his fellow-exiles, his own familiar friends, who had so long suffered cheerfully for his sake, had turned against him. Truly his soul was passing through the midst of the shadow of death; but still he feared not, for he knew that his Lord was with him, and that if all men should forsake him, He would only take him the more tenderly into His care, and cling the more closely to him. Notwithstanding the contempt and reproach which met him on every side, he preserved his gaiety and cheerfulness, nor could the least change be detected in his countenance. No doubt this equanimity came the more easily to him, because the reproaches were directed only against his own reputation, while the Church was untouched by them.

That evening S. Thomas and his party reached Montmirail before the King of France, who had escorted the King of England part of his way on his return; but when at length Louis arrived, he did not call, as was his custom, at S. Thomas's lodgings. Early the next morning S. Thomas and his friends set out for Chartres on their way back to Sens, but without taking leave of Louis, who was in bed, and was not disposed to see the saint. As they rode along, the people would come out to look at them, and would ask who they were; and when they were told it was the Archbishop of Canterbury and his suite, they would point him out to each other, and say, "This is the archbishop who yesterday kept true to his God, and would not give up His honour for the sake of the kings,"— for the news of the conference had spread far and wide. Such remarks would be often overheard by S. Thomas, and this touching tribute of sympathy from the poor and simple, was a great consolation to him.

All hopes of a reconciliation had not yet been abandoned by those who had brought about the late meeting, and who now believed that the archbishop's arrogance was the only impediment. His intimate friend, the Bishop of Poictiers, was therefore sent after him and overtook him at Etampes, where he renewed his entreaties to him, for peace sake to place himself unreservedly in the king's hands. S. Thomas answered, as he had ever done, that he would do so saving God's honour and the liberty of the Church. However, the bishop, apparently with good intentions, so modified this answer in reporting it to Henry, as to lead him to suppose that the obnoxious reservation would be given up, and under these circumstances he joyfully consented to another meeting on the feast of S. Peter's Chair, January the 18th. But when the bishop told S. Thomas what he had done, the saint was much distressed, and wrote to him in strong but affectionate terms, refusing decidedly to attend any more conferences till Henry had obeyed the Pope's mandate and restored the property of the Church, lest the delay in doing so should be laid to his charge.

The Pope's envoys, too, attempted once more to make peace, but as they utterly failed to effect a reconciliation on February 7th, they gave Henry the Pope's second letter, which warned him that at the beginning of Lent S. Thomas's powers would be restored. This they did at a second meeting of the kings. When Henry heard what were the contents of the letter, he refused to receive it, and it was with difficulty that he was at last persuaded to do so. When the envoys asked for his reply to it, he answered in a shifting and evasive style, so that it was impossible to elicit from his words the least assurance that he would obey the Pope's mandate; but when they pressed him more closely, he at last told them plainly, that the archbishop should never enter England till he had promised to observe what others had observed, and he himself had formerly promised to do. When the envoys reported this answer to S. Thomas, his reply was equally conclusive; for he said that he was ready to do what the king required saving his order, and he could not promise otherwise, because the Pope, in reproving him at Sens for his former unconditional promise at Clarendon, had said, that not to save his life ought a bishop to bind himself except "saving God's honour and his order"; and, moreover, without authority from his Holiness, he could not make changes in a formula which was acknowledged by the whole Western Church, and which was even contained in the oath of fealty prescribed by those very usages on account of which he was banished. The envoys were now compelled to acknowledge that their mission had proved a total failure. The Prior of Montdieu wrote to Cardinal Albert that, by the king's own confession, the liberty of the Church was the real barrier between him and the archbishop, and so long as the latter resisted usages subversive of it, peace between them was impossible. Bernard de Corilo also said to Herbert, "I would rather have my foot cut off than that your lord the archbishop should have made peace at that conference, as I and all others advised him." Thus ended the conferences, and thus, after five years of contention, all came back to those three little words out of which the whole affair had sprung. S. Thomas had seen from the first that the very existence of the Church in England hung on those three words, and thoughtful men now perceived that he had always been in the right.

As soon as the conferences were closed, the kings parted, and Henry returned to his dominions much elated at the favourable terms which he had obtained from the King of France, and even more so at the discomfiture of S. Thomas, whose expulsion from France now seemed inevitable. His joy and triumph were manifested in a way characteristic of him. Before many days had elapsed, he threw all his engagements to the winds, broke the treaty with the Bretons and Poitevans to which the King of France had been a party, committed many acts of violence and rapine, and, among others, put to death Robert de Silli, one of the nobles of Poitou, with whom he had exchanged the kiss of peace, and for whose safety he had pledged his word. Thus did he fully justify the prudence of S. Thomas in refusing to hold further parley with him, till he should have proved by acts of restitution the sincerity of those promises, which he habitually found equal facility in making and in breaking.

S. Thomas and his fellow-exiles had now returned to the Abbey of S. Columba, and had resumed their usual tranquil life. Three days after their arrival, they were sitting together talking over plans for the future, for they were daily expecting to be banished the King of France's territories. S. Thomas was as cheerful as though nothing unusual had happened, and he answered the condolences of his followers with quiet laughter and pleasantry. "Be not so alarmed," said he, "I am the only one aimed at; when I am disposed of, they will not persecute you, at least not so seriously." They assured him that he was the only one for whom they were concerned. "Oh," he replied, "I commit myself to God's keeping, now that I am shut out of both kingdoms. I cannot betake myself to these Roman robbers; they are always despoiling the miserable. Let me see; I have heard that they are a more liberal people in Burgundy, near the river Saone. I will go there on foot with one companion; perhaps when they see us, they will take compassion on our forlorn condition, and give us subsistence for a time, till God interposes for us. God can help His own in the lowest misery, and he is worse than an infidel who distrusts God's mercy." No sooner was this said, than the mercy of God appeared at the very door. A servant of the King of France summoned the archbishop to the court. "In order to expel us from the kingdom," cried one of the party. "You are no prophet," said S. Thomas, "nor the son of a prophet; do not forebode evil." They went accordingly in obedience to the summons.

When they arrived, Louis was sitting, and looking downcast; nor did he rise up, as was his custom, to meet S. Thomas. This was an ominous beginning. After a long silence, the king bent his head down as if he were reluctantly meditating the archbishop's expulsion, and everyone was in painful suspense expecting the announcement; when all at once he sprang forward, and to the astonishment of the whole party, and with sighs and tears, threw himself at the saint's feet. S. Thomas raised him up; and when he had recovered himself, he said, "my lord, you were the only clear-sighted one amongst us!" He sighed and repeated, "O my father, you were the only clear-sighted one amongst us! We were all blind, and gave you advice repugnant to God's law, and surrendered God's honour to the pleasure of a man. I repent, my father; I deeply repent. Pardon me, and absolve me from this fault. I offer myself and my kingdom to God and to you; and I promise henceforward, as long as I live, not to fail you or yours." S. Thomas gave him absolution, and Louis ever after kept his word. Then S. Thomas and his suite returned to S. Columba's in great joy.

CHAPTER XX. EXCOMMUNICATION OF THE BISHOPS,

LENT at last arrived and S. Thomas's powers were fully restored. The Bishops of London and Salisbury, expecting to be now publicly excommunicated, anticipated the sentence by appealing to the Pope, and fixed the 9th February, A.D. 1170, for the term of their appeal. S. Thomas, however, took no notice of the appeal, because having been made in order to evade justice it was invalid.

On the following Palm Sunday, A.D. 1169, S. Thomas assisted at the High Mass and procession in the famous monastery of Clairvaux; and at the close of the function he solemnly excommunicated the Bishops of London and Salisbury, and many other persons, both clerics and laymen, among whom were all who had been excommunicated at Vezelay, and who had since been irregularly absolved on John of Oxford's authority; and he warned Geoffrey Ridel, Archdeacon of Canterbury, and five others whom he named, that on Ascension Day he would pronounce a similar sentence on them, unless they should meanwhile make satisfaction for their outrages against the Church. Geoffrey and the others neglected to make reparation, and, accordingly, on Ascension Day they were excommunicated.

It was, however, no easy matter to get these sentences promulgated in England; for the ports were strictly watched, and imprisonment and the usual sanguinary penalties awaited all who should attempt to bring them into the kingdom, or to publish them. Meanwhile the report of them had arrived, and the Bishop of London summoned the Bishops of Exeter and Salisbury and some others to Westminster, to consult on the emergency. Bartholomew of Exeter sent him a message, warning him, as being excommunicated, not to offer him the usual kiss of salutation; but when, notwithstanding, Gilbert did offer it with characteristic timidity he did not dare to refuse it. As for Joceline of Salisbury, not much more than four years before he had been one of S. Thomas's supporters, and had incurred personal risk at Northampton in his defence; but since then a change had come over his spirit, and he boldly defied his archbishop's authority. "If Buinard the archbishop," said he, "or any fool of an archbishop of mine, order me to do anything that I ought not to do, do you think I should do it?"

Mattel's stood thus when Ascension Day came round. Among the crowd who flocked on this great festival to the old Cathedral Church of S. Paul's, was a young man called Berengarius, illiterate and of low station, but possessed of high courage and an ardent zeal for God's service, for which he was ready to lay down his life; and in his company was another layman, William Bonhart, who shared his heroic spirit. The Gospel and the sermon were over, and many of the congregation who had heard Mass elsewhere were beginning to leave the church, when Berengarius walked up to the altar and knelt down. The celebrant, by name Vitalis, thought he was about to make an offering, and stretched out his hand to receive it; when Berengarius placed two letters from S. Thomas in it, and holding the hand firmly closed on them, bade him read them aloud to the people, and afterwards deliver one to the bishop and the other to the dean, at the same time calling on William of Norhall, the deacon, and Hog, the sub-deacon, to bear witness to what he had done, and not to assist at Mass till the letters were read. Then turning to the people, he cried in a loud voice, "Know all of you, that Gilbert, Bishop of London, is excommunicated by Thomas, Archbishop of Canterbury and Legate of the Apostolic See!"

Instantly there was a great uproar, some insulting Berengarius, others trying to seize him, others rushing hither and thither to see what the stir was about, or to escape from the tumult, while a few near the altar asked Vitalis if the city were placed under an interdict, and hearing that it was not, did not trouble themselves further. In the general confusion Bonhart threw his cloak over Berengarius, and mingling in the crowd which was pouring out of the church, they escaped to Bonhart's lodgings; and though search was made for

Berengarius, he managed to go to York, where he delivered letters from the Pope, and finally he escaped safely out of the country. Meanwhile Vitalis did not wish to continue the Mass till the letters were read; but the deacon went to Nicholas, the archdeacon, who said, "Would the priest stop his dinner if a messenger were to bid him cease to eat in the archbishop's name?" Encouraged by this irreverent query, they finished the Mass, and the letters were only read privately.

Gilbert was in the country, at Stubbehuthe, now Stepney, when he heard what had happened in his cathedral. He hurried to town, and on the following Saturday he met the chapter, and by their order Vitalis delivered the letters to the bishop and dean. The bishop read his aloud, knitting his brows, and in a voice almost choked with emotion; and when he had finished it he made a speech attacking the several points in it, and wound up by saying that the archbishop had no power over him or his see, because London had been the archiepiscopal see till the right was taken from it by a pagan invasion, and on this ground he renewed the appeal to the Pope which he had made at the beginning of Lent. The dean, archdeacon, canons, and priests of S. Paul's joined in the appeal, but the canons of S. Bartholomew's, S. Martin's, and Holy Trinity refused to do so.

The bishops met at Southampton on Trinity Sunday, when the Bishop of London tried to persuade them to join him and the Bishop of Salisbury in their appeal. But the Bishop of Durham, who spoke first, said evasively, "that he would consult his metropolitan, the Archbishop of York, and, after due deliberation, would do what he might, saving God's honour and his own." The Bishop of Exeter objected, that if they appealed, they would be uniting with excommunicates, and placing themselves in a danger which nothing should induce him to encounter; adding, that if any sentence of his superior against himself should come to his knowledge, he would bear it obediently—a suggestion which Gilbert treated with ridicule and contempt. The venerable Henry of Winchester, being unable to attend, wrote, "I, who am worn out with age and infirmities, am summoned by the Lord, and am therefore unfit for appeals to an earthly tribunal; and I pray you to excuse my joining in appeals which may bring me under an anathema;" and he further published the letters of excommunication as soon as he received them. All the other bishops declined to join in the appeal, and the Bishops of Norwich, Lichfield, and Chichester published the letters.

Gilbert's only resource now was the king. From him he easily obtained leave to appeal, and even to go to the Pope if he wished it; in which case Henry offered to provide an honourable retinue, and bear all the expenses of the journey. He also wrote to the Pope, complaining bitterly of the excommunication of his friends, treating it as a personal injury to himself, "who," he said, "am a devoted son of the Church of Rome, ever ready to submit to justice."

The excommunication of so many persons did indeed cause great uneasiness throughout the country, and especially at the court. For all who intentionally or accidentally held any friendly communication with the excommunicates, incurred the minor excommunication; and as the circle widened, it became hard to know who was, or was not free from the Church's anathema, the awful penalties of which even the careless shrank from incurring.

For instance, it happened one day when Henry was sitting out in a meadow by the chapel at Caen, Richard of Ilchester approached. Some Templars who were standing by advanced to meet him, and, taking off their helmets, were going to kiss him, when Henry called out to them to keep at a distance, as he did not wish them to kiss an excommunicate.

On another occasion Henry was not equally considerate. For the Bishop of Worcester having gone to Mass with the king, just as Mass was beginning Geoffrey Ridel came in, whereupon the bishop left the chapel. Henry, in astonishment, sent to ask why he had gone away; and Roger having stated his reason, he sent him an angry message, bidding him leave the kingdom with all speed. Roger, immediately mounting his horse, and ordering his servants to follow with his baggage, returned the answer that his foot was already in the stirrup. After a while Henry broke out into insults and threats, on which one of the bystanders took courage to expostulate:—"My lord, what have you done? You have banished a bishop who is closely united with you in faith and blood. You have given the archbishop what will please him best; and the Pope, who has had as yet no reason for blaming you, will now have a cause to do so, placed in his way by yourself. You grieve your friends and rejoice your enemies by banishing an innocent man, not to say a bishop." Touched by the suggestion as to the impolitic bearings of his conduct, Henry sent a horseman to recall the bishop, but he refused to come; whereupon he sent others, and finally he sent a large party to bring him back whether he would or no. Then Roger returned, but he spoke his mind plainly out to the king, and henceforth Geoffrey Ridel was forbidden to enter the chapel when Roger was at court.

Meanwhile Henry's letter had reached the Pope, and though it had no effect on the permanent state of affairs, it was the cause of a great mortification to S. Thomas.

When Henry, as already stated, had received the Pope's letter of warning from his Holiness's envoys, he had perceived there was no chance of obtaining his object from them. He had therefore secretly sent messengers to Italy to see what bribery could effect. He offered 3,000 marks and a thorough repair of their fortifications to the Milanese, 2,000 marks to the citizens of Cremona, and 1,000 each to those of Parma and Bologna, if they would obtain the deposition or translation of S. Thomas. To the King of Sicily he offered his daughter in marriage; and he had the audacity to try to bribe the Pope by offering to release him from the demands of the Romans, to give him 10,000 marks besides, and to allow him to appoint whom he would to the See of Canterbury and all the other Sees in England which had long been vacant. But his character for veracity was so low, and his position was so evidently unjust, that his messengers were everywhere repulsed. The utmost they could obtain was a promise from the Pope that he would once more send envoys to mediate a peace.

It was at this moment that the news of the bishops' excommunication and Henry's indignant letter, reached the Pope. He was surprised and greatly distressed at S. Thomas having used his newly-recovered powers so soon. But as he had acted under his general authority he could not blame him. He wrote to him, however, on the 19th June, expressing his regret that he should have acted without specially consulting him while envoys from both himself and Henry were still at his court; and adding, "As we are unwilling that your sentence should be revoked but by your own deed, we advise, counsel, and exhort you, as a beloved brother, that in order to mitigate the king's displeasure, you of your own will suspend it till such time as you learn from our envoys whether the said king is willing to be reconciled and to realise the promise of your recall. It becomes ourself and you to await with patience, and to tolerate him with all gentleness of spirit for the space of two or three months, that we may leave him without excuse. If you do not think fit to accede to this our request, and things turn out not according to your wish and expectation, but, which God avert, to the contrary, you must attribute the result to yourself and not to us. But if, according to our wish and suggestion, you suspend the sentence till the arrival of our envoys, and the king still persists in his obstinacy, in that case you shall be at liberty before the departure of the envoys unhesitatingly to revive the sentence without incurring the risk of our displeasure yea, rather, you may look to us for every support and assistance."

On the receipt of this letter S. Thomas immediately suspended the sentences of excommunication. It should be noticed that though he would be in an agony of distress at any measure derogatory to the dignity of his office or to the Church's authority, he habitually received with equanimity what threw discredit only on himself; his humility, no doubt, leading him to acquiesce in the justice of such mortifications, and even to rejoice in them as destructive of self-love.

CHAPTER XXI. THE POPE'S SECOND ENVOYS.

THE envoys whom the Pope now sent, in fulfilment of his promise to Henry to make a final attempt to mediate a peace, were Gratian, a nephew of Pope Eugenius III., and sub-deacon and notary of the Holy See, and Vivian, Archdeacon of Orvieto and advocate of the Roman Court. Both of them were men of considerable reputation, and Vivian was moreover distinguished by his great legal acquirements. Their appointment was very agreeable to S. Thomas, because both of them, and especially Gratian, were known to be very honest and incorruptible. Moreover, they were bound by a solemn oath to abide by prescribed terms of peace which they were on no account to exceed, and not to remain beyond an appointed day, nor to allow Henry to defray their expenses unless peace was actually concluded. Henry, too, had bound himself, both by word and writing to obey the Pope's advice and mandate. But though the written promise was in S. Thomas's hands, experience had taught him not to rely confidently on Henry's words till deeds should prove their truth.

On the feast of the Assumption, the 15th of August, 1169, letters from these new envoys were delivered to Henry at Argenton. He was much troubled at their contents. Geoffrey Ridel and Nigel de Sacville, two of the excommunicates who were with the court, were alarmed, and departed in haste. On the 23rd of August the envoys arrived at Domfront, a town of Maine where Henry then was. Late that evening, on his return from hunting, he called on them before going to his own house, and received them with all honour, reverence, and humility. While they were exchanging compliments, Prince Henry, who had been hunting with his father, came to the door with his young companions, blowing their horns, and bringing the stag which they had killed as a present to the envoys.

The next morning at about six o'clock, Henry called again on the envoys, and took them with him to the apartments of the Bishops of Seez and Rennes, where, after a little time, they were joined by John of Oxford, now Dean of Salisbury, and by the Archdeacons of Salisbury and Llandaff. Here they remained in conversation together till three in the afternoon, all standing—sometimes speaking gently, and sometimes loudly and angrily. Henry's object was to obtain the absolution of the excommunicated clerics, without their taking the usual oath. Just before sunset he came out, very wroth, complaining bitterly that the Pope had never listened to his requests, and saying with defiance, "By God's eyes, I will do something else!" "Threaten not, my lord," answered Gratian, mildly; "we fear no threats, for we come from a court which is accustomed to dictate to emperors and kings." Then a convocation was held of all the barons and white monks who were in attendance, and nearly all the chapel royal; and Henry called on them to bear witness to the greatness of the offer he had made; namely, the restitution of the archbishopric and the restoration of peace. At last he left them somewhat pacified, and he appointed that day week for giving a definite answer.

On the appointed day, the 31st of August, the envoys had another audience, and in the presence of the Archbishops of Rouen and Bordeaux, and all the bishops of Normandy, presented to Henry the Pope's letters, praying for the archbishop's return and reconciliation. Henry answered by a tirade against S. Thomas, and concluded by saying, "If I grant any of his lordship the Pope's requests for that person, I shall deserve many thanks for it."

The next day the envoys had another audience, at a place called Le Bur. As soon as they arrived the king entered the park, attended by the bishops, who had now been joined by Roger of Worcester. Henry began by asking in private to have his clerics absolved without the prescribed oath. This the envoys positively refused; whereupon Henry mounted his horse, and swore, in the hearing of all, that he would never again listen to the Pope or anyone else in the archbishop's behalf. The bishops then entreated the envoys for the love of God to give up this point, which they did most reluctantly. Henry accordingly dismounted, and soon after he said that he wished them all to know that it was not through him that the archbishop had left England; that he had often recalled him that he might explain his conduct, but he had always refused to come; notwithstanding, in compliance with the Pope's prayer and commands, he would restore his archbishopric to him, and allow all who had been banished on his account to return. This concession he made about three in the afternoon, and afterwards he was very cheerful and went through much other business.

At a later hour he returned to the envoys, and asked them to go to England, or at least to send one of their clerics to absolve the excommunicates who were there. This Gratian refused, and Henry shouted angrily, "Do what you will, I care not for you or your excommunication one egg." He then mounted his horse and rode off, but the bishops following and remonstrating, he returned. It was then resolved that the bishops should write to the Pope, and tell him that the king was ready to comply with every command of his Holiness, but that the envoys raised difficulties. Much time was wasted in composing this letter, and at last Henry, quite out of patience, was going away; but the bishops told him that the envoys had shown them a mandate from the Pope, commanding every one to obey whatever they should decree. "I know," answered Henry, "I know they will interdict my kingdom; but shall not I, who can take a strong castle a day, be able to take one cleric if he publishes the sentence?" However, when one or two points were conceded, the storm blew over, and Henry said, "Unless you make peace this night, you will never again get to this point." Then calling them all together, he said, "It behooves me to do much at the request of my lord the Pope, who is my lord and father; and therefore I restore his see to the archbishop, as well as my favour to him and all who are banished on his account." The envoys and all who were present returned him thanks, and he added, "If I have been deficient in anything to-day, I will make it up to-morrow."

The next day, September the 2nd, they met again at noon at the same place. After a long discussion about the absolution of the king's clerics, it was agreed that Geoffrey Ridel, Nigel de Sacville, and Thomas FitzBernard, should place their hands on the Gospels, and declare, in the word of truth, that they would obey the instructions of the envoys. Henry next demanded that all the Church property which he had alienated, should remain with its present owners; but this was positively refused. After this the bishops committed to writing the terms of the peace to which Henry had consented; when he insisted on its being inserted, "that the archbishop should hold his church to the honour of the king and his posterity," and to this unmeaning formula the envoys saw no objection. But when the conference was about to break up, at nine at night, Henry insisted that the words, "saving the dignity of his kingdom," should be inserted, thus showing plainly what meaning he had attached to the former unmeaning words, and that he had hoped, under cover of their ambiguity, craftily to establish the claims which he had brought forward at Clarendon. To this reservation, however, Gratian refused to consent on any terms; and thus the conference ended.

On the feast of our Lady's Nativity, September the 8th, the envoys retired to Caen, whither several bishops and laymen followed them to renew the negotiations. The envoys now offered to accept Henry's clause, "saving the dignity of his kingdom," provided the words, "saving the dignity of the Church," were also inserted. To this, however, Henry would not consent, and consequently his deputies were obliged to give up his phrase, "saving the dignity of his kingdom." But when the deputies returned to their master, he refused to ratify this concession; and thus the negotiations were once more brought down to the point from which the dispute had sprung, and here they were once more broken off.

The envoys gave the king till Michaelmas to reconsider the matter, warning him, that, if by that time peace were not concluded, the sentence on the excommunicates, whose absolution had been only conditional, would come again into force. The time of grace passed; Henry remained impenitent; the anathema fell once more on his friends and advisers; and thus this mediation ended as all the preceding ones had done.

The envoys now set out on their return to Italy, and the Archbishop of Sens accompanied them. On their way they stopped to see S. Thomas, and Gratian told him that in every particular about which they had talked to Henry, they had never met such a turncoat and crafty dissembler, as he had proved himself to be, for he was always seeking how he might contrive to delay the business, so as to justify his own cause and injure that of the saint.

But when Henry heard that the envoys were accompanied on their return by the Archbishop of Sens, a prelate of great reputation whom he considered his strongest opponent, he was much alarmed, fearing that the legatine authority over his continental dominions might be given to him. He, therefore, sent messengers again to the Pope; and with the view of engaging Vivian on his side, he wrote to him, entreating him to return, and promising to make peace on the terms prescribed by him and the Pope. And in order to secure his aid more effectually, "he caused letters to be written, and affixed his seal to them, in which he promised that, for the love of his lordship the Pope, he would restore to" S. Thomas "the Church of Canterbury and all his confiscated possessions in peace and security;" adding, "that if S. Thomas would make peace on the terms he wished, he would make him the head of his kingdom, and suffer him to want in nothing." Vivian, who had not the same insight into Henry's character as Gratian, allowed himself to be deceived by this letter, and was induced, contrary to the Pope's orders, to return to Henry's court.

CHAPTER XXII. THE CONFERENCE AT MONTMARTRE.

DELAY was, indeed, Henry's principal weapon, and so skilfully had he handled it, that he had now protracted the contest for six long years from its first opening at Westminster, and its termination still seemed as distant as ever. He had also managed so craftily to fetter his adversary, that it was only at short periods during these long years, that he was at liberty to use his spiritual weapons. For either the Pope, deceived by Henry's plausible professions, recommended S. Thomas to wait and try the effect of gentleness, or he actually suspended him, or an appeal was pending, or legates or envoys were negotiating; and it was only in the brief intervals between these various circumstances, that S. Thomas was at liberty to act. One of these brief intervals of freedom recurred when Gratian and Vivian had closed their mission. S. Thomas waited till there could be no further hope of Henry's repentance, and then he resolved to take the step which alone, he had foreseen from the first, would bow the proud and obdurate Plantagenet. He accordingly issued letters to the bishops and other officials of the different dioceses, and to all the religious houses of England, ordering them, by his own authority and that of the Apostolic See, to publish the interdict which he laid upon the kingdom, unless the king should repent and make amends to the Church before the feast of the Purification, the 2nd of February, 1170. These letters also denounced those who were already excommunicated, and added to the black list John of Oxford and four others, unless they should make satisfaction before Christmas.

Henry met this alarming measure with fierce defiance. The precautions at the ports to prevent the Letters being brought into the kingdom were redoubled, and cruel penalties were enacted against anyone who should bring them. If he were a monk his feet were to be cut off; if a cleric, he was to be blinded and mutilated; if a layman, he was to be hanged; and if a leper, to be burned. An oath was ordered to be administered throughout the country, promising that the letters of the Pope and the archbishop would neither be received nor obeyed; and the bishops and abbots were summoned to London by Geoffrey Ridel and other officials, in the king's name, to give security that they would carry this edict into effect.

But none of the bishops obeyed the summons, nor any of the abbots except Clarembald, the intruded abbot of S. Augustine's, Canterbury. Henry of Winchester publicly declared, that so long as he lived, he would, at all costs, obey the decrees of the Pope and the archbishop, to whom he had sworn fealty and obedience; and he charged his clergy to do the same. Bartholomew of Exeter followed his example, and then retired to the sanctuary of a religious house till the storm should pass. The Bishop of Norwich, even in the presence of the royal officials, excommunicated Hugh, Earl of Norfolk, and the others, as S. Thomas had ordered; and when he came down from the pulpit, he placed his pastoral staff upon the altar, saying, he would see who would dare to extend his hand against the Church and its possessions; after which he too sought safety in a cloister. The Bishop of Lichfield also declared himself ready to obey the commands of the Pope and the archbishop, and then took refuge in the Welsh parts of his diocese. Matilda, Countess of Devonshire, flatly refused to take the oath, or to allow any of her vassals to do so; and even Roger of York resisted it.

The bold attitude which S. Thomas had now assumed, the better spirit which the English bishops were beginning to show, and the presence of Gratian and the Archbishop of Sens at the Papal court, all told upon Henry. He began to fear, that at last he should be compelled to make peace with great loss both of money and reputation. He determined, therefore, to try once more whether he could improve his prospects through the mediation of the King of France. He did not, however, dare to ask for another meeting with Louis, because he had broken the promises which he had made at Montmirail; but assuming an appearance of humility, he gave out that he was going to make a pilgrimage to the tomb of S. Denys, the martyr and apostle of France, and to see his young lord, Louis's son, Philip Augustus, who was then a boy; and he was in hopes that, when Louis heard of his arrival, he would come to meet him, and would bring S. Thomas with him. He also made Vivian write to S. Thomas, and urge him to attend the meeting. In reply, the saint expressed great indignation that Vivian should thus unauthorized assume anew the office of mediator: and he warned him that he would become a joke and a laughing-stock to the nobles, since hardly anyone had been able to escape the king's snares, or to make way through the subtleties and circumlocutions in which he was such an adept. Notwithstanding, he consented out of respect to the Holy Church and to himself personally, to go to the Chapel of the Martyrdom, between Paris and S. Denys.

Matters turned out as Henry had hoped. He entered the French territory as a pilgrim; Louis met him at S. Denys, where they held an amicable conference, in which it was arranged that Henry should give his second son, Richard, to be educated by Louis, who, on his part, promised to summon the court of S. Gilles to Tours to do homage to Richard for the county of Toulouse; and after this, the two kings went together to Montmartre. S. Thomas had not yet arrived, so they waited for him in a plain beyond the chapel; and when he came, he went into the Chapel of the Martyrdom while they remained outside, thus avoiding all personal communication till peace should be concluded.

S. Thomas had taken the precaution to put the terms on which he could make peace into writing, in the form of a petition, which was approved of by all for its moderation; and this petition the Archbishop of Rouen and the Bishop Seez presented to Henry, while at the same time Vivian reminded him of his promises to himself, and urged him to fulfil them. But Henry now retracted his word, and showed himself in such colours, that Vivian, who felt his own honour implicated, reproved him plainly to his face, as the circumstances justified his doing; and then, going back to S. Thomas, told him publicly that he did not remember to have ever seen or heard of a greater liar. The King of France and his nobles seconded Vivian in the attempt to bring Henry to reason, going backwards and forwards as mediators between him and S. Thomas; and at last, after much discussion and argument, all difficulties seemed to be smoothed down. The Constitutions of Clarendon were virtually withdrawn, full effect was given to the liberties of the Church; and Henry only stipulated that S. Thomas "should return to England, and there discharge his metropolitan duties in all respects as before, submitting to all the royal customs and prerogatives; and that he should not, under the plea of the Church, usurp what belonged to the king, nor would the king, under plea of the royal prerogative, claim any privileges which belonged to the Church." As "there was now no wish shown to subject the Church in ecclesiastical matters to the king's will," S. Thomas considered it unnecessary to retain the phrase, "saving the honour of God," which had formerly caused so much difficulty, and it was therefore omitted.

The next point to be considered, was the restoration of the property of which S. Thomas and his clerics had been deprived, which he valued at about 30,000 marks (£20,000), and some particulars of which were specified in his petition, though his long absence from England rendered it impossible for him to tell precisely what the king or his officials had alienated. S. Thomas reminded the mediators of "that divine precept, by which restitution is enforced before absolution can be given, adding, that it was unbecoming the royal magnificence to confiscate to his own use the goods of the poor and of the Church, and equally unlawful of him to make grants out of what was not his own: which was the same as if one should make an offering to one altar out of what he had robbed from another, or as if one should crucify Peter to redeem Paul." The King of France and the other mediators, however, argued, "that if every other impediment were removed, a holy and righteous pastor would not persist in opposing a reconciliation, and alienating himself any longer from his Church, for the sake of a pecuniary consideration; he ought rather to embrace the Church as his spouse in the two arms of his love, and do his duty to her, no matter how torn or tattered might be her condition." However, the mediators readily went to Henry and spoke to him on the subject of restitution. Henry answered in English, "but in so involved and intricate a style, for he had abundance of words at his command, that while plain men would take for granted that he yielded everything, the more acute hearers saw that this assent was qualified by certain most perverse and intolerable conditions." In fact, the substance of his reply was, that S. Thomas should enjoy in peace all that his predecessors had enjoyed and all his own possessions, by which phrase, as those familiar with the circumstances could perceive, he excluded the Church property which S. Thomas had recovered soon after his consecration, and the benefices which had fallen vacant during his exile. Still, the answer was so cleverly turned, that so long as Henry's intention was believed to be sincere, S. Thomas could not make any reasonable objection to it; and he accepted it the more readily, because he had resolved from the first not to "refuse any terms that might be at all tolerable to the Church."

Thus every storm seemed to be blown away, and the exiles were rejoicing, thinking that they were on the point of entering the harbour of peace. Now it happened that S. Thomas, with his usual prudence, had lately consulted the Pope as to what guarantee for Henry's sincerity he should require. And the Pope had answered, that as a Churchman and a priest he could not exact a pledge or oath from the king; and that as the cause between them was one of justice and the peace of the Church, for which, whether in open quarrel or after peace was made, it was precious to give one's life, he ought to be satisfied if the king would give him a kiss of peace. Accordingly, S. Thomas asked through the mediators for the kiss, as a token of reconciliation. But Henry answered, that he should have been glad to give it, had he not formerly sworn that he would never kiss the archbishop, and his wish not to break his oath was the sole cause of his now refusing to kiss him.

When the King of France and the mediators heard this, they began to suspect that they had been deluded by Henry's honeyed words. But they did not express their suspicion or make any comment, and hastening back to S. Thomas, who was waiting in the Chapel of the Martyrdom, merely repeated to him Henry's words, just as he had spoken them. As soon as S. Thomas heard the answer he became alarmed, and the first words which he uttered, showed at once that he saw far into the future. For he did not wait to consult anyone, but answered decidedly, that at present he would not make peace with the king, unless, according to the advice of the Apostolic Pontiff, it was ratified by the kiss of peace. Louis immediately said that he would not advise him, for his weight in gold, to return to England without receiving in public the kiss of peace. Count Theobald of Blois added that it would be perfect madness; while many of those present whispered to each other, that Robert de Silli had not found even the kiss of peace a sufficient protection.

S. Thomas's decided answer, to which Henry did not reply, cut short the conference. As night was coming on, the kings mounted their horses and set out for Mantes, twelve leagues off, where they were to spend the night. As they rode along Henry repeatedly cursed S. Thomas, reckoning up the various annoyances and causes of vexation that he had given him. On their way to Mantes little Prince Philip was brought to Henry, but he received him with a melancholy look, and when he had spoken a few words to him, hastily sent him away. The next day the kings rode together to Passy, where Louis expected to receive Prince Richard into his charge. But Henry said that he would consign him to Louis's care at their next meeting at Tours, which, it was generally thought would never take place. Louis now perceived that Henry had been acting a double part throughout, and thus they parted worse friends than they had met.

When S. Thomas heard that the kings had left Montmartre, he prepared to set out for Paris. As he was quitting the Chapel of the Martyrdom one his followers came up to him and said, "My lord, to-day we have treated of the peace of the Church in the Martyrdom, and it is my belief that by your martyrdom alone will the Church attain peace." The saint briefly answered, "Would to God, that even by my blood she might be freed. That night the exiles lodged in the Temple, the same house, belonging to the Templars, just outside the walls of Paris, in which S. Thomas had been received, when, as chancellor, he had visited Paris with such a magnificent suite.

As for Vivian, the abrupt termination of the conference had completely opened his eyes. When Henry, soon after, sent him fifty marks, requesting him again to interest himself in making peace, he scornfully rejected the gold. He took every opportunity of publicly expressing his opinion of Henry; and in writing to the Pope, he said, "He is sophistical and captious in every word he says about the Church." Thus was Henry unmasked by one who had been prepossessed in his favour, and who for a time had been his warm partizan.

CHAPTER XXIII. FRESH OUTRAGES.

WITHIN the last few weeks a great change had come over the state of affairs. Peace on almost any terms was desired by both parties by Henry, because he saw that excommunication and an interdict were imminent, and by S. Thomas, because the constitutions and the illegal oath having been abandoned, the liberties of the Church were secured; and this great object being attained, he cared not what might befall himself through Henry's duplicity. Under such circumstances, it would naturally be supposed that peace would have been speedily and easily concluded; but so hardened was Henry in his pride and impenitence, that while he really wished for peace, he was ready to catch at every straw which seemed to give him the least chance of delaying or avoiding the necessary concessions. One effect of this mutual desire for peace, however, was, that when the feast of the Purification arrived, S. Thomas did not publish the letter declaratory of the king's contumacy, which was necessary in order to give effect to the interdict which he had formerly pronounced; and thus the anathema still hung over the kingdom, suspended, as it were, by a single hair, which might at any moment be broken.

Not very long after the conference at Montmartre, an interview between the king and the archbishop was arranged by the Norman bishops; and S. Thomas had travelled as far as Pontisare, on his way to the place of meeting, when word was brought him that Henry had broken off the engagement. This sudden change was brought about by the return from the Roman court of the messengers, whom Henry had sent thither after Gratian's departure, and who now brought him exaggerated reports of their success in obtaining the absolution of the excommunicates. He was so elated by this little triumph that he thought no more of peace, but turned his attention to the coronation of his eldest son, Prince Henry; and for this purpose he suddenly returned to England at the end of February, 1170.

The mission of Henry's messengers, however, had not been so successful as their master had been willing to believe. Its only result was, that the Pope gave authority to the Archbishop of Rouen and the Bishop of Nivers to absolve the excommunicates on two conditions, namely, that they should take the usual oath, and that there should be a *certain hope* of reconciliation. At first an exception was made as to the Bishop of London; but he hurried off to the Papal court, and pleaded his cause so well, that he also was allowed to benefit by the powers conferred on the two prelates. These prelates were further instructed to urge Henry to fulfil his promises at the late conference; and if he refused to do so, they were ordered, after a notice of forty days, to lay an interdict on the kingdom.

Thus the Holy Father had done all that the laws of the Church and justice to S. Thomas demanded; but the event proved that Henry's exultation was not quite unfounded. S. Thomas warned the Bishop of Nivers, that in the execution of his commission, he would have "to *fight with beasts*"; that Henry would probably "refuse to hear anyone, or to do anything till his friends were absolved; that till he carried this point he would perhaps affect moderation, hold out great expectations, and, as if under the influence of religious feeling, would confess sin, to obtain credit for innocence, and expose spots in his conscience, which he could easily wipe out by affected virtues. But immediately the absolution should be granted, he would resume his inveterate hardness, and would show himself inaccessible to entreaty." Notwithstanding this warning, the two prelates allowed themselves to be overcome by Henry's imperious will, as he had foreseen they would be, and they absolved all the excommunicates without regard to the prescribed condition, that there should be an immediate prospect of peace. Even Gilbert was absolved by the Archbishop of Rouen on Easter Day, A.D. 1170. But as if to prove how deficient he was in the contrition and resolution of amendment, which, in all cases, are indispensable to the validity of absolution, one of his first acts immediately after, was to celebrate, in open contempt of S. Thomas's office, a pontifical Mass in the saint's own church of Canterbury.

Though these absolutions were irregular, and therefore invalid, yet they were a great mortification to S. Thomas, because they encouraged sin and impenitence, and created scandal. He expressed these feelings with his usual clearness and decision in the following letter to his friend Cardinal Albert. This letter is the more interesting, because it seems to have been the last of those powerful remonstrances which S. Thomas poured forth at various times during his exile; and it has the solemn tone of a farewell address from one who felt that his race was well-nigh run, and that the crown of victory would soon be within his grasp.

"I would, my beloved, that your ears were within hearing of my countrymen, and that you knew the contemptuous sayings against the Church of Rome, which are being chanted in the street of Ascalon! . . . . I know not by what fortune it has come to pass, that the side of the Lord is always sacrificed at the court of Rome: Barabbas escapes, and Christ is crucified. By the authority of the court, our exile and the sufferings of the Church have been protracted to the end of the sixth year. Your lordships have condemned the wretched and homeless, and for no other reason, I speak from my conscience, than because they are feeble and Christ's little ones, and will not recede from the justice of the Lord. On the other hand, you have absolved the sacrilegious, the murderer, the robber, persons who have not repented, and whose absolution, I say it freely, Christ being my authority, would not hold in the sight of God, though S. Peter pronounced it. In S. Luke's Gospel our Lord commands, that 'if thy brother sin against thee, rebuke him; and *if he is penitent*, forgive it him; and if seven times a day he sin against thee, and seven times a day he turn to thee, *saying, I repent,* forgive it him.' Think you the words of Christ are idle where He says, '*if he is penitent*,' and '*if he turn to thee, saying, I repent*'? Surely in the day of judgment He will not admit that his words were idle; nor will He pass over those uncondemned, who, against the form he prescribes, presume, by vain absolution, to justify the wicked without confession or penance, and to save alive the souls that should not live. I for my part will never grant remission to the impenitent who have plundered the Church of God. Yet for that Church we are prepared to die. If all the cardinals rise up against us, and arm not only the English King, but all the world to our destruction, I will never, with God's blessing, either in life or death, withdraw from my fidelity to the Church.

"And now I have done. For the rest I commit to God His own cause, that God for whom I am proscribed and exiled. Let Him act by me as He sees best. It is my intention to give the court no further trouble in this matter. Let those seek its protection who are strong in their iniquity, and who, after trampling justice underfoot and leading innocence captive, return glorying in the shame of the Church."

Triumphant at having obtained the absolution of his friends, Henry proceeded in his course of defiance. Anticipating that the threatened excommunication could not be much longer deferred, he resolved to make it in great measure powerless, by crowning his eldest son, Prince Henry, and transferring to him the sovereignty of England. The chief obstacle to this was, that it was an undoubted prerogative of the Archbishop of Canterbury to crown the sovereign. Reginald, Archdeacon of Salisbury, suggested that Henry should ask the Pope to empower some other bishop to perform the ceremony. Henry answered that it would be impossible to obtain such a favour; but Reginald replied, "Our lord the Pope will act like a dolt and a fool if he does not grant your petition." There are extant two letters from Pope Alexander, empowering Roger of York to crown the prince; but they are supposed to be forgeries; and this seems to be proved by the fact, that Henry did not afterwards refer to them in his own justification, but rested his excuse on a different ground. It happened that when the See of Canterbury was vacant after Theobald's death, Henry had first thought of crowning the prince; and fearing that Roger of York, who was then out of favour with him, would claim his right to officiate during the vacancy of the See of Canterbury, he obtained permission from the Pope to have the ceremony performed by any bishop whom he should choose. It was of this old permission that he now availed himself in favour of that very Roger, for whose exclusion it had been obtained, and of whom he had said that he would rather his son were beheaded than that Roger's "heretical hands" were laid upon him. This is what he himself told S. Thomas, when the latter asked him, after their reconciliation, why he had driven the bishops into disobedience when "they had received the prohibition of our lord the Pope."

As soon as S. Thomas heard what Henry was proposing to do, he applied to the Pope for letters forbidding Roger and the other bishops to officiate. He obtained three, dated respectively, November, 1169, February the 26th, and April the 5th, 1170. But the ports were so well guarded that he could not manage to get a copy of them conveyed to their destination till Saturday, June the 13th, which was the day before the one fixed for the ceremony. They were then delivered to Roger and the Bishop of London, but both prelates disregarded them. The young prince was crowned by Roger on Sunday, the 14th of June, and the Bishops of London and Salisbury also officiated. As if to add to the outrage, not only was the ancient and usual coronation oath, which guaranteed the liberties of the Church, omitted, but another maintaining the royal customs was substituted for it.

One morning about this time, as S. Thomas lay sleepless after matins, he was thinking about the king's wonderful prosperity, and musing especially about what might be the future fate of his former pupil—"our Henry," as he was wont tenderly to call him—and of one of his brothers, either Richard or Geoffrey, when, as he was dropping off to sleep, he heard a voice which said,

"Mors tulit una duos, tulit altera sed male patrem."

As S. Thomas had never learnt to make verses, and had never written a line of verse, he mentioned to Herbert at the time what had been suggested to him, and Herbert remembered it in after years when he saw the fulfilment of the prophecy. The sin that was committed at Westminster on that coronation day, brought its own punishment; for it inspired Prince Henry and his brothers with ambitious pretensions, which involved the king during the rest of his reign in quarrels with his own children, and at last brought his gray hairs in sorrow to the grave.

As soon as the prince was crowned the king returned to Normandy. As he approached Falaise, the Bishop of Worcester came out three miles to meet him. Henry had summoned Roger to the coronation; but when the latter went to Dieppe intending to cross the Channel, the queen and Richard de Humet, the Justiciary of Normandy, who feared he would stand up for S. Thomas's rights, forbade him to go, and ordered the provost of Dieppe and the shipowners not to give him a passage. Henry seems not to have been aware of this, for as soon as he saw Roger, he burst into one of his habitual fits of rage, and loaded the bishop with opprobrious epithets. "Now I know," said he, "that you are a traitor. I myself ordered you to be present at my son's coronation, and though I named the day, you have chosen to be absent; you have shown plainly that you have no love for me, nor for my son's promotion. I see that you favour my enemy, and hate me and mine. But you shall no longer have the revenues of your bishopric. I will take them away from you, for you have shown yourself unworthy of bishopric or benefice. Truly you never were the son of the good Earl Robert, my uncle, who brought you and me up in his castle together, and had us there taught our letters and our manners." Roger explained the cause of his absence, but Henry would not believe him, and cried out in a violent passion, "The queen is in the castle at Falaise, and Richard de Humet is not far off; do you quote them as your authorities?" "Certainly not the queen," answered Roger; "for, if through fear of you she were to suppress the truth, you would be in a greater rage with me, and if she were to confess it, you would be shamefully mad with that noble lady, and I am not of sufficient consequence, that for my sake she should hear one rough word from you. It is well that I was not present at that coronation, which was offensive to God, not on the prince's account, but the prelate's; and if I had been there I would not have suffered it to be performed. You say that I am not the son of Earl Robert. Whether I am or not, I cannot tell; but you do not show by your gratitude that that same Earl Robert was your uncle." Then Roger narrated how badly Henry had behaved to all Earl Robert's family, and he added, "As for your threat of taking away the revenues of my bishopric, take them if you are not satisfied with those of the archbishopric and six vacant sees and many abbeys, which you receive to the peril of your soul, and turn to secular uses the alms of your fathers and the patrimony of Jesus Christ." A knight of Aquitaine who was by and did not know the bishop, asked who he was, and on being told, he replied, "It is lucky for him that he is a Churchman; if he were a soldier, the king would not leave him two acres." Another, thinking to please the king, reproached the bishop bitterly; but Henry turning on him, loaded him with the foulest abuse, saying among other things, "You vile fellow, do you think that because I say what I like to my cousin the bishop, you or any other person may insult or threaten him? I can scarcely keep my hands off your eyes. It is too bad for you and the others to abuse a bishop." They had now arrived at their lodgings; and after dinner the king and the bishop talked apart amicably about a reconciliation with S. Thomas.

CHAPTER XXIV. THE RECONCILIATION.

MEANWHILE the Archbishop of Rouen and the Bishop of Nivers had shown no haste to obey the Pope, and urge Henry to a reconciliation. The Bishop of Nivers had indeed made a feeble attempt to cross to England, but he and his colleague were easily persuaded to await Henry's return to Normandy. The Archbishop of Sens wrote to the Pope, and consequently fresh letters were sent, ordering them to bring Henry to a conference within twenty days, and then, if he did not submit, to lay the kingdom under interdict within forty more. These letters were sent in the first place to S. Thomas, who, not wishing to precipitate extreme measures, did not deliver them, but allowed their contents to be generally known, with the view of spreading terror and intimidating his opponents.

Henry now perceived that further delay and resistance were both alike impossible. An additional motive for a reconciliation was suggested by one of his friends, who wrote to him, "Why is the archbishop kept out of the kingdom? He had far better be kept in than kept out." The hint was given to one who would not be slow in interpreting it. He no longer avoided the Archbishop of Rouen and the Bishop of Nivers, but forthwith arranged a conference to treat of peace, and conceded everything which before he had refused.

A meeting between the Kings of France and England was to take place shortly on the borders of Maine and Chartrain, between the castles of Viefui and Freitval, and the Archbishop of Sens tried to persuade S. Thomas to go thither in company with himself, the Archbishop of Rouen, and the Bishop of Nivers. At first S. Thomas was very unwilling to attend the conference unbidden, but at last he consented to go, and the three archbishops and the Bishop of Nivers set out together.

The Kings held their conference on the 20th and 21st of July, and concluded their business without mentioning S. Thomas, so that his clerics greatly feared that they who had come unbidden would retire disgraced. The prelates who had accompanied him, had, however, been interceding with Henry, and at last he consented to an interview with the saint on the following day. He promised to abide by the Pope's commands on every point except the matter of the kiss, adding, on his oath, that he did not refuse it from any design against S. Thomas; and calling God to witness this, he prevailed on the Archbishop of Sens to pledge himself for its truth. He even said that he would yield this point, however reluctantly, rather than part at variance with his lordship of Canterbury. The Archbishop of Sens, therefore, returned to S. Thomas, and told him how gracious the king had been, both in manner and words, and entreated him not to mar the prospect of returning kindness by insisting on the kiss; adding, that Henry had said publicly, "Let him wait till I am in my own dominions, and I will kiss him to his satisfaction on his mouth, and his hands, and his feet; and I will hear his Mass too. For the present, I must be excused; it will be an act of greater grace afterwards." These professions met with scant credence; but, as the saint's followers remarked even then, Christ's champion "was prepared to lay down his life for his sheep"; and being "eager for peace, and not afraid of death, he did not demand the kiss, but accepted the terms as they were offered, influenced rather by charity than by fear of death."

That night the King of England was the guest of the King of France. In the course of conversation, Henry said, "To-morrow that thief of yours shall have peace, and a good one too." "What thief, pray, by the saints of France?" asked Louis. "That Archbishop of Canterbury of ours," answered Henry. "I wish he were ours as well as yours," replied Louis; "you will please God and man if you make a good peace with him, and I shall be ever grateful to you."

The next morning, being the feast of S. Mary Magdalen, the 22nd of July, the King of England, with a vast multitude in his train, repaired at dawn of day to a verdant meadow, which in old times was called Traitors' Meadow. The King of France, though near the spot, absented himself purposely from the conference, in order that Henry's advances might appear the more spontaneous and sincere. S. Thomas, attended by the Archbishop of Sens and Earl Theobald, arrived rather later. The other French who had attended the previous conferences also came in great crowds to the spectacle.

Henry, as soon as he caught sight of S. Thomas, spurred forward from the midst of his party, and darted straight up to the saint with head uncovered, so as to be the first to salute. They exchanged greetings, offered right hands, and embraced. Then Henry retired with the two archbishops, and S. Thomas addressed him about the injuries done to himself and the Church, in a discourse which the Archbishop of Sens declared to be most touching and pertinent. After this, to the amazement of all, Henry drew S. Thomas apart and talked to him as familiarly as if they had never quarrelled, and for so long a time that the anxious bystanders were wearied; and it was noticed, that even S. Thomas shifted from side to side in his saddle as if he were tired out; which they afterwards found was in consequence of the irritation caused by his long hair-shirt. In the course of the conversation, S. Thomas exhorted Henry to repent and make open compensation to the Church for the injuries inflicted by him, while Henry listened with attention and kindness, and promised amendment. S. Thomas then urged him to make reparation for his late grievous injustice to the Church of Canterbury, in having caused his son to be crowned by the Archbishop of York. For some time Henry was unwilling to assent, and excused his conduct by various arguments; but at last he said, "I doubt not the Church of Canterbury is the noblest of the churches of the west, and so far from wishing to deprive her of her rights, I will do as you advise, and take measures for her relief and restoration to her ancient dignity. But, as for those who up to this time have betrayed the interests of both of us, I will, with God's help, answer them as traitors deserve"; adding that S. Thomas should crown Margaret, the French princess, who was betrothed to his son; and as an acknowledgment of the rights of his Church, he should repeat the coronation of the young king. At this promise S. Thomas was so overjoyed that, to the great surprise of the beholders, he leapt from his horse, and would have knelt to the king, but Henry, taking hold of his stirrup, forced him to remount, saying with tears in his eyes, "My lord archbishop, what more! Let us renew our old intimacy; let us henceforth be friends, and forget our past enmities. Only I beg of you to give me honour in the sight of those who are standing by."

Henry then passed over to his party, and casting a glance on the late fomenters of discord, said aloud, "Now that the archbishop has shown such good intentions, if I, in my turn, did not show as good, I should indeed be the worst of men, and should verify all the evil that has been said of me. I believe I can do nothing wiser or better than try to surpass the archbishop in kindness, charity, and good offices."

Henry then withdrew to a short distance, and left S. Thomas with the bishops and his fellow-exiles, to whom he related all that passed between him and the king. By their advice he drew up in writing all his claims, and then advancing towards Henry, presented his petition through the Archbishop of Sens. Henry received it graciously, and promised, in the hearing of all, to restore to S. Thomas, the Church of Canterbury, and to the other exiles, all their possessions as described in the petition; and further, as Theobald, Earl of Blois, who was present, wrote to the Pope, he gave him free and lawful power over the bishops who had dared to place the young king on the throne against the right and honour of the Church of Canterbury, that, at his Holiness's pleasure or his own, sentence might be pronounced against them. And now all the exiles who were present, came forward and knelt at the king's feet, and he restored to each his possessions with peace and the royal favour.

After all was over, Henry and S. Thomas talked together till evening as familiarly as in the days of their friendship. On parting, it was agreed between them that S. Thomas should return to pay a visit of thanks to the King of France and his other benefactors, and to arrange his affairs; that he should then go and stay with Henry in Normandy before embarking for England, in order to show how thoroughly he was restored to the king's favour and intimacy; and that, meanwhile, he should send one of his clerics to England with letters to the young king and the officers of state, to receive his possessions and those of his friends.

As S. Thomas was about to retire, Arnulph, Bishop of Lisieux, as if unable to conceal his vexation at the termination of the quarrel, attacked him and demanded the absolution of the king's friends. Geoffrey Ridel, too, stepped in, and began some insulting remark, whereupon Henry drew the saint aside, and begged him not to mind what such persons said, but to go home quietly in God's favour and his own. He then asked the archbishop's blessing. Thus the conference ended, and. S. Thomas and the exiles returned to S. Columba's.

CHAPTER XXV. FEARS AND WARNINGS.

The news of the reconciliation was received at the Roman court and elsewhere with very mixed feelings. In the midst of their joy all distrusted Henry's sincerity, for, as Cardinal Albert wrote on the occasion, "We discerned that the Ethiopian does not easily change his skin, nor the leopard his spots." Hard as restitution and reparation must almost always be, Henry had made them harder by surrounding himself with those who, having long fattened on the spoils of the Church, would be losers by his repentance, and would, therefore, encourage him to violate his engagements.

In conformity with the arrangement at Freitval, S. Thomas sent Herbert and John of Salisbury to the king, who was then in Normandy, to ask for the necessary letters to the young king and the officers of State in England, ordering the restoration of the property which had been alienated. On their arrival in Normandy they found that Henry was confined to bed with tertian fever, and they had to wait a considerable time for an audience. When at length they were admitted to the royal presence, great difficulties were made about the restoration of several farms, and especially of the Castles of Rochester and Saltwood, which last was in the hands of Randolph de Broc. In reply to their exhortations. Henry put them off again and again, and at last, when they became very urgent, he said, as his final answer to John of Salisbury, who was spokesman, "O John, I shall by no means deliver up the castle to you until I see you behave to me differently from what you have yet behaved." Letters to the young king, though not such as had been promised, seem, however, to have been afterwards given, and S. Thomas sent messengers with them to England.

On their arrival, these messengers found that almost all to whom they spoke, were much attached to S. Thomas and were looking anxiously for his return, but were afraid to show their feelings or to obey his mandates. The only person who dared to co-operate with them was Robert, the Sacristan of Canterbury. In the first instance, all who had been appointed by Henry to benefices which had fallen vacant during the saint's exile, were ejected, and S. Thomas's nominees took possession; but before long the latter were turned out, and the intruders were reinstated. Not only were the Michaelmas rents collected by the royal officers as before, but even those due at Christmas, were seized in the king's name by anticipation. And when they sought redress from the young king, the only answer to their complaints was that all had been done by Henry's orders, and a distant day was appointed for looking into the matter of the restoration. It was even said on good authority that Henry had issued briefs, ordering Roger of York and the Bishops of London and Salisbury, to the prejudice of the archbishop's rights, to elect bishops for the vacant sees, and send them to be consecrated by the Pope. No wonder then that Randolph de Broc and his agents committed all sorts of violent outrages on the property of S. Thomas and his clerics, and carried off all they could lay hands on into the Castle of Saltwood, in order that on his return he should find only dismantled houses, dilapidated barns, and naked threshing-floors; and, not content with this, Randolph openly declared, that before S. Thomas should eat a loaf of bread in England, he would take away his life.

As soon as the Pope heard from S. Thomas how matters stood, he sent letters to the Archbishops of Rouen and Sens, and the Bishop of Nivers, ordering them to threaten Henry with an immediate interdict, and all holders of Church property with excommunication, unless restitution were made forthwith. He also suspended Roger of York, and all the bishops who were present at the coronation, and replaced the Bishops of London and Salisbury under the sentence of excommunication from which they had been conditionally absolved. The publication of these sentences he intrusted to S. Thomas's discretion, and full powers as apostolic legate were lodged in his hands, the persons of the king, queen, and princes only being excepted.

S. Thomas followed up the Pope's remonstrances by a letter from himself to Henry, in which he pointed out how the Church, as well as Henry's own honour and his soul, were suffering from the conduct of his officials; and he concluded with the following prophetic words:— "Forasmuch, however, as there are plain indications that, through hatred of our person, the mother of the British Churches is in danger of perishing, we, in order to save her from this fate, are prepared, God willing, to surrender our life into the hands of Randolph and his accomplices in persecution; yea, and to die a thousand deaths for Christ's sake, if His grace enable us. I had intended, my lord, ere now to have returned to you, but the necessities of the afflicted Church draw me to her side. With your favour and permission I purpose returning to her—perhaps, unless your timely pity ordain it otherwise, to die for her. Yours, whether we live or die, now and ever in the Lord."

S. Thomas had determined to remain in France till restitution of the Church property was actually made, for this was the best guarantee of Henry's sincerity that he could have; but the Pope now urged him, in spite of Henry's violation of his promises, to return without delay to England. Obedience, in things great and small, was the rule and practice of S. Thomas's life; and he therefore hesitated not to obey the holy father. With this view, he hastened to complete the arrangements of his journey; and, thanks to the liberality of the French nobles, who vied with each other in providing him with every requisite, he was soon prepared to start with more than one hundred horses in his train.

His parting from the generous friends who had ministered for many long years to his wants, was deeply mournful; for all felt that his days were numbered, and he himself shared the impression. His last words to the Bishop of Paris were, "I go to England to die." At his farewell visit to his magnificent host, the King of France, he said, "We are going to England to play for heads." "So it seems," answered Louis. "My lord archbishop, if you followed my advice, you would not trust yourself to your king; and as long as King Louis lives, the wine, the food, and the wealth of France shall never fail you." "God's will be done," was the saint's reply. Then, after many words of mutual affection, and of gratitude too warm and too deep for words to express, they parted with tears.

S. Thomas left Sens on the feast of All Saints, the 1st of November, on which day the sixth year of his exile was completed. Before crossing the Channel, he wished to see as much as possible of Henry, in the hope of ingratiating himself with him. He therefore determined to attend a meeting between Henry and Theobald, Earl of Blois, which was to take place at Tours on the 12th of November. He arrived the evening before; and though Henry went out to meet him, it was noticed that he did not look kindly on the saint and his companions; a coldness which was easily accounted for by the fact, that he was attended by Nigel de Sacville, who had been excommunicated, and who even now usurped S. Thomas's church at Harrow. The next morning, at the suggestion of Nigel, Henry ordered a black Mass to be said, in which the kiss of peace is not given. After Mass, the "Salve Sancte Parens" was said as usual in honour of our Blessed Lady; after which the priest kissed the text of the Gospel, and carried it first to the archbishop, and then to the king, to kiss; whereupon S. Thomas said, "My lord, I have come to you in your own dominions: give me the kiss now according to your promise." But Henry answered, "Another time you shall have enough."

On another occasion, when Henry was at the Castle of Chaumont, near Blois, S. Thomas paid him an unceremonious visit, and was well received. As they were talking familiarly together, Henry said to the saint, "Why do you not do my will? I certainly would put everything into your hands,"—language which, Herbert said, reminded him of the words of Satan to our Blessed Lord, "All this will I give thee, if thou wilt fall down and worship me."

At their last meeting, Henry's parting words were, "Go in peace. I shall follow you, and see you either at Rouen or in England, as soon as I can." S. Thomas answered, "My lord, my mind tells me that I am parting from you as one whom in this life you will not see again." "Do you think me a traitor?" replied Henry. "My lord, that be far from you," was the saint's rejoinder.

It had been agreed that S. Thomas was to go to Rouen to meet the archbishop, who would pay his creditors all the debts he had contracted, account to him for the rest of the revenues of the archbishopric, and afterwards escort him to England. On arriving at Rouen, S. Thomas found that no arrangements had been made with the archbishop, either for paying the money or accompanying him to England. The archbishop, however, gave him three hundred pounds as a gift, and said, that as all was safe enough in England, it was not necessary that he should go with him. Henry also had led him to expect an interview with him at Rouen; but he excused himself from coming, on the plea of an unfounded report that the King of France was about to make an inroad on Auvergne, to repel which the inhabitants had asked his assistance. He wrote strongly urging the saint not to delay his journey. "Inasmuch," said he, "as many things are told me respecting your lordship's delay, which perhaps are not true, I think it expedient for you to take your departure for England with all speed." He also sent the notorious John of Oxford to be his escort. S. Thomas accepted this affront with perfect humility, and only said on seeing John, that times were indeed changed, when the Archbishop of Canterbury was to receive protection from him.

Under John of Oxford's escort, S. Thomas journeyed to Wytsand, or Ouessant, in the territory of Boulogne, whence he intended to embark. From this place he sent the Pope's letters of censure to the bishops by one Osbern, and that to the Archbishop of York by Idonea, a nun, whom he encouraged to attempt this hazardous task by a beautiful letter, from which the following extracts are taken.

"God hath chosen the weak things of the world to confound the mighty. The pride of Holofernes, which exalted itself against God, when the warriors and priests failed, was extinguished by the valour of a woman; when apostles fled and denied their Lord, women attended him in His sufferings, followed Him after His death, and received the "first fruits of the Resurrection. You, my daughter, are animated with their zeal: God grant that you may pass into their society. The spirit of love hath cast out fear from your heart, and will bring it to pass that the things which the necessity of the Church demands of you, arduous though they be, shall appear not only possible but easy."

He then instructed her to deliver the letter to the archbishop, in the presence of the bishops if possible; but if not, in the face of all who were present; and, moreover, lest the letter should be suppressed, she was to give a copy of it to the bystanders, and to inform them of its intention—all of which would necessarily take time, and expose her to greater personal risk. Finally, he concluded thus: "My daughter, a great prize is offered for your toil—remission of sins, a fruit that perisheth not, the crown of glory which, in spite of their past lives, the blessed sinners of Magdala and Egypt have received from Christ their Lord. The Lady of Mercies will attend on you, and will entreat her Son, whom she bore for the sins of the world, God and Man, to be the guide, guard, and companion of your steps. He who burst the bonds of death, and curbed the violence of devils, is not unable to restrain the impious hand that will be raised against you. Farewell, bride of Christ, and ever think on His presence with you."

Before S. Thomas embarked, he had the satisfaction of hearing that his messengers had found the archbishop and the bishops at Dover, on the point of embarking to go to the king in Normandy, and had delivered the letters to them.

S. Thomas was kept waiting at Wytsand several days by an unfavourable wind, during which warnings of the danger which awaited him in England came from various quarters. Milo, Dean of Boulogne, went to him and said, "I have a message to you from the Count of Boulogne; he bids you beware, for the English coast is beset with soldiers, who will either murder you or make you prisoner as soon as you land." But S. Thomas answered, "Did you tell me I was to be torn limb from limb, I would not regard it; for I am resolved that nothing shall hinder my return. Seven years are long enough for a pastor to have been absent from the Lord's sorrowing flock. I will only ask my friends (and a *last* request *should* be attended to) that, if I cannot return to my church alive, they will carry me into it dead."

One day they walked down to the beach to look at the vessels in which they were to cross, and while they were there a ship arrived from England. They asked the sailors what was said there about the archbishop's return, and they were told that everyone was very much pleased. But the captain took Herbert aside, and said to him, "Wretched people, what are you doing? Where are you going? Certainly to your death: so say all who know anything about it, and everybody expects it. Besides, there are soldiers in the very port where you are going to land, waiting to take the archbishop and those who are with him." Herbert then went to S. Thomas, and told him what the captain had said. Gunter de Winton, a good, simple soul, who had been very faithful to the saint, overheard their conversation and remarked, "If my advice were asked, I should recommend our waiting till this storm blows over; for, if the country is moved now, what will it be when the king hears of the suspension of the bishops?" "And what do you say, Herbert?" asked S. Thomas. "My lord," answered Herbert, "it is difficult for me to hazard an opinion. But it seems to me that, if we go back after having said farewell to our friends, and received the Pope's blessing, it would redound to our dishonour; whereas death in such a cause will be a glorious martyrdom." S. Thomas replied briefly, "Your speech seems faithful; but it is hard, and who shall fulfil it?" After a pause he added, "Truly, Gunter, I see the land, and, by God's help, I will enter it, though I know for certain that my death awaits me."

CHAPTER XXVI. THE RETURN.

AT length, on Tuesday, the 1st of December, very early in the morning, S. Thomas and his fellow-exiles, accompanied by John of Oxford, embarked for England. As they were hurrying on board, one of the clerics said to S. Thomas, "Look, my lord, there is England." To which the saint replied, "You are very eager to go, but before you have been there forty days you will wish yourself anywhere else."

In consequence of the various warnings S. Thomas had received, he ordered the captain to steer for Sandwich, which was his own port, from which he made his escape more than six years before. As the vessel in which he was entered the harbour, the cross of Canterbury was erected at the prow. As soon as the people on shore caught sight of it, they flocked in crowds to the beach to welcome him; some rushed into the water to meet him the sooner; others knelt for his blessing; many wept for joy; while all around there rang the cry, "Blessed is he that cometh in the name of the Lord, the father of the orphans, and the judge of the widows."

The retainers of the Archbishop of York and the Bishops of London and Salisbury, under the command of Randolph de Broc, Reginald de Warenne, and Gervase de Cornhelle, sheriff of Kent, also hurried from Dover to meet him, giving out that they would behead him if he dared to land. When they saw him they scarcely saluted him, but asked rudely why, on his very first entrance into the kingdom, he had suspended and excommunicated the king's bishops. S. Thomas answered quietly, that he had the king's permission to punish the injury to his Church which they had committed. On hearing the king's name they were more moderate, but they demanded the absolution of the prelates. This matter he postponed till he should be at Canterbury; and John of Oxford protesting in the king's name against all violence, they prepared to retire. But before they went, Reginald de Warenne tried to force Simon, archdeacon of Sens, as being a foreigner, to take the oath of allegiance to the king; but as there was no mention of the Pope in the oath, and it was not usual to impose it upon the clergy, S. Thomas would not allow Simon to take it.

When it became generally known that the archbishop had landed, the whole country was in a tumult of joy. His journey to Canterbury was a triumphal procession. People from far and near, great and small, came to meet him; the parish priests led out their flocks to welcome him; the poor pressed round him; cries of "Blessed be he that cometh in the name of the Lord," rent the air; and so great was the throng, that though the distance to Canterbury was only six miles, it was late in the evening before he could arrive there.

In his own city the joy knew no bounds. The cathedral and the streets were decked out; a public entertainment was prepared; the rich put on their finest silks and most costly garments, the poor donned their holiday garb, and all went out in joyous procession to conduct him into the town; the churches resounded with chants and anthems, the halls with trumpets, and signs of rejoicing appeared on every side. S. Thomas went straight to his own cathedral church, and as he entered it his face was seen to shine, as if reflecting by its outward splendour the fire of holy love and gladness which burned in his heart. Seating himself on his throne, he received his monks with the kiss of peace, while all the bystanders wept for joy. Then Herbert said to Him, "We do not now mind when you may have to leave the world; for this day the Spouse of Christ has conquered in you." S. Thomas answered only by a look full of expression. In the chapter-house he preached a most forcible sermon on the text, "We have here no abiding city, but seek one to come." At its conclusion he retired to his palace, with mingled feelings of joy, of thankfulness, and of most solemn awe.

The next morning Randolph de Broc and his soldiers, accompanied by the chaplains of the bishops, came to demand their absolution. "You have not come in peace," said they, "but in fire and sword, treading your fellow-bishops underfoot, and treating them as your footstools, uncited, unheard, unjudged. Your suffragans had gone to the sea to receive you, but they have unexpectedly and undeservedly found themselves dressed in certain black garments, of which, if your lordship pleases, they must be ridded before they can present themselves." S. Thomas answered, "The peace of sinners is no peace; for there is no true peace except to men of goodwill. Jerusalem, abounding in luxury and self-indulgence, said to herself, 'It is peace'; but our Lord in His pity wept over her, because the vengeance of God hung over her and was hidden from their eyes." He also reminded them that the sentences were passed by the Pope, and it was not for them to call the acts of his Holiness in question. Still, however, they were very urgent for the absolution; so at last he promised, that after ascertaining the king's wishes, and consulting the Bishop of Winchester and others of his fellow-bishops, he would consent, for the sake of peace, to receive the excommunicated bishops as brethren, on condition of their taking an oath to obey the judgment of the Pope. As this oath was no more than what the Pope had himself required at their former absolution, the Bishops of London and Salisbury, after some hesitation, were disposed to submit; but Roger of York said, "My coffers still contain .8,000, and I will spend every farthing of them in beating down Thomas's insolence. Do not let him get over you, but let us set off to the king, who has all along stood by us, and, if we let him, will do so to the last." Then the three prelates hurried off with all speed to the king in Normandy; but they left behind them Geoffrey Ridel, archdeacon of Canterbury, whom they sent to the young king to seize every opportunity to poison his mind against the saint, to whom he was much attached.

When S. Thomas had been a week at Canterbury, he set out to pay a visit to the young king, who was then at Woodstock. He had previously despatched Richard, Prior of S. Martin's, Dover, to the young king, to tell him that he was about to come and pay his homage to him as his new sovereign, and to present to him three magnificent high-stepping charges, richly caparisoned, which he had brought for him from Flanders. On his way to London, he passed through Rochester, where the bishop, his old friend Walter, brother to Archbishop Theobald, came out in procession with his clergy to receive him with suitable honour. When he was three miles from London, another procession of three thousand poor scholars from the various churches in the city, together with a vast multitude of clergy and laity, both men and women, came out to welcome him; and when they caught sight of him, they all struck up the "Te Deum." S. Thomas bowed to the crowd as they saluted him, and he scattered money to the poor, which made them redouble their acclamations. Thus he passed on to the Church of the Canons Regular of S. Mary's, Southwark, where the canons in procession received him at the porch; and as they intoned the "Benedictus Dominus Deus Israel," the crowd outside took up the chant, and continued the canticle. But in the midst of the general joy, a well-known crazy woman named Matilda, kept calling out, "Archbishop, beware of the knife! Archbishop, beware of the knife!"

After leaving S. Mary's, S. Thomas took up his abode in the palace of his attached friend, the Bishop of Winchester, who had consecrated him and had always been faithful to him, and here he spent the night of the 13th of December. Of this palace there now remains only an ancient fireplace, a pointed doorway, and an old wall remarkable for its thickness, all of which stand about one hundred yards from the west end of the modern Church of S. Saviour's, Southwark.

The day after S. Thomas's arrival in London, Joceline of Louvaine, younger brother to Henry the First's queen Adeliza, came to him with a message from the young king, forbidding him to make processions about the country, and recommending him to return to Canterbury. S. Thomas asked whether it was the young king's intention to exclude him from his presence and his confidence. "His commands are what I told you," answered Joceline haughtily, and left him. As he was going out, he met a rich citizen of London going in. "And are you going to see the king's enemy?" asked Joceline. "I advise you to go home quickly." "We do not know," answered the citizen, "whether you reckon him the king's enemy; but we have heard and seen the letters of the king, who is over the water, respecting the reconciliation; if there be anything more behind, we know nothing about it."

Randolph de Broc and Gervase de Cornhelle also summoned the priors of the churches and the citizens of London to answer for having made a procession in honour of the king's enemy; but the priors did not attend, and the citizens refused to give bail, because they had not received any warrant either from the king or his justices.

In the midst of the general exultation, the saint's own spirit was sorrowful, for he was passing through that last conflict with human infirmity which was to prepare him for his triumph. He wrote at this time to a friend, Simon, the Abbot of S. Alban's, to meet him at Harrow, his own manor which Nigel de Sacville still usurped, and his letter concluded with the words, "that he had never needed consolation so much as now." Their meeting was touching and impressive. S. Thomas was deeply affected at seeing his old friend, embraced and kissed him tenderly; and then, quivering with emotion, he pressed him to go to Woodstock to make a last attempt to procure him admission to the young king, who he knew was much attached to him, but was being prejudiced against him by his attendants. The abbot went, but failed in his mission. S. Thomas, on hearing this, heaved a deep sigh, and shaking his head mournfully, said, "Let be—let be. Is it not so, is it not so, that the days of the end hasten to their completion? My lord abbot, many thanks for your fruitless labour. The sick man is sometimes beyond the reach of physicians, but he will soon bear his own judgment." Then turning to his clerics, he added, "Look you, my friends, the abbot, who is bound by no obligations to me, has done more for me than all my brother bishops and suffragans." After they had talked over all that the saint had undergone abroad, the abbot said, "By God's grace it is all now happily ended." S. Thomas sighed, and taking the abbot's hand under his cappa and pressing it, he said, "My friend, my friend, I will tell you my case as to another self; things are very different with me to what men think. New persecutions are beginning. The king and his son (who is my only hope) are devising fresh injuries." The abbot said, "How can this be, holy father?" With a deep sigh, and looking up, S. Thomas answered, "Well enough, well enough, I know to what matters are tending." When the day of parting came, the abbot, with clasped hands, entreated S. Thomas to spend Christmas and the feast of S. Stephen at his abbey. But the saint answered, shedding tears as he spoke, "Oh, how gladly would I come, but it has been otherwise ordered. Go in peace, dear brother, to your church, which may God preserve; but I go to a sufficient excuse for my not going with you." They rode together to the high ridge of the hill of Harrow, and as they parted, S. Thomas bade the abbot pray for him to his holy martyr-patron, and promised to remember him in his prayers. "I will go," he added, "and celebrate such a feast in my church as the Lord shall provide for me."

After a few days, S. Thomas returned to Canterbury. As the roads were unsafe, he took with him five soldiers, whom he dismissed on reaching Canterbury. His enemies, however, caught hold of this to represent to both the kings that he was marching about England with a great army, besieging towns, and intending to drive the young king out of the country.

The first night of his journey home S. Thomas stopped at Wrotham, where a poor priest, called William, who said Mass at Chidingston, came to him, and asked for a private audience. When they were alone, William said, "My lord, I bring you the relics of S. Lawrence, S. Vincent, and S. Cecilia, as S. Lawrence, in a vision, told me to do." "Brother," asked S. Thomas, "how do you know that they are the relics of those saints?" "My lord," answered William, "in my vision I asked S. Lawrence for some sign; for I said that otherwise you would not believe me; and S. Lawrence told me that you lately put your hand to your breast, and found the hair-shirt torn which you wear next your skin; and while you were deliberating whether you should have that one repaired, or a new one made, you soon put your hand in again, and found it whole." "In virtue of obedience," replied S. Thomas, "I command you to tell nobody as long as I live." "So be it," rejoined William; "I am a poor man, and serve in another's church; think of me, my lord." "Come to me," answered S. Thomas, "four days after Christmas, and I will provide for you." William then took his leave.

When S. Thomas arrived at Canterbury, he found himself in a trying position in consequence of the wicked conduct of the De Broc family, who having long administered the revenues of the archbishopric, were now unwilling to give up the profit which they had made out of the spoils of the Church. They kept illegal possession of his Castle of Saltwood, in the neighbourhood of Canterbury, and from this stronghold they did all they could to provoke S. Thomas, or to get up a quarrel with his dependents. While S. Thomas was in London, Randolph de Broc had seized a ship laden with his wine, cut the cables, carried off the cargo and anchors, killed some of the sailors, and shut up the rest in Pevensey Castle. On hearing of this outrage, S. Thomas sent the Prior of S. Martin's and the Abbot of S. Alban's, with a complaint to the young king, who at once ordered the ship to restored, and the sailors to be set free. Notwithstanding, the De Brocs continued their depredations. They hunted without leave in a chase belonging to the archbishop, killed a stag, and carried off several of his dogs. They also lay in wait by night in the roads near Canterbury to attack passers-by; and the day before Christmas, Robert de Broc, who after being a cleric and a monk, had broken his vows and returned to the world, captured a train of the archbishop's packhorses, and made his nephew, John de Broc, cruelly cut off the tail of one of the horses to the stump. The anxiety and peril in which S. Thomas and his followers lived, is most graphically described by John of Salisbury, in a letter to the Abbot of S. Remy, in which he says, "The archbishop received an order from the young king to return to the precincts of his cathedral church. To those with him, orders were given not to leave the kingdom, but as they valued their safety, to be on their guard. On the publication of this order, the archbishop and his followers returned to Canterbury; and there, in much danger, we are now waiting for the day of the Lord. No way seems now open for our consolation and safety, unless the prayers of yourself and the saints can deliver us from the snares of those, who would wipe us utterly away from the face of the earth. Yet, although the persecution is most grievous, and few among the rich and honourable come near the archbishop, he himself, with the dignity of a bishop, does justice for all that come to him, laying aside all consideration of person."

Meanwhile the Archbishop of York, and the Bishops of London and Salisbury had crossed the sea, and found the king at Bur, near Bayeaux, in Normandy. He had already heard about the suspension and excommunications, and he had been told that the archbishop was travelling about the country at the head of a large body of soldiers. The bishops repeated the whole story, charging S. Thomas with treason, and artfully placing every circumstance in the light best calculated to irritate the king. "By God's eyes," cried he, "if all who were concerned in my son's coronation are to be excommunicated, I shall be one of the number. What would you have me to do?" "It is not for us to advise," they answered; "your barons will do that." At length some one said, "My lord, so long as Thomas lives, you will not have good days, nor a peaceful kingdom, nor quiet times." At these words such a fit of passion seized the king, that his eyes flashed fire, his whole look was disordered, and in his blind fury he exclaimed, "A curse upon all the false varlets I have maintained, who have left me so long exposed to the insolence of this low-born cleric, and have not attempted to relieve me of him!" Saying which, he left the council-chamber.

On hearing the king's rash words, four knights went out from the royal presence, and after swearing to execute their fatal purpose they parted, and travelling by four different routes, all arrived at Saltwood Castle on the self -same day and hour. Their names were Reginald FitzUrse, William de Tracy, Hugh de Morville, and Richard Brito, or the Breton. After their departure the king summoned the barons to his chamber, and laid before them his complaint for the imaginary wrongs he had received from S. Thomas; when, far from trying to pacify him, they only encouraged his evil passions. Engelgere de Bohun, uncle to the Bishop of Salisbury and himself excommunicate, said, "I know not what you can do with such a man, except you bind him and hang him on a cross." William Malvoisin, nephew to Eudo, Earl of Bretagne, said, "Some time ago I was at Rome, on my return from Jerusalem; and on questioning my host concerning the Popes, I learnt that a Pope had once been killed for his intolerable haughtiness and insolence."

When the debate was over, Henry sent William, Earl of Mandeville, Seiers de Quincy, and Richard de Humet in search of the four knights, who, it was said, had gone to seize S. Thomas. The two first remained at the French coast, watching for him if he should attempt to fly, and Richard de Humet crossed the sea, and watched the English coast with a similar intention. Richard also ordered Hugh de Gundeville and . William Fitz John, the young king's guardians, to bring the household troops without his knowledge to Canterbury.

Christmas had now come round. On Christmas night S. Thomas sang the gospel of the Nativity after matins, according to the Benedictine rite, and celebrated the midnight Mass. He also sang High Mass on Christmas Day; and before it he preached a beautiful sermon on the text, "On earth peace to men of goodwill;" and as he was speaking of the holy fathers and confessors of the Church of Canterbury, he said they had one archbishop who was a martyr, S. Elphege, and "it was possible that they might soon have another." At these words, tears burst from his eyes, sobs choked his utterance. All in the church were moved, sobs and groans broke forth, and a low murmur was heard, "Father, why do you desert us so soon? To whom do you leave us so desolate? But soon checking his tears, the saint resumed his discourse. As he proceeded, his plaintive strain gradually rose to the high tone of apostolic reproof and holy indignation, so that "you would have thought," says Herbert, who was present, "that you were looking at the prophetic beast which had at once the face of a man and the face of a beast"; till at last, as the climax of his denunciation, in a loud, clear voice he excommunicated Geoffrey Ridel and Nigel de Sacville, who retained possession of his churches of Thierlewd and Harrow, and also Robert de Broc, who having been summoned by a messenger to do penance, had sent back for answer by David de Ruminel, a soldier, that "if he were excommunicated he would act as an excommunicate."

Christmas Day, that year, fell on Friday, and after Mass S. Thomas went to the refectory, and as the Church permits, ate meat, thinking it more religious to do so in honour of the joy of Christmas than to abstain.

On the two following days, the feasts of S. Stephen and S. John the Evangelist, he also sang Mass. On the former day he sent Herbert with letters to the King of France, the Archbishop of Sens, and others of his friends. As his retainers had been forbidden to leave the kingdom, Herbert had to go privately by night. He shed many tears at parting, for his own forebodings were confirmed by the saint's words, that "he who had borne so much with his master, would never see that master's face again on earth." He also sent Alexander Llewellyn, his cross-bearer, and Gilbert de Glanville with a letter to the Pope, in which, after relating what had happened since his return to England, and the pretexts that were being sought to rekindle animosities, he concluded with the words, "May your Holiness fare well for ever, dearest Father." He also sent Richard, his chaplain, and John Planeta with letters to the Bishop of Norwich, and Hugh Bigod, Earl of Norfolk, about the absolution of some priests in Earl Hugh's domains, who had incurred the minor excommunication. Their pardon seems to have been granted as a special favour to Earl Hugh, in return for the admirable spirit with which, when he was excommunicated for usurping Church property, he had made restitution without delay, "not only with kindness, but with magnificence."

The saint did not forget the poor priest who had come to him at Wrotham. He sent William Beivin, who knew him, to enquire whether he had arrived at Canterbury; but as he was not to be found, he intrusted to William Beivin for him, a deed conferring on him the Chapel of Penshurst, and excommunicating all who should hinder its fulfilment—in virtue of which deed the poor priest received the benefice after the martyrdom, for the young king said he would not incur the saint's excommunication.

Reports of an alarming character now poured in fast. On Sunday, S. John's Day, S. Thomas received a letter from a friend at court, warning him of his coming fate. A soldier in the service of the conspirators, told Richard, a cellarer of the monastery, that S. Thomas, would not see Tuesday night. Richard repeated this to S. Thomas, who smiled and said "They are threats." Reginald, a citizen of Canterbury, also told S. Thomas that the murderers had landed and were making their preparations; on hearing which the saint shed tears, and said, "They will find me ready to die: let them do what they like. I know, my son, and I am certain that I shall die a violent death; but they will not kill me outside my church."

CHAPTER XXVII. THE MARTYRDOM.

THE four knights from the court arrived at Saltwood Castle on Monday the 28th of December, the feast of the Holy Innocents. They spent the night in consultation with their infamous host, Randolph de Broc, and his family. At an early hour the next morning the whole party repaired to S. Augustine's Abbey, outside the walls of Canterbury, where they were received by Clarembald, the intruded abbot; and here they spent the day. There, on that soil hallowed by the mortal remains of S. Augustine, King Ethelbert, S. Dunstan, six other archbishops, and a host of saintly monks—that soil of which S. Dunstan had said, that every footstep was planted on the grave of a saint—even on that holy soil, they shrank not from making their last preparations for the deed of blood and sacrilege.

The neighbouring castles had for some time back been kept in a state of defence, and to them they now sent to collect soldiers, whom they dispersed about the town; with orders to prevent the people stirring out of their houses. Finally, in the afternoon they rode from the abbey with about a dozen men-at-arms, and made their rendezvous at the house of one Gilbert, not far from the gate of the archbishop's palace.

The preceding midnight the saint had said matins in his own room with several clerics and monks. After the office he opened a window, and for some time stood looking out silently into the night. Suddenly turning to his companions, he asked the hour, and whether it would be possible to reach Sandwich before dawn. They answered that it was yet very early, and there was time to go much further. But, repelling the temptation, he said to himself, "God's will be done in me; Thomas will wait for whatever God has in store for him in the church over which he presides."

That last morning of his life on earth he assisted at Mass in the cathedral. He went to confession, and his spirit of contrition and his obedience in doing his penance were remarked. He received the discipline three times in the course of the day; and he spent several hours in the chapter-house, in spiritual conference with two monks who were remarkable for their piety. At three o'clock in the afternoon he dined. His dinner consisted of a pheasant, and one of the monks said to him, "Thank God, I see you dine to-day more heartily and cheerfully than usual." The saint replied, "A man must be cheerful who is going to his Master." When dinner was over and grace had been chanted, the saint retired to his private room, where, seated on his bed, with his clerics and some of the monks on either side, he conversed, as was his custom, on spiritual subjects. The crowd of persons, chiefly the poor, who had dined with him, still loitered in the court-yard, and the servants who had waited at his table were seated at their dinner in the hall.

Such was the state of things in the palace when, at four o'clock, the four knights, attended by Randulf, an archer, entered the open, hospitable doors, and asked for the archbishop. FitzNigel, the archbishop's seneschal, recognising that they were the king's servants, received them respectfully, and offered to show them the way to the archbishop's room. As they passed through the hall, those who were at dinner invited them to join them, but they declined. FitzNigel, preceding them, entered the archbishop's room, and told him that four knights from the king were without, and wished to speak to him. "Let them come in," answered S. Thomas, and went on talking to those around him. As they entered, those near the door saluted them, but they only muttered an indistinct answer. Then, going up to the archbishop, the knights sat down on the floor at his feet without saluting him, and Randulf, the archer, sat on the floor behind them.

After a pause, the saint, scrutinizing them, saluted them peacefully; but they took no notice, and looked at each other in silence, till at length FitzUrse answered contemptuously, "God help you." The colour rose to the saint's face, for he saw that they were come for an evil purpose. FitzUrse, who seemed to be their leader and the most daring among them, breathing fury against the saint, then said, "We bring you a message from the king: tell us if you wish it to be delivered in public." John of Salisbury said, "My lord, let us discuss this in private"; and FitzUrse made the same request. Accordingly S. Thomas ordered everyone to leave the room; and the doorkeeper ran up and opened the door, so that those who were in the next room could see both S. Thomas and the knights. As the others were going out, FitzUrse began to speak about the absolution of the bishops; whereupon S. Thomas said, "These things must not be spoken in private;" for he feared lest they should misrepresent his words. He therefore called to the doorkeeper, and ordered him to send back the clerics, but not to admit any laymen. So bent were the miserable men on murdering him, that, had they been left alone with him, they would have killed him, as they afterwards confessed, with the shaft of his cross, which was standing by.

When the clerics had returned, S. Thomas said humbly to the knights, "Now, you may tell your lord's will in their presence." FitzUrse answered, "My lord the king says, that he made peace with you in all cordiality, but that you have not kept it. He has heard that you have gone through his cities with bands of armed men; and you have excommunicated the Archbishop of York and the other bishops for crowning the young king. You must go to Winchester, and do your duty to your lord and king." "And what am I to do?" asked the saint. "You ought to know better than we," answered FitzUrse. "If I knew," replied the saint, "I would not say I did not know; but I believe I have done my duty towards him." "By no means," retorted FitzUrse; "there is much to do, much to mend. The king's commands are, that you go to the young king and take the oath of fealty, and swear to make amends for your treason." The saint said, "What am I to swear fealty for? And what is my treason?" "The oath of fealty," answered the other, "is for the barony which you hold of the king; and all your foreign priests, too, must take the same oath of allegiance." S. Thomas replied, "For my barony I will do my duty; but neither I nor my clerics will swear any more oaths. There are enough perjured and censured already. But, thank God, I have already absolved many, and I hope, by God's help, to free the rest."

FitzUrse rejoined, "We see that you will not do anything we propose. The king further orders you to absolve the bishops." "I did not suspend nor excommunicate them," answered S. Thomas; "it was done by the Pope, and you must go to him." "But it was done through your means," exclaimed FitzUrse in great fury. "I do not deny," said the saint, "that it was done by my means; but it is beyond my authority to loose those whom my lord the Pope has bound. As to my suffragans of London and Salisbury, I have already sent them word that I would absolve them, on their promising to submit to the judgment of the Pope; but they have refused. The same I am now ready to do. All that was done was under the king's permission, which he gave me on the day of our reconciliation. I was on my way to the young king when I received his orders to return; for which I was sorry. So far from wishing to uncrown him, I would gladly give him three crowns and broad realms."

Reginald FitzUrse cried out insultingly, "What is that you say? It is an unexampled and unheard-of treachery if the king has given leave to suspend the bishops, who were present at the coronation only at his own command. It never came into his mind. Yours is an awful crime, in feigning such treachery of our lord the king." "Reginald, Reginald," answered the saint, "I do not accuse the king of treachery. Our reconciliation was not so secretly done; for archbishops and bishops, many men of rank and many religious, and more than five hundred knights were there and heard it; and you yourself, Sir Reginald, were there." "I was not there," replied Reginald. S. Thomas said quietly, "God knows it; for I am certain that I saw you there." FitzUrse swore he was not there, and repeating that it was a strange and unheard-of thing to accuse the king of treachery, added, "This cannot be borne any longer, and we, the king's liegemen, will not bear it any more." Then the other knights broke silence for the first time, swearing again and again by God's wounds, that they had borne with him far too long already.

John of Salisbury interposed, "My lord, speak in private about this." But S. Thomas answered, "There is no use; they demand things that I neither can nor ought to do."

FitzUrse continued, "From whom do you hold your archbishopric?" "Its spiritualities," answered S. Thomas, "from God and my lord the Pope; its temporalities from the king." "Own yourself to be the king's altogether," rejoined FitzUrse. "We are commanded," replied S. Thomas, "to render unto Caesar the things that are Caesar's, and unto God the things that are God's." Then they gnashed their teeth at him. But he continued, "Since I have landed under the king's safe-conduct, I have suffered many threats, insults, and losses. My men have been made prisoners, and their property taken from them. Robert de Broc has mutilated one of my horses, and Randolph de Broc has violently detained my wine, which the king sent himself to England through his continental dominions. And now you come to threaten me. I must say I think it very hard." Hugh de Morville said, "If the king's men have injured you or yours, why did you not tell the king, and not excommunicate them on your own authority?" "Hugh! how you hold up your head!" answered S. Thomas. "If anyone injures the rights of the Church, and refuses to make satisfaction, I shall wait for no one's leave to do justice." FitzUrse exclaimed, "These threats are too much." One of them shouted, "Threats, threats! will he put the whole land under an interdict, and excommunicate us all?" Another joined in, "With God's favour he shall not do it; he has excommunicated too many already."

Thereupon all the knights leaped up, twisted their gloves, flung about their arms in wild excitement, and altogether behaved like madmen. One of them rushing up to S. Thomas, said, "We warn you that you have spoken to the peril of your life." FitzUrse also said, "Thomas, in the king's name, I distrust you." But the saint answered firmly, "I know that you are come to kill me; but I trust in the God of heaven, who died on the cross for me. You threaten me in vain. If all the swords of England were pointed against my head, your terrors could not move me from the observance of God's justice, and the obedience of our lord the Pope. You will find me foot to foot with you in the battle of the Lord. I have already fled once from my duty, and will do so no more for ever. If I am allowed to perform my office in peace, it is well for me; if not, God's will be done. Besides, I wonder the more at your deportment, considering what there is between you and me." He spoke thus in allusion to the fact that Reginald FitzUrse, William de Tracy, and Hugh de Morville had made themselves his liegemen when he was chancellor. But they cried, "There is nothing between us against the king." FitzUrse adding, "We can well threaten the archbishop; we can do more. Let us go."

Most of the archbishop's household, clerics and soldiers, were now collected, alarmed at the loud voices. Turning to them, FitzUrse said, "We enjoin you in the king's name, whose liegemen and subjects you are, to leave this man." As they did not move, he said, "Ho, you clerics and monks, we order you, in the king's name, to seize this man, and not to let him escape." "The task will not be difficult," replied the saint. "I will not go away. Here you will find me; here I will await you," at the same time raising his hand to his head, as if by presentiment marking the place where he should receive their strokes.

As they were rushing out he called to Hugh de Morville, who was the most gentle of the party, hoping to save him at least from the guilt of the impending crime; but Hugh heeded him not. On their way the knights seized William FitzNigel, the seneschal, and Ralph Morin, a soldier of the archbishop's. FitzNigel cried out, "My lord, see what they are doing to me." S. Thomas answered, "I see; this is their strength and the power of darkness." He followed them a few steps, and gently asked them to let FitzNigel go, but they would not.

Then they rushed through the hall and the court, shouting out, "Arms, men, arms!" One of their soldiers having removed the porter and taken his place, the great door was opened for them as they came pouring out, and immediately after it was closed, the wicket alone being left open. FitzNigel and Simon de Croil, a soldier of the Abbot of S. Augustine's, they stationed to keep guard on horseback in the court.

When the knights went to S. Thomas's room, they had their armour on under their capes and tunics. These they now threw off under a mulberry-tree in the orchard, and put on their swords. FitzUrse armed in the porch before the hall, and forced Robert Tibia, the archbishop's shield-bearer, to help him. As soon as the knights had finished their equipment, they once more rushed along, shouting, "The king's soldiers, the king's, the king's!" till they came to Gilbert's house, where they had left the rest of their party. Then Osbert and Algar, and others of the archbishop's servants, seeing what they were doing, shut all the doors, and fastened them securely.

When the knights had retired, S. Thomas returned to his seat, and consoling his clerics, exhorted them not to fear; and it seemed to those who were present, that though he was the only one among them whose life was threatened, he alone was nevertheless as calm and undisturbed as if he had been invited to a wedding. Then John of Salisbury, with his wonted affectionate boldness, began to reprove him for not having called on his council to answer the knights, "for," added he, "they only try to make you angry, to catch you in your words; for they seek nothing but your death." But the saint, who well knew that his death had been predetermined unless he would forsake the cause of the Church, answered, "Counsel is already taken. I know well enough what I ought to do. We must all die, and the fear of death must not turn us from justice; I am more ready to die for God and justice, and the liberty of God's Church, than they are to inflict it on me. God's will be done." Those around him, in thinking over what had occurred, took different views of it. Some believed there was no ground for fear; that the knights were intoxicated, and would speak differently when sober; that as it was the festival of the Nativity, Christ's peace could not be broken; and that, moreover, the king's word was pledged for the saint's safety. But most thought that the knights would surely return and fulfil their threats.

And now a loud noise was heard, a crashing sound of hacking and hewing, and things falling; and there was a general rush of the servants through the hall down the steps towards the church, as if flying from armed men; and there came from the church a loud wailing sound, from those who had heard the knights calling on their soldiers to arm. Some people rushed into the saint's room, crying out, "My lord, my lord, they are arming!" But he answered quietly, "What matter! let them arm." The monks, many of whom were present, urged him to take refuge in the church; but he answered, "Be not afraid; monks are given to see dangers at their worst." Still they pressed him, and still he refused; for he wished to redeem his pledge, to await his murderers; and, moreover, he now saw that the hour of his martyrdom, for which he had so long sighed, was approaching, and he feared lest it might be delayed, if not pass away altogether, if he retired into the church. But the monks persisted, some trying to drag him with them; while others reminded him that he ought not to absent himself from nones and vespers, which ought at that moment to be chanted. On hearing this, he no longer refused, but ordered his cross to be brought; and Henry of Auxerre, a cleric, bore it before him. They first tried to pass by the usual way through the orchard to the cathedral; but the court and orchard were full of armed men; then they turned through a room to a private door, that was seldom used, leading into the monks' cloisters which adjoined the church. As they were hurrying along, they met with a sudden obstacle, for the door was locked, and they had not got the key; and as the murderers were now close at hand, there seemed no chance of escape. But Richard and William, two cellarers of the monastery came up through the monks' cloister on the other side of the door, and tore off the bolt; so that, to the surprise of the fugitives, it flew open, as if by a miracle.

When they had got into the cloister, the monks wished to shut the door behind them. At this the saint was displeased; and he made them all go before him, walking himself last and slowly; nor could the least sign of fear be detected in his dress or deportment; his exterior was as calm as his heart was fixed. Twice he stopped to reassure his companions, and once he looked over his right shoulder; it might have been that he thought of pursuers, or, perhaps, he wished to assure himself that no one had loitered behind and shut the door. He lingered, too, in the place of less reverence where he was standing, for having caught a glimpse of his happy consummation, he feared lest the greater sanctity of the church should deter his murderers from their purpose, and cheat him of his heart's desire. Thus they passed along the north and east sides of the cloister, and reached the lower door of the north transept of the cathedral.

Vespers had just begun when two boys rushed into the church, and told, with trembling accents, that soldiers were breaking into the palace and monastery. Then came the noise of the armed men, and the terrified people rushing into the church threw the monks into confusion, and broke off the service. Some of the monks continued in prayer, and others ran to meet the saint, thanking God that he was not killed, as had been reported, and saying to him, "Come in, father; come in, that we may suffer together, and be glorified together. Console us by your presence." He answered, "Go on with the divine office." As they lingered about the door, he said, "As long as you remain in the entrance, I will not go in." Then they gave way, and the people who were crowding forward, being pushed back, he said on the threshold, "What are these people afraid of?" They answered, "Armed men in the cloister." He replied, "I will go out to them." The monks who, through the open door, had caught a glimpse of the knights entering the cloister by the same door as S. Thomas, and approaching along the west and south sides of the cloister, now wished to close the door of the transept, regardless of the throng of servants and others who were flying before the knights. But the saint forbade them, saying, "It is not right to make a fortress of Christ's church, which is a house of prayer; it is able to protect its own, even if the doors be open, and we shall triumph over our enemies by suffering rather than by fighting; for we came here to suffer, not to resist." Still the monks tried to fasten it; whereupon going to the door he said, "Let my people in"; and, drawing in those who were outside, he said, "Come in, come in quickly—faster, faster"; and when all had come in, the door was left open. Those around him now carried him along with them into the church, and they wished him to seek safety in the sanctuary; but he refused, and went towards the High Altar, where he usually sat while the office was chanted.

Meanwhile the knights, after collecting all their followers who were at Gilbert's house, returned to the palace, and found the hall-doors closed and barred, so that they could not enter. But Robert de Broc, who knew the place well, because his brother Randolph had so long had possession of it, offered to take them in another way. He led them through the orchard, thinking to go by that entrance straight to the archbishop's room; but that door also being closed, he brought them through the ambulatory, where the wooden steps were under repair, and the carpenters' tools were lying about. FitzUrse seized an axe, and the others took hatchets, and with these they hewed down a wooden partition which barred their way; and then breaking through a door and window, they got into the hall, and after wounding the servants who had closed the great doors, they opened them again; then they rushed over the palace, and not finding the archbishop in his own room, they followed him through the cloister to the church, which they reached just after S. Thomas had been persuaded to leave the door and go inside.

The saint had gone up four steps of the High Altar, when Reginald FitzUrse appeared at the door on the right side, in a complete suit of armour, with his sword drawn; and immediately behind him, on the left side, were the three others, armed at all points, but with their visors up, and all held in their left hands the carpenters' tools which they had picked up. FitzUrse shouted, "This way to me, king's men!" and there followed him Hugh Horsea, a subdeacon, Robert FitzRanulph, three other knights, and a number of soldiers armed, though not in coats of mail, and some of the townspeople whom they had forced to join them. And the door having been left open, they entered without impediment, whilst their very looks and the rattle of their arms, struck terror into all beholders. Then there was a great commotion, the monks and clerics, and John of Salisbury among them, flying for safety, some to the altars, and some to places of concealment, all except Robert, Prior of Merton, William FitzStephen, and Edward Grim, the cleric. These three tried to drag S. Thomas up the steps which led from the transept to the choir; but the saint said to them, "Leave hold of me, and go away; there is nothing for you to do here; let God dispose of me according to His will."

It was now five o'clock, the short winter's day had closed, and it being dark, with a long night coming on, the saint could easily have taken refuge in the crypt, where there were many recesses for concealment, or he might have fled by a winding staircase to the lofts and vaulting above the church; and thus he might possibly have escaped pursuit altogether; or something might have happened in the meantime. But he chose none of these things. He withdrew not, entreated not, uttered not a murmur or complaint; but awaited his hour, for Christ's sake and for the Church, with resolution of soul and calmness of voice and deportment; and as became a true martyr, he endured unto the end.

As the ruffians entered, one of them cried to the monks, "Do not move." Another exclaimed, "Where is Thomas, traitor to the king?" As there was no answer, FitzUrse said to one against whom he had run, "Where is the archbishop?" The saint, moving his head slightly to the monks, instantly answered, "Here I am no traitor, but archbishop. What do you want with me!" Some one exclaimed, "Your death." He replied, "And I meet it gladly. I am ready to suffer in the name of Him who redeemed me with His blood. But I charge you by His authority that you touch none of mine." As he spoke he came down the steps, and passing FitzUrse and turning towards the right, he stood by a pillar which had hidden him from their sight as they entered, having the altar of our Blessed Lady on his right, and that of S. Benedict before him. The knights, startled by his sudden appearance in his white rochet in the gloom of twilight, fell back some paces, but they soon recovered themselves. Then some one struck the saint on the shoulders with the flat of his sword, saying, "Fly, or you are a dead man." But he answered, "I will not fly." The four knights now came up, and with them Hugh Horsea, surnamed Mauclerc on account of his irreligiousness, all calling out, "Absolve the bishops whom you have excommunicated." He said, "I will do nothing more than I have already done." Then turning to

FitzUrse, he added, "Reginald, I have done you many favours: do you come against me with arms?" "You shall know it," answered FitzUrse. "I will tear out your heart; are you not a traitor?" FitzUrse laid hold of his robe, knocking off his cap with his sword, and saying, "Come, you are my prisoner." But the saint pulled his cappa out of FitzUrse's hand, and answered, "Do with me *here* what you will." Then they tried to place him on William de Tracy's shoulders and carry him out of the church, but he stood firm in his place, with Edward Grim alone standing by him and assisting him, for Robert of Merton and FitzStephen had fled to the altars. He pushed De Tracy away so that he almost fell on the pavement; and as FitzUrse pressed on him he thrust him back, saying, "Touch me not, Reginald, you profligate wretch; you are my man, and owe me fealty and submission." FitzUrse answered, "I owe you neither, contrary to my fealty to the king."

FitzUrse, finding that they could not drag him out of the church, and fearing the interference of the townspeople, who were crowding into the church, threw down the axe which he had hitherto carried, and waved his sword over the saint's head, crying out, "Strike! strike!" Seeing that his hour was come, the invincible martyr, bowing his head in the attitude of prayer and raising his clasped hands to heaven, said, "I commend myself to God, to Holy Mary, blessed Denys, and S. Elphege." Scarcely had he uttered these words when De Tracy aimed a blow at him. But Grim, who still held S. Thomas in his embrace, threw up his arm covered with his cloak to shield the saint, who exclaimed, "Spare this defence." The blow fell on Grim's arm, and nearly severed it, so that he was forced to retire to one of the altars close by. The sword then glanced off to S. Thomas's head, shaving off its crown, which had been anointed with the holy oil at his consecration, and resting upon his left shoulder, cut through his vestment to the flesh. The saint wiped with his arm the blood that was falling from his head, and giving thanks to God, said, "Into Thy hands, O Lord, I commend my spirit." A second blow upon his head was dealt, probably by FitzUrse, but he still stood unshaken. The third blow from William de Tracy, brought him to his knees, and then joining and stretching out his hands to God, he fell on his face before the altar of S. Benedict, at the same moment breathing in a low voice his last words, "For the name of Jesus and the defence of His Church, I am ready to die."

Even in falling his attitude was composed, as of one prostrating himself in prayer, so that not even his pall was disarranged. As he fell Richard de Brito gave him a fourth blow with such violence, that the sword broke against his skull and the pavement, and the whole of his ample tonsure was shorn from his head, Richard saying as he struck, "Take that for the love of my Lord William, the king's brother," in allusion to an incestuous marriage between William and the Countess de Warrene, which the saint had prevented. Then Hugh Horsea put his foot upon the saint's neck, and with the point of his sword drew out the brains and scattered them over the pavement, exclaiming, "Now, soldiers, let us be off; he will never get up again." Hugh de Morville alone had struck no blow, but had contented himself with keeping back the people who would have interfered to stop the bloody deed. Tracy afterwards confessed to the Bishop of Exeter that although they had gone to the Church with all alacrity, and even rejoicing, yet the deed was no sooner done than the ground seemed to yawn beneath them as if it would swallow them up. Quickly, however, they smothered conscience, and rushed from the church, by the same door as they had entered, brandishing their swords and shouting out as before, "The king's men! The king's men!" They and their followers ran over the palace, breaking open the coffers, desks, and treasuries, forcibly removing the horses from the stables, wounding the servants, and pillaging all that came to hand. They carried off the chalice which the saint used at Mass, his ring with a costly sapphire in it, a knife said to be "worth a city's ransom," besides rich stuffs for vestments, gold, silver, books, clothes, and other spoil, to the value of 2,000 marks, which they divided among them. Among other things they found, to their great surprise, two hair-shirts, at sight of which some of the band muttered, though with bated breath, for fear of their companions, "Truly this was a righteous man!" and beating their breasts they left the palace. But the rest cast aside such things as rubbish, and of no value to them. Such was the mood in which, when satiated with blood and pillage, they turned their steps to Salt wood Castle.

CHAPTER XXVIII. THE BURIAL.

EVEN before the bloody deed was completed, the alarm had been given in the city, and people began to flock to the church. All were thunderstruck at the awful event, and rushed to the spot, beating their breasts and clasping their hands in agony, for the loss of him who had always been the father of the orphan, the protector of the widow, and the consoler of those who mourned. They threw themselves upon the holy corpse as it lay on the floor, kissing with the utmost reverence his hands and feet.

Before long, the monks dismissed the multitude, and closed the doors of the church. Osbert. the saint's chamberlain, cut off a piece of his surplice and threw it over his head, and for a short space the body lay deserted, while all waited in terror, listening to the noise and uproar made by those who were ransacking and pillaging the palace. At length night came on, and the ruffians departed. Then the clerics, the monks, the servants, and some of the townspeople, assembled round the saint. He lay on his face, as if he were still in prayer; the red blood, issuing forth, mingled itself with the whiteness of his brains; and thus blended together, they stained the pavement with the colour of the lily and the rose, typifying at once the life as well as the death of God's martyr and confessor. The blood, too, had congealed round his head in the form of a crown, as if in token of his sanctity; but his face was entirely free from stains, save one slender stream which had descended diagonally from the right side of his forehead to the left side of his neck. While the body still lay on the pavement, some of them signed their eyes and forehead with the blood; others brought bottles and carried off secretly as much of it as they could; while others, again, cut off shreds from their garments, and dipping them in the blood, kept them as relics. After a time the monks raised the body, and placed it on a bier before the high altar. They replaced his scalp, which was hanging from his head and attached to it only by a small piece of skin; and as blood still oozed from the wound, they put a dish to catch it; they collected the scattered brains and blood; and the spot which had been hallowed by his martyrdom, they reverently railed round with benches to protect it from the tread of passers-by. In moving him, they found beneath him the axe which FitzUrse had thrown away, and by his side were the fragments of De Brito's sword.

That night there was a violent thunderstorm; and amid the rolling peals of thunder which echoed through the vaulted aisles, and the bright flashes of lightning which lit up the church, the monks kept watch around the bier in deepest sorrow and lamentation. Though so much blood had flowed from the wound, yet the face was not paler or thinner than before; the forehead was not more wrinkled, nor were the eyes more sunk; the neck was not emaciated, nor were the shoulders fallen; the body retained its elasticity, and the skin its firmness. The beauty of his countenance still remained, and even in death he bore upon his lips that calm and holy smile which had characterised him through life. He seemed, in fact, not so much to have breathed his last, as to have closed his eyes while the fresh colour was still upon his cheeks, and to have fallen into a sound slumber.

Then Robert of Merton, his confessor, thrust his hand into the saint's breast, and showed the monks what none had before suspected, that he wore next his skin a hair-shirt, and over that the habit of a monk. At this sight the monks exclaimed, "See, see! he was a true monk, and we did not know it." In an ecstasy of spiritual joy they prostrated themselves before him, they kissed his hands and feet, and they invoked him as "S. Thomas, God's holy and glorious martyr."

Then they watched till dawn; and as the first faint streaks of light appeared in the horizon, it seemed to the mourning monks that the corpse waved its right arm and slowly made the sign of the cross, as if blessing his faithful friends. But when the day broke, it came as a harbinger of fresh tribulation. For a body of armed men assembled outside the city walls, and Robert de Broc came to the convent with a brutal message from his brother Randolph, commanding the monks to "remove that disloyal traitor out of the way as fast as possible, and to throw him where nobody would know him; or else, he warned them that he would drag him out by the feet, and tear him in pieces for the dogs and swine."

In extreme alarm they carried their treasure down to the crypt, and prepared to bury it. They undressed him, and beheld, to their great astonishment, the unusual length of his hair-shirt, reaching down to his knees and full of vermin, and also the marks of the many stripes which he had received even up to the preceding morning. Once more they raised their voices in joyful chorus, magnifying God for their archbishop's double martyrdom, the voluntary one of his life, and the violent one of his death, and all flocked to gaze upon the new attire of the once splendid chancellor. Out of reverence they did not wash off the blood which had bathed the body, nor did they anoint him with balsams, as was customary for the archbishops of Canterbury; but they dressed him in his hair-shirt and the Cistercian habit which the Pope had given him, and over these they placed the pontifical vestments in which he had been consecrated, with his pall, gloves, ring, sandals, and pastoral staff. Then they laid him in a new marble coffin in the crypt, before the altars of S. John the Baptist and S. Augustine the Apostle of England, and the vessel containing the brains and the blood was placed before it. After this the crypt was closed, and none ventured to enter it except by stealth.

But miracles in honour of the martyr became frequent; and as the fame of them spread abroad, people came to visit the scene of the martyrdom, and begged, but in vain, to be allowed to venerate the holy relics. At length the monks yielded to the universal wish; and on the 2nd of April, which was the Friday in Easter-week, the crypt was thrown open. Crowds of pilgrims from far and near flocked to the holy shrine, and the number of miracles increased. When all this came to the ears of the De Brocs, their hatred to the martyr revived, and the monks were told that they were making preparations to carry off the precious relics by force. The monks were terrified, and in great alarm they took the body out of the marble coffin, and putting it into a wooden one, hid it behind the altar of our Blessed Lady. Once more, amid peals of thunder and flashes of lightning—for again there was a violent thunderstorm—they watched through the livelong night. But the ruffians did not come, for they saw it was folly to dream of checking the devotion, since, as they were forced to say, "all England had gone after him." The monks soon found, however, that it was all in vain for them to hope to hide the blessed martyr's relics; for the next day two miracles took place, one of them at the very altar where they had concealed him, and thus their secret was publicly revealed. So they took courage, and carried him again down to the crypt, and put him once more in the marble coffin, round which they built a strong wall of large wrought stones clamped with iron and lead, which may still be seen; and over the whole, at a distance of about a foot from the top of the coffin, they placed a roof, in which were two openings, through which pilgrims might touch and kiss the coffin.

During all this time, and for many months after, no Mass was said in the cathedral; the altars were stripped, the crucifixes were veiled, and the monks assembled in the chapter-house to say their office, but without any chanting. Thus the Church remained in mourning for the deed of blood by which it had been desecrated, till at the expiration of a year within a few days from the martyrdom, on the feast of S. Thomas the Apostle, December 21st, it was reconciled with the usual ceremonies by the Bishops of Exeter and Lichfield, to whom the Pope's legates transferred the necessary powers, which they had themselves received for that purpose from the Holy Father.

CHAPTER XXIX. THE EXCOMMUNICATION—THE ABSOLUTION.

MEANWHILE the news of the sacrilegious murder spread abroad, and was received throughout Christendom with feelings of horror, which no words can be found to express. When the young king heard it, he raised his hands and eyes to heaven, thanking God that he knew nothing about it, and that none of his followers were there; and he mourned deeply for the saint, to whom he was sincerely attached. He had had no share in the harsh acts which had lately been done by his guardians in his name, and it had been noticed that he received the saint's messengers with great cordiality whenever his guardians were not present. As for the Bishop of Winchester, his first exclamation was, "Thank God, it was my privilege to consecrate him!" But when, in the following August, a few days before his death, Henry paid him a visit, he reproved him severely for his share in the martyr's death.

In France, where the saint was so loved and honoured, the sensation was very great. The Archbishop of Sens, who had just received legatine authority, at once placed an interdict on Henry's continental dominions, and he wrote to the Pope in the strongest terms, denouncing Henry and the guilty bishops as the virtual murderers. The King of France and many distinguished persons in the realm wrote to the same effect, all of which letters were taken to the Pope by Alexander Llewellyn and Gunter, whom the saint had despatched two days before his death with his own last letter to the Holy Father. When his Holiness received the news, he shut himself up for eight days, not seeing even his own suite. An order was given that no Englishman should be admitted to his presence, and it was generally believed that on Maundy Thursday he would solemnly excommunicate Henry, and lay an interdict on his kingdom.

Henry was at Argenton when the news reached him. At the first words of the messengers he burst into loud lamentations, and exchanged his royal robes for sackcloth. At times he would cease his cries and become stupefied, and then he would burst again into cries and lamentations louder than before. For three whole days he shut himself up in his room, refusing all food and consolation; and for forty days more he remained in seclusion, in penance and fasting, seeing no one, holding no councils, hearing no causes, heeding not the affairs of the state, but ever repeating again and again, "Oh, that it should have happened! Oh, that it should have happened!" For he was alarmed lest, on account of his long enmity to the saint and his late rash words, it should be supposed that he had been privy to the deed. He sent orders to Canterbury that the saint should be properly buried, and he also despatched messengers plead his cause with the Pope.

Only a few weeks previously, messengers had gone to the Papal court to obtain the absolution of the excommunicated bishops, and they were on the point of success when the news of S. Thomas's death arrived, and threw everything into confusion. The second embassy, after a perilous journey, reached Tusculum where the Papal court then was, on the Saturday before Palm Sunday; but to their great dismay they found that the Pope would not admit them to his presence, the cardinals would hardly speak to them, and no one would show them any attention. At length, after much difficulty, the Abbot of Valace, and the Archdeacon of Lisieux, who were the least suspected of the party, were admitted to an audience; but no sooner did they begin to speak of their master "as a devoted son of the Church "than the whole court exclaimed, "Hold! Hold!" as if his very name were offensive in their ears. Late in the evening of the same day, they again saw the Pope, first privately, and afterwards in the presence of all the cardinals, and also of Alexander Llewellyn and Gunter; but they failed to make any favourable impression, because, though they could not deny that their master's words had been the immediate cause of the murder, their instructions from him were limited to "recalling the favours which the king had conferred upon the archbishop, and the excesses which the latter had committed against the king's dignity." Maundy Thursday was now at hand, and there was no doubt that the Holy Father would then publicly, and with the usual impressive solemnity, excommunicate Henry by name, and lay all his dominions on both sides of the sea under an interdict. In this emergency, they acted with the same unscrupulous zeal that had throughout characterised Henry's messengers. "Feeling it our duty," as they say in a letter to their master, "not lightly to suffer this severity to fall on your majesty's person and kingdom, we adopted a plan for averting the impending sentence, and took all the hazard upon ourselves, from a firm conviction that things would turn out agreeably to your wishes, and to what we think ought to be your wishes. For in our alarm we signified to the Pope through the cardinals, that you had instructed us to swear in his presence that you would abide by his decision, and that you will ratify this by your personal oath." Accordingly on the same day, namely, Maundy Thursday, about three in the afternoon, Henry's messengers and those of the bishops, all swore to this effect in full consistory. The Pope, therefore, omitted Henry's name in the public excommunication, and excommunicated in general terms only, the murderers of S. Thomas, and all who had given them counsel, approbation, or assistance, or who had harboured them. After Easter, the Bishops of Worcester and Evreux, who were associated in Henry's embassy, arrived, but they refused to take the oath which the others had so recklessly volunteered. A fortnight later the Pope confirmed the interdict which the Archbishop of Sens had already laid on Henry's continental dominions; and he further forbade Henry to enter a church till the legates whom he would send to see if he was truly humbled should permit him to do so.

The Archbishop of York remained under suspension till the 6th of December, A.D. 1171, and the Bishop of London till the 1st of May, 1172, though he had been freed from excommunication in the preceding August. The Bishop of Salisbury probably received absolution about the same time.

As for the murderers, before long they were again at court, and were on familiar terms with the king and constantly joined him in hawking and hunting. Generally, however, they were shunned. No one would speak to them, or eat or drink with them, and the remains from their table were thrown to the dogs; and even they, it is said, after tasting them rejected them. Conscience, however, at last awoke, and within a year after the martyrdom De Morville, FitzUrse, and Brito set out on pilgrimage to Jerusalem, where they performed a long course of public penance. But though they had thus made their peace with the Church, so deep was their contrition for the sin they had committed, that the image of their sacrilege was constantly before their eyes, and though they were young men and had hitherto been strong and healthy, within the short space of three years they all died on their way home, incessantly praying for forgiveness, and the intercession of S. Thomas the martyr.

De Tracy, De Morville, and FitzUrse had all been doubly guilty, because they had sworn fealty to S. Thomas when he was chancellor. De Tracy, moreover, bore the guilt of having struck the first blow at the saint. Notwithstanding he continued impenitent for several years. At last, about A.D. 1174, his heart was touched, and filled with compunction he made a pilgrimage to Rome, whence he set out for Jerusalem. But on his journey he was seized at Cosenza in Calabria by a horrible and loathsome disease, and died miserably, after making his confession to the bishop of the place.

On his death-bed he signed a deed of gift, one of the witnesses to which is the Abbot of S. Euphemia, a convent within twenty miles of Cosenza, making over to the See of Canterbury the manor of Daccombe, or Dockham, in the parish of Moreton Hampsted, South Devon, for the maintenance of a monk to say Mass in the Cathedral "for the love of God, and of his soul and the souls of his predecessors, and for the love of Blessed Thomas, the archbishop and martyr of venerable memory." The chapter still holds this manor in virtue of this deed.

Among the archives of Canterbury, together with this deed, is a document which states that William Thann, "before his departure to the Holy Land with his master," made his wife swear to render up to the Blessed Thomas and the monks of Canterbury all the lands given him by his lord William de Tracy. He died on his journey. His wife married again, and her second husband prevented her fulfilling her vow. But she survived him and she then gave the lands to S. Thomas and the see.

In Devonshire where the De Tracys had large estates, there still remain nine parish churches dedicated to S. Thomas in reparation of his death, which prove the sincerity of the murderer's contrition and the devotion of his family to the martyr.

Under the long promontory, still called S. Thomas's Head, which juts into the Bristol Channel, may be seen the ruins of the Priory of Woodspring, founded in 1210 by William de Courtenay, probably the son of the murderer's daughter, who married Sir Gervase de Courtenay, in honour of the Holy Trinity, the Blessed Virgin, and S. Thomas of Canterbury. This Priory held lands bequeathed to it by Maud the daughter, and Alice the grand-daughter, of Richard Brito, the murderer, praying for the intercession of the glorious martyr for Alice and her children.

In the course of the year 1171, Cardinal Albert, the saint's old friend, and Theodwine, Cardinal of S. Vitalis, arrived in England as legates from the Pope. But so far was Henry from being humbled or contrite, and so little intention had he of ratifying the terms to which his envoys had sworn in his name, that the legates could not get access to him, and the usual precautions of guarding the ports and issuing sanguinary threats, were taken to prevent the publication of any sentence, or even the delivery of any letter to himself. It was also believed that one of his motives for the invasion of Ireland at this time, was to keep himself out of the way of ecclesiastical censures. At length, however, on the Tuesday before the Rogation season, he met the legates at Gorham, and on the following day he gave them a second audience at the Abbey of Savigny. But after a long conference he refused to take the oath they required of him, and left them in great anger, saying, "I shall return to Ireland, where I have many things to attend to; and you may go anywhere you please in my dominions, and exercise your legation as you think proper." But through the mediation of Arnulf, Bishop of Lisieux, and others of his friends, he was brought to reason; and at a third meeting, which took place at Avranches on the following Friday, he promised to do all that the cardinals desired.

Accordingly, on the following Sunday, being the fifth after Easter, the legates rode into Avranches in company with Henry and his son, the young king. They all went together to the cathedral, where, with his hand on the gospels, Henry swore that he had never commanded, nor wished that the archbishop should be put to death, and that when he heard of it he grieved rather than rejoiced, adding of his own accord, that he grieved more than for the death of his father or mother; and as he admitted before all, that the archbishop's death had taken place entirely through him, he swore to perform to the letter whatever penance or satisfaction the cardinals should require of him. Then the legates made him swear obedience to Pope Alexander and his successors; that he would take the cross for three years and go in person to the Holy Land, unless the Pope gave him leave not to go; and that he would find two hundred knights, and maintain them for a year at the rate of three hundred guineas each, to fight against the Saracens under the command of the Templars. He further swore that he would renounce the Constitutions of Clarendon, and all other bad customs which had been introduced against the Church in his time, and would allow all other bad customs which had been introduced before his reign to be examined and modified by the Pope and a body of religious men; that he would not hinder appeals in ecclesiastical causes to the Church of Rome; that he would restore the possessions of the Church of Canterbury as they existed the year before the saint's exile, and make restitution to all clerics and laics who had been deprived on his account. There were beside private penances of fasting and alms, which were not published. The young king also swore that he would observe all that his father had sworn, and should his father die without fulfilling the penances, he would, if he survived, himself perform them.

Then the legates, to leave nothing undone, led King Henry out of the church; and there, kneeling upon his knees, he received absolution, and was introduced anew into the Church, from which he had been interdicted for above a year.

Ten days later, on the Tuesday after the Ascension, Henry publicly repeated the above oaths at Caen, in the presence of the Archbishop of Tours and his suffragans; and he affixed his seal to the documents which the legates had drawn up and sealed.

The great Norman cathedral of Avranches was erected on the brow of a high ridge, overlooking "the wide bay, in the centre of which stands the majestic rock of S. Michael, crowned with its fortress and chapel. Of this vast cathedral, one granite pillar alone has survived the storm of the French Revolution; and that pillar marks the spot where Henry performed his first penance. It bears an inscription with these words: '*Sur cette pierre, ici, à la porte de la cathedrule d'Avranches, après le meurtre de Thomas Becket, A rchévêque de Cantorbery Henry II., Roi d'Angleterre et Due de Normandie, reçut a genoux;, des leyats du Pape, l'absolution apostolique, le Dimanche, xxii. Mai, MCLXXII.*'"

One more task still remained for the legates. They had been ordered by the Pope to inquire into, and examine juridically, the numerous miracles which were reported to have taken place through S. Thomas's intervention from the very day of his martyrdom. This they had done, and the result was, that on Ash Wednesday, the 21st of February, 1173, Pope Alexander solemnly canonized S. Thomas of Canterbury as a martyr for the cause of the Church of God, and ordered his festival to be observed throughout the world on the 29th of December, the day of his martyrdom. Accordingly, on the 7th of July, at a council held at Westminster to elect the saint's old friend, Richard Prior of S. Martin's, Dover, to succeed him as archbishop, for S. Thomas was actually canonized before his see was filled, the bull of canonization praising his life as well as his death was read, and a Te Deum was sung. Then all the bishops who had opposed him in life, confessed their fault; and one of them, in the name of the rest, intoned the prayer, *Adesto Domine*: "Hear, O Lord, our petitions; that we, who of our iniquity acknowledge ourselves to be guilty, may be freed by the intercession of blessed Thomas, Thy bishop and martyr."

The Holy Father, in his letter announcing the canonization to the chapter of Canterbury, ordered them to remove the martyr's body in solemn procession, and place it on an altar, or elevate it in a chest suitable for the purpose. The erection of a chapel and shrine befitting so great a saint, was a work of time, and about fifty years elapsed before they were completed. The site chosen for the purpose was the chapel of the Blessed Trinity, where he said his first Mass, which he generally preferred for his subsequent Masses and private devotions, and which was already hallowed by the remains of S. Odo, S. Wilfrid, and Archbishops Lanfranc and Theobald. This chapel was pulled down, and in its place was erected a splendid structure, to contain the shrine of S. Thomas. Hither the holy relics were removed with a ceremonial of extraordinary magnificence, on Tuesday the 7th of July, 1220, on which day the Church in England has ever since kept the festival of S. Thomas's translation.

It would be long to tell how rapidly and widely the devotion to S. Thomas spread, not only through England, but throughout Catholic Europe. Kings and nobles, bishops and priests, monks and laymen, and most of all the poor and afflicted, whom he had so loved in life, now flocked to his shrine; and for many a century no pilgrimage was deemed more efficacious, and no intercession more powerful, than that of the martyr, S. Thomas of Canterbury. Rich gifts, too, were heaped upon the shrine, so that its beauty and magnificence were unrivalled. A Venetian who visited it about A.D. 1500, describes it as exceeding all belief. Notwithstanding its great size, it was covered with plates of pure gold, which were so encrusted with precious stones, sculptured gems, and cameos, that the gold was scarcely visible; but the beauty of all else was far surpassed by a ruby of marvellous brilliancy, the size of a thumbnail, or small hen's egg, which was known as the Regale of France, having been offered on the shrine by the saint's valued friend, Louis VII. of France, when he made the pilgrimage of Canterbury to obtain the restoration to health of his son, Philip Augustus.

CHAPTER XXX. THE VOLUNTARY PENANCE—CONCLUSION.

THUS was penance won for the Church by the blood of S. Thomas, her undaunted champion and glorious martyr. Thus too was peace with the Church regained through contrition and penance, by those who were guilty of his blood. What was the exact measure of Henry's complicity is known only to God. That he was the immediate cause of the murder he fully admitted; that he meditated some act of violence, is evident from the measures he took to seize S. Thomas in case he should attempt to fly; but that he premeditated the murder he always denied. On the other hand, Giraldus Cambrensis deliberately states, that William de Tracy confessed to Bartholomew, Bishop of Exeter, that the four knights had been bound *by the king* by oath to kill the archbishop, and that they therefore reproached Hugh de Morville for not taking a more active part. A sergeant of the king's court also told a priest, Richard de Halliwell, in confession, that he had with his own hands sealed letters written by Nigel de Sacville, which were sent to England to command the archbishop's death. It seems, however, more in accordance with Henry's usual double-dealing to suppose, that, trusting to the zeal of his unscrupulous tools, he would merely suggest the crime, and thus secure for himself the privilege, which on so many other occasions he claimed, of disowning the actions of his own agents. The sincerity of his contrition when he was reconciled to the Church at Avranches, must be left to the judgment of Him who alone can fathom the depths of the human heart. But a deeper contrition and a severe penance yet awaited him, and these were brought about by the just providence of God, and the hidden grace of the Holy Spirit.

The coronation of his son, which Henry planned as a gross insult to S. Thomas, and in defiance of the Church's authority, eventually became the instrument of his punishment. The young king, elated at his elevation, claimed independent power, and by a strange retribution, his first un filial act was a protest against the election of S. Thomas's successor, as having been made without his permission. Before long he flew to arms; his brother Richard joined him; Louis King of France, and Philip, Earl of Flanders, took their part; and it was as much as Henry could do, to defend his Norman dominions. But before long news came that William III., King of Scotland, had crossed the border, taken Carlisle, and laid waste all the north; and that many of the principal English barons had declared for the young king, who was only waiting for a fair wind to invade England. Messenger after messenger arrived in quick succession, urging Henry's immediate return, till at last the Normans said in jest, "The next thing the English will send will be the Tower of London."

Henry lost no time in embarking, taking with him his queen Eleanor, his son's queen Margaret, his son John, and his daughter Jane. It was very stormy, but Henry prayed aloud for a good passage only if his arrival would promote peace with both clergy and laity. He landed at Southampton on Monday, the 8th of July, A.D. 1174. Notwithstanding the dangerous crisis, he deferred all public business, and set out at once on a pilgrimage to S. Thomas's tomb, fasting strictly on bread and water. On the following Friday he came in sight of Canterbury, when he leaped from his horse and went the rest of the way on foot. From S. Dunstan's church, outside of the city, he walked barefoot and clad in the coarse woollen garments usually worn by pilgrims, and the blood which flowed freely from his feet, bedewed the street. At the church-porch he stopped to pray; then he visited the spot of the martyrdom, which he watered with his tears; after which he said his *confiteor* before the bishops who were present, and went with much reverence to the tomb, where he remained a very long time in prayer. After a while Gilbert, Bishop of London, spoke in Henry's name to all who were present, saying, that the king knew that his angry words had caused the martyr's death, though he never intended it; that he also felt that he had been very wrong in his persecution of him during his life; and that he had therefore come to make full satisfaction, trusting that his humble penance would be acceptable to God and S. Thomas, for which he begged their prayers. He that day restored in full all the dignities and rights of the Church of Canterbury, and whatever, in that or other lands, the Church had freely held in past times; and he also made an offering, as a gift to the martyr, to keep lights burning at the tomb. When the bishop had concluded, the king ratified and confirmed all that he had said. Gilbert must have shared his master's humiliation in making this speech, and it may be charitably inferred that he also shared his contrition; for he granted special indulgences to all who should contribute to build the hospital in Southwark, then about to be erected "in honour of God and the Blessed Martyr S. Thomas."

After the close of Gilbert's speech, Henry's shoulders were bared, and having bent his head down to one of the openings of the tomb, he received five strokes from each of the prelates present, and three from each of the monks, who were above eighty in number; and after he had been absolved, he watched by the tomb through the night, fasting and kneeling on the bare ground in prayer. After matins and lauds he visited the altars and relics of the saints in the upper church, and then returned to the crypt. At daybreak he asked for Mass; and after assisting at it, and drinking some water in which a drop of the martyr's blood had been diluted, he returned to London, taking with him a small phial of the same.

On the same day and at the very same hour that Henry was hearing Mass at S. Thomas's tomb, his troops took Alnwick Castle, and made the King of Scotland prisoner at Richmond, On the following Thursday at midnight a messenger from the army arrived in London. With difficulty he gained admission to the royal chamber, and waking the king, told him the glorious news. Henry was stupefied, and scarcely believing that he heard aright, he said, "Tell me again." Then he asked, "Have you brought letters?" When they were produced, he glanced at them; and then leaping from his bed, with tears in his eyes he gave thanks to God and S. Thomas. Within three weeks after Henry's pilgrimage and penance the rebellion was quelled, and peace reigned throughout England.

S. Thomas, during his exile, had told Herbert that it had been revealed to him in a vision, that he should yet render Henry assistance in some of his troubles. Thus was the promise of this vision now fulfilled.

.   .   .   .

And now, once more, the blood of the martyr became the seed of the Church a seed which budded and grew amidst showers, and storms, and gleams of sunshine, and in due season brought forth the fruit of liberty and peace. S. Thomas's death and Henry's voluntary penance ushered in a new era; for though the Church's rights were still often outraged by lawless and tyrannical monarchs, yet her supernatural powers were not again endangered, and S. Thomas's name gave courage to her defenders, while it paralyzed the strength of her oppressors. In 1176 a council again met at Northampton, and formally confirmed the jurisdiction of the ecclesiastical courts, decreed that bishoprics and abbeys should be filled up within a year of their falling vacant, and freed the clergy from other grievances. A few years later, in 1186, S. Hugh having refused to enter on the See of Lincoln, because he had been elected by the king's command elsewhere than in the cathedral, Henry acquiesced in this canonical objection, which was directly opposed to the twelfth constitution of Clarendon; and he permitted a second and free election to be made by the canons in Lincoln Cathedral before S. Hugh was enthroned. About thirty years after, in January 1215, John, after having resisted for five years the election of Stephen Langton to the See of Canterbury, and having thereby subjected his people to an interdict, voluntarily granted the clergy the right of free election; and a few months later, in June 1215, he signed Magna Charta, the first article of which secured to the Church her liberties, and the property which she held in trust for God and the poor. Thus, as in the days of Ethelbert, of Alfred, and of S. Edward, English liberty and law were placed on the firm basis of religion, and society was held together by spiritual and moral bonds rather than by mere physical force. And as happier days arose, and justice and order took the place of violence and despotism, the Church was enabled to exercise her sacred functions freely, and to spread the blessings of faith and holiness over the land. On a hundred thousand altars the Holy Sacrifice was constantly offered up. In thousands of sanctuaries, Jesus dwelt in the Blessed Sacrament in the midst of His faithful and loving children, and the voice of prayer and praise rose day and night in union with the angelic hosts, who ever worship before the throne of God. In spite of wars, famines, and pestilences—the heritage of a fallen race—it was universally acknowledged that no other nation was so happy and prosperous, or lived in such comfort and abundance as the people of fair and merry England. And though, according to our Lord's promise, the poor were not wanting in the land, since the poor are the treasures of the Church, yet starvation and misery were unknown. For the whole country was thickly dotted over with houses, where supernatural charity had taken up its abode, and where dwelt those, who, in imitation of their Lord, had made themselves poor that others might be rich, and now devoted their strength, their substance, and their whole lives to ministering to the wants of the poor and afflicted, in whom they beheld the image of that Lord, to whose love and service they had vowed themselves.

Thus nearly four Gentries passed away, when at length there sat upon the throne of England another Henry, who inherited at once the blood and the spirit of Henry Plantagenet. He, too, began his career as "a devoted son of the Church, and won the proud title of Defender of the Faith. But in course of years wicked passions obtained the mastery over him, and finding it impossible to bend the law of God to his sensual will, he resolved to throw off its yoke. The times were then even more evil then they had been in S. Thomas's day, for heresy and infidelity were added to schism; and Henry Tudor could strike at the root of religion more directly than the Plantagenet had ever dared to do. While he still hesitated, his unprincipled minister, Thomas Cromwell, suggested that all his difficulties would vanish, if he would take into his own hands the authority hitherto held by the Pope, and declare himself head of the Church in England; for then the clergy, being sensible that their lives and fortunes were at his disposal, would become the obsequious ministers of his will. Then was enacted a scene parallel to that at Northampton, but with a far different result. A false charge was trumped up against the whole body of clergy, that they had appeared without the royal permission before Wolsey as Papal legate, though the permission had actually been granted under the great seal; and on this false plea, their persons and property were declared to be at the king's mercy, unless, as the condition of their pardon, they would acknowledge him to be "the only supreme head of the Church and clergy of England." For three days they hesitated; but at length, trembling for their lives and possessions, both Houses of Convocation unanimously consented to acknowledge Henry as "the chief protector, the only and supreme lord, and, *as far as the law of Christ will allow*, the supreme head of the Church and clergy of England; but four years later, the qualifying clause was withdrawn, and they took an oath to recognise him absolutely as the supreme head of their Church.

When England was thus cut off from Christian unity, the consequences that S. Thomas had foreseen at Clarendon, quickly ensued. The Church's jurisdiction was transferred to the king. The convocation promised not to make any laws for the government of their flocks in faith, morals, or other spiritual matters without his authority. Appeals were henceforth made, not to the Holy Father, the sure refuge of the oppressed, but to the king, too often himself the chief oppressor. New articles of faith were ordered to be believed on the king's authority; and the penalties of heresy were decreed against all, who should teach or maintain any opinion contrary to such doctrines as he should then or hereafter publish.

The Church's spiritual jurisdiction also was transferred to the king. Henry appointed as his vicegerent, Thomas Cromwell, a layman, whom he invested with his own supreme ecclesiastical jurisdiction, and who in turn appointed lay deputies. Thus the lay government of the Church by its lay Head was fully carried out. Then, in order to prove that the author and source of spiritual jurisdiction in the kingdom was not God, but the king, the spiritual powers of the archbishops and bishops were suspended; and only after the interval of a month, and on their own petition, were they given leave to resume them. But they were required to sign a commission from the king, declaring that they received their authority from him alone, during his pleasure only, and as his deputies.

The possessions of the Church also passed into the king's hands; and it soon appeared, as S. Thomas had said at Clarendon, that the king's treasury was not the fit place for the property of Christ's poor. In the course of a few years the poor were robbed of their inheritance, the provision for their subsistence and relief was squandered on profligate and servile favourites of the court, starvation and misery fell on the land, and poverty, instead of being honoured and cherished, as hitherto, for the sake of our Blessed Lord, came to be treated as a disgrace and a crime. But in spite of cruel enactments, of hangings, whippings, and imprisonments, in spite of selfish and hardhearted legislation, in spite even of the noble though spasmodic efforts of individual benevolence, the hydra-headed monster has ever gone on multiplying, and still stalks forth boldly in defiance of every attempt to arrest and exterminate it. And it is only reasonable that it should be so. For in a fallen world, natural means must always prove inadequate to the cure of human woes, and supernatural charity, endued with power from on high, alone can suffice to meet and alleviate the heavy burdens of suffering humanity.

When the evil work was done, and the Church of England was trampled under foot, Henry was still unsatiated. For he deemed his triumph incomplete so long as S. Thomas's shrine at Canterbury stood as a silent witness against him, or S. Thomas's name rose in prayers to heaven, or S. Thomas's memory lived in the hearts of his flock, or even the watermen of London doffed their caps to his statue as they passed the niche in which it stood at Lambeth Palace. Accordingly, with impious arrogrance, he caused the saint to be formally cited on the 24th of April, 1538, to appear before the king's tribunal; and after a mock trial with all regular form of law, on the 11th of June sentence was passed on him as having "been guilty of contumacy, treason, and rebellion," and it was ordered "that his bones should be publicly burnt, to admonish the living of their duty by the punishment of the dead; that the offerings made at his shrine should be forfeited to the crown; that he should not be esteemed or called a saint; that all images, and pictures, and statues of him should be destroyed, the festival in his honour be abolished, and his name and remembrance be erased out of all books." In the following August this sentence was carried into execution. The precious stones alone of the shrine filled two chests, which it took seven or eight men to carry, and twenty-six carts were laden with the rest of the spoil; and when the tomb had been demolished, the relics were disinterred and burnt, and the ashes were scattered to the wind.

This act of Henry's can be compared, for brutal ferocity, only to that of the Pagans of Lyons, who threw the ashes of the martyrs into the Rhone, in order to prevent their resurrection to eternal life. And it was equally impotent. For Henry dreamt not of the truth which modern science has revealed, that matter is indestructible; and little did he think that by that sacrilegious outrage, he was only spreading wider and wider the blessed influence of the saint. For wherever that fine dust rested, or that impalpable aroma was wafted, it was the salt of the desolate and blood-stained soil, the odour of a sweet sacrifice, a fructifying seed, which, as the storm and the breeze bore it from place to place, brought strength to the martyr, and courage to the confessor, and peace to the bereaved and fainting mourner. Thus has it come to pass, that the tyrant's impotent rage has been overruled to the greater glory of God; for the whole of England has become the shrine of S. Thomas, and her soil like that of Rome, may claim to be hallowed by the dust of the martyr and the saint.

NOTES.

NOTE A.

The story that S. Thomas's mother was a Saracen princess first appears in a work known as the Quadrilogus, a compilation from four of the original biographies, which was made about A.D. 1220, on the occasion of the translation of S. Thomas, by Cardinal Langton. There are two copies of the Quadrilogus, but only one of them is entitled to the name, because it alone is compiled from the four lives of Herbert de Bosham, John of Salisbury, and Alan and William of Canterbury, while the other contains quotations also from FitzStephen and Grim, besides several unauthenticated details, among which is the legend of the Saracen princess. The latter compilation, however, is generally called the First Quadrilogus, apparently because it was the first to be printed in Paris, A.D. 1495, under the title of "Vita et Processus S. Thomas," while the other was not published till A.D. 1682, by Lupus, at Brussels. Both Canon Robertson and Father Morris, S.J., however, are of opinion that the latter was the earlier work, because it is strictly a compilation from four biographies, and it does not contain unauthenticated details, which would probably have been added at a later date.

See "Materials for History of Thomas Becket," iv., Introd. p. 20; "Life and Martyrdom of S. Thomas Becket," by the Rev. John Morris, S.J., p. 523, Ed. 1885.

NOTE B.

At the dissolution of the monasteries the precious reliquary in which the Apostle's hand was kept, was carried off and broken up, but there is no record what became of the hand. Some years ago, however, a Protestant physician found in the ruins of Reading Abbey a hand, black from age and exposure, with a sword-cut across the fingers, but free from the least trace of corruption. He placed it in his museum and labelled it as the hand of S. James the Apostle. About 1855 the museum was broken up and its contents were sold, when the hand was bought by the late Mr. Mackensie, of Findon, Rossshire. On his death soon after, it passed into the possession of the late Mr. Scott Murray, of Danesfield, whose family now have it. It may fairly be presumed, positive proof being unattainable, to be really the hand of the Apostle.

NOTE C.

In connexion with Gilbert's claim to independence of Canterbury, John of Salisbury writes to the Chapter of Canterbury (Epp. Jo. Sar. ii. p. 212): "He relies on a prophesy of Merlin, who, under some impulse, I know not what, foretold, before the coming of S. Augustin into England, that 'when the dignity of London should be transferred to Dover, the Christian religion should be destroyed and restored again.' " FitzStephen, in his description of the city of London, affixed to his Life of S. Thomas, says: "It was once the metropolitan see, and is thought likely to become so again, . . . unless, perhaps, the archiepiscopal title of S. Thomas, the martyr, and his bodily presence in the Church of Canterbury, shall secure the dignity of it for ever where it now is "(FitzSt. iii. 2). These predictions have been curiously fulfilled by the recent restoration of the metropolitan dignity to London, under the title of Westminster, Canterbury having lost at the Reformation the "bodily presence" of S. Thomas.

NOTE D.

This account of the martyrdom is compiled from the contemporary biographies. Four of these—Grim, FitzStephen, John of Salisbury, and the anonymous author of the Lambeth MS. were eye-witnesses of the martyrdom. Three others—Gervase, Benedict, and William of Canterbury—were on the premises, and the others, especially S. Thomas's intimate friends, Herbert and the anonymous writer known as Roger of Pontigny, would naturally have learnt every particular from the eye-witnesses. Giraldus Cambrensis mentions, with a tone of special authority, several details which he had not found in the other biographies (Angl. Sacra, ii. 423); and Gamier, we know, took great pains to collect his materials from the friends and relatives of the saint.

NOTE E.

Grim thought it was FitzUrse who struck the first blow.

But Tracy boasted on his return to Saltwood that he had cut off the arm of John of Salisbury, for whom in the dim light he mistook Grim.

NOTE F.

The history of the murderers as given in the text rests on contemporary and documentary evidence, and is therefore strictly historical. It is supported by the facts that De Morville, who was Justice Itinerant in Northumberland and Cumberland, vacated that office the year after the murder, and FitzUrse in the same year made over his estate of Willeton, in Somersetshire, no doubt as an expiatory offering, one half to the knights of S. John and the other half to his brother Robert, who built the chapel of Willeton.

The deed of gift of the manor of Daccombe to the See of Canterbury is not dated, but its proximate date is fixed to the year 1174 by its confirmation at Canterbury by Henry, which is attested by "Richard elect of Winchester," and "Robert elect of Hereford," 1174 being the only year that Henry was in England, while Richard and Robert were respectively bishops elect of Winchester and Hereford.

The nine parish churches in Devonshire dedicated to S. Thomas are at Bridford, Kingswear, Lapford, North Lew, Newton Stacy, Exeter, Thorverton, Plympton, and Bovey Tracy. The seven first are dedicated to him alone. That at Plympton is dedicated to S. Maurice and S. Thomas of Canterbury, and that at Bovey Tracy to S Peter and S. Paul and S. Thomas of Canterbury. (Report of Devonshire Association for the Advancement of Science, Literature, and Art, vol. xiv., July 1882, p. 304.)

Besides the historical evidence many local traditions are handed down about the murderers, which, however, are not always very correct. Tbe boatmen of Ilfracombe point out a huge rent, or cavern, called Crook Horn, in which Tracy, they say, hid himself for a fortnight immediately after the murder, and was fed by his daughter. Another tradition marks an old farmhouse close to Morte Bay, still called Woollacombe Tracy, as the spot to which he was banished, being condemned to make "bundles of the sand and binds (wisps) of the same." He is also said to have "lived in this neighbourhood" a private life when wind and weather turned against him"; or, as another local tradition expresses it, since the murderer's departure for the Holy Land was delayed by contrary winds,

"The Tracys
Always have the wind in their faces."

The villagers of Morthoe point out a tomb with an inscription to "Sir William Tracy," in which they say lies the murderer who founded the church. But documentary evidence proves that the tomb and transept are of the reign of Edward II., and the figure carved on it represents Sir William Tracy, rector of the parish, in his sacerdotal vestments, who died in 1322. Local histories also confuse the murderer with a baron of the same name, probably his son, or grandson, who took part in the wars of 1216 and 1222, when the murderer would have been ninety years old.

Nichols, in his "Pilgrimage of Erasmus," says, that Hugh de Morville, another of the murderers, was party to a deed in 1199. But there is no proof that it was not his son who executed the deed, which is the more probable because Hugh was a family name, which was also borne by the founder of Dryburgh Abbey.

Fuller has asserted that FitzUrse went to Ireland and was the ancestor of the McMahons of the north apparently with no other foundation than the fact that McMahon is the Celtic translation of FitzUrse, or "bear's son." This assertion is so obviously absurd that it is noticed only because Dean Stanley has thought it worthy of repetition. Not only is it undoubted that all the Irish families whose names begin with O or Mac are descendants of the Milesians, who came to Ireland in pre-historic times, but in records which modern Irish scholars and antiquarians accept as authentic, the settlement of the McMahons in the County Louth, where their descendants are still to be found, is shown to have taken place before the arrival of S. Patrick.

(See Stanley's "Historical Memorials of Canterbury," pp. 70, 106.)

NOTE G.

The full particulars of this transaction will be found in Strype's "Memorials," Burnet's "History of the Reformation," Collier's "Ecclesiastical History "and Wharton's "Specimen of Errors."

Gardiner and some of the other bishops insisting that they had received their spiritual jurisdiction from God, and could not part with it to the king (Strype, i. pt. i. p. 215, Fol.), Legh and John ap Rice, two of Cromwell's deputies suggested that the king should suspend their spiritual juris diction temporarily, because without this interruption of their functions they could pretend they had received their authority from some other source than the king. But if they were obliged to ask his majesty to restore them the power to exercise their spiritual functions, they would thereby acknowledge and publicly declare, that the king was the sole source of all power within the realm, and that all kinds of jurisdiction were derived from him alone. (Strype, i. pt. i. p. 208, Fol.; pt. ii. Rec. 57, p. 145, Fol.)

Accordingly on the 18th September, 1535, the king sent Cranmer letters of inhibition, to be forwarded to the Archbishop of York and all the bishops and archdeacons, strictly forbidding them, in virtue of his spiritual ecclesiastical authority, to presume to exercise their spiritual jurisdiction in any way during the visitation of all the churches and religious houses in the realm which he was about to make (Collier, ii. 22, Fol.; Rec. No. 31). After the lapse of about a month he wrote to each of the archbishops and bishops separately, saying that moved by his humble supplications he committed to him and gave him leave in his stead, and in the way and form hereafter described, to confer orders on suitable persons and to exercise all other branches of ecclesiastical jurisdiction (which were specified), in his stead, in his name, and by his authority, besides and beyond what are declared in Holy Writ to have been committed to him. (Collier, ii. 33, Fol.; Rec. 41.) Each archbishop and bishop was required to accept this commission from the king before he could resume the exercise of his spiritual jurisdiction ("Specimen of Errors," p. 51), and again on his translation to a new see (Burnet, i. p, 267; Rec. No. 14, p. 184, Fol.; or Vol. iv. p. 410, Ed. Pocock).

Made in the USA
Coppell, TX
22 July 2020